Good Moanin'

The Best of Bob Talbert

Detroit Free Press

Published by the Detroit Free Press
321 W. Lafayette
Detroit, Michigan 48231

Good Moanin'
The Best of Bob Talbert
Copy editing: Sue Chevalier, Pat Dunphy
Book design: Bill Diem
Cover design: Milt Kelsey
Keyboarding: Marsha Banks, Winnie Carpenter,
    Terri Sosnowski
Project coordinator: Jon Pepper

Manufactured in the United States of America.

ISBN 0-9605692-3-5

Introduction

It's funny how I remember every single column, exactly what emotions prompted each one.

And I remember your reaction, or lack of, to each one.

I'm not just talking about the 100-plus columns included here. I'm talking about more than 5,000 columns I've written for the Detroit Free Press in the past 16 years.

It's not that I have such a great memory or anything like that. It's just that columns are your babies, your children.

I'm still right proud of the way some of them turned out. And some, considering the years and changing times, embarrass me now.

That I remembered them all in detail was my biggest surprise as I began reviewing 16 years' worth of columns to help select the ones to go into this "Good Moanin' " selection.

A pleasant surprise. Tells me how much I've enjoyed writing a daily column for the Detroit Free Press since that first one in August 1968.

When Executive Editor David Lawrence suggested this collection, I thought it would be a simple task to pick my favorites.

But as I went through the library files, it became apparent I would be incapable of making the final selection. I liked too many too much.

I picked about 500 columns and maybe 5,000 Monday Moanin's and turned it over to Features Editor Chip Visci and Jon Pepper, who coodinates Free Press special publications such as this, and they made the final picks.

Even as I write this I don't know what they selected. I know what the cover looks like — an ego trip for me — and I know the final "moan" in the book.

I didn't want to know which columns and moans they picked because I didn't want to argue about the ones they left out.

I know that there are highly personal columns about me and my family.

Some critic once said I write a gossip column about myself

and my family. I do. In 16 years I haven't let a major emotion or event pass that I didn't write about.

I've tried to share everything with you every day. All those various column pictures on the cover indicate the changes I've gone through with you over the years. It's almost been like keeping a daily diary. Highs and lows, ups and downs, the good and the bad.

My life has been an open column, you might say.

I've written columns about two good marriages and a good divorce. That's right, a good divorce. My first wife, Beryl, and I decided to get a divorce so a good marriage wouldn't turn into a bad one — and we went on a second honeymoon to Spain to celebrate the parting. When Lynn and I got married, Beryl was there along with my children, Dafna and Jason.

One week about four years ago, Lynn acquired three firsts in her life: a home, a teenage son and a pet dog. She survived to write about it, which I have a hunch she does somewhere in "Good Moanin'."

I also have a hunch there'll be some "babies" in this thing about how "ah tawk wif a Suh-thun ak-sin," about discovering new life-styles and reminiscing about old ones soon to be forgotten.

And the Monday Moanin's — there must have been 30,000 million of 'em by now. It's the most popular column I write. An identifying thing. Trademark, if you will.

Every Monday Moanin' I dump out all my thoughts, observations, rah-rahs, boo-hisses, one-liners and assorted nonsense from the preceding week into the top left corner of the Free Press' Feature Page.

While every essay in this book pulled in its share of the mail from readers, the Monday Moanin's generated the most mail every week. So at the end of each chapter, there are some Monday Moanin's for you.

Thank you's? There are plenty. To David Lawrence, for his constant support. To Sue Chevalier, who painstakingly edited each and every column. To family and friends, who don't mind me writing about them and asking them so many questions. And most of all, to the Detroit Free Press and its readers, who've let this barefoot hillbilly become a Detroiter.

I'm dying to see which columns they picked. So, if you'll excuse me, folks, I've got a book to read . . .

Bob Talbert

GOOD MOANIN'

DETROIT, MICHIGAN

Kennedy Square at noon: A new circus is in town

They come to Kennedy Square at High Noon. It's a tradition in Detroit, a tradition that started yesterday.

They pop from their concrete cocoons like madras-coated and mini-skirted butterflies. They come down out of their steel and glass hives to preen and sun and be seen. They wander up from the subterranean cavern, seeking the sun. They drift over from traffic-ripe thoroughfares to watch and be watched.

In Detroit, which the policeman said has "no exact downtown, actually," a new heart has grown from a raw wound that once cradled the Old City Hall. You can't see the $4 million underground parking lot, but you can see the $700,000 plaza and its shifting circus of people, dancing about the shallow pool and climbing the curving stairs.

In a little less than a year, it has become all things to all people — a place for watching and being watched. A place to park the mind and body. A place to pose, peruse or just pause.

There are all kinds, there for all kinds of reasons. But like colored bits of glass in a kaleidoscope, they make a pattern.

And from the pattern emerges the differing types . . .

THE PREENERS — The girls come in all ages, all colors and all sizes. The boys are peacocks in their green-on-green tight suits. Nehru jackets and sparkling medallions. Aloof and proud, they move through the plaza like sleek canoes slithering through their own private lakes.

THE BROWN-BAGGERS — Just a few blocks from fancy restaurants, these budgeting secretaries and junior executives peel the brown paper off homemade goodies — cream cheese on datenut bread, bologna with mayo on white — far tastier than the Seersucker-Suit Set's two drinks and $4.50 special.

THE LONELY — Tough, tired faces atop little lumpy bodies, hopefully looking at each passerby. On second glance, they're not really old, just defeated by the times and the struggle and the action. They stare at nothing a thousand miles away, or as close as the next bench. Her toothless mouth works the gum over like a small red fist. They would rather sit alone than talk with someone as far away as they.

THE SHOPPERS — For these short-timers, it's a place to count their money and change. A perfect "I'll meetcha there at noon" place. A spot to air those Dr. Scholl's toes and give the corns a break. A shortcut between sales and the banks. She gives her girdle a secret tug or two, checks her straps, buttons and zippers and moves on.

THE MYSTERIOUS — Sunglasses the size of ashtrays. Sketch pads and writing tablets and the Japanese cameras. Day-glo clothes and drip-dry beards. Could be hippies or poets or artists. That tall one in the sport coat — a TV newsman. Maybe an actor or singer or celebrity or some other role-player. But somebody, for sure.

THE SMALL FRY — There are two kinds. Youngsters blossoming at the ends of mothers' hands, hurrying on churning legs to match Mom's modern pace. And the gaggle of drifting sub-teeners, parentless, aimless and restless.

THE ESCAPISTS — Grabbing that precious, private hour away from the dull, the drudge, the grinding sameness of routine. She reads "In Cold Blood," a far cry from selling $3.95 blouses to bargain hunters. Some just smoke a pipe or two. Others sit and guess what the others are sitting and guessing.

THE GIRL-WATCHERS — From professional lechers with sear-thin mustaches to the self-conscious amateur peekers with downy cheeks, they come to look at the girls. Innocent closet voyeurs, fantasizing in the noonday sun.

There are others, of course, hundreds of them. The Hustlers, the Hairdos and the Hi-theres. The Regulars, the Resters and the Reciters. The Teasers, the Tipplers and the Time-passers.

— Bob's first column in the Free Press, Aug. 10, 1968

Some favorite things: Let's make them official

Michigan ranks near the bottom in having State Things. We have a State Tree (white spruce), a State Fish (brook trout), a State Bird (robin), a State Flower (apple blossom), a State Stone (Petoskey) and that's about it.

I know those folks in Lansing have a lot more to worry with than Things and don't want to clog the legislative machine with trivia.

But we really don't have enough State Things. Other states show us up.

Take Maryland. (What do you mean you wouldn't take it on a bet? Are you trying to start something?) Maryland has a State Sport — jousting. I'm not sure what that is, but it has a nice ring to it. I think a worthy candidate for Michigan's State Sport would be striking, followed closely by picketing.

California has a State Insect — the California dogface butterfly. Since there don't seem to be any Michigan dogface butterflies around, I would suggest the gnat. Do I hear a second?

New Mexico has two State Vegetables — the chili and the frijole. Class, eh? I really didn't know the chili and the frijole were vegetables until I looked it up, to tell you the truth. I was all set to nominate the mushroom as the Michigan State Vegetable, until someone suggested I look that up, too. The darned thing's a fungus. So let's make the mushroom the State Fungus. How many other states have a fungus.

I do not have to tell you that Tennessee has a State Horse. In Michigan, as far as I can tell, it's a four-way race between the quarter horse, the thoroughbred, the trotter and the pacer. If no winner emerges, I suggest as compromise selecting the State Jackass. I have a list of 96 people who could qualify.

Virginia has a State Dog, the American foxhound. Michigan should adopt the hound dog, which would give us a State Song ("You Ain't Nuthin' But a . . . ")

While we are called the Wolverine State, I can find nowhere that the wolverine is the official State Animal. And I have never met the first wolverine who claimed us.

For a State Mineral, my wife nominates mud or sand. She says we could mix them together and make a brick which would give us an alternate State Rock.

Wisconsin, smirking over there to our west, has a State Fossil, the mastodon. I hesitate nominating a Michigan State Fossil since we've already elected several of them to office.

Michigan should have a State Scapegoat. Prime candidates include the mayor of Detroit, any policeman, and your neighborhood and principal.

There is only one candidate for the State Excuse: the Weather.

There are lots of states with State Colors. Michigan should have one. Red is out because some carper would cry about Communist infiltration. Throw out pink for the same reason. In fact, all pastels have to go because no self-respecting state can show up in lavender or fawn. Blue has to go because some civil libertarians would claim it denotes a police state. Yellow conjures up the image of cowardice. And you have to be very careful today when you speak of black or tan or brown. Maybe we could settle on green, which would please the outdoorsy set and tourist traps whose motto is "Keep Michigan Green — Bring Money."

The State Snack is a contest between the Coney Island (with onions) and the Hot Soft Pretzel (with mustard). Except in the Upper Peninsula, where it's the pastie.

As to a State Drink, the candidates include the Cold Duck, the Bullshot and Red Pop.

I hesitate to nominate a State Car. Personally, I'd hold out for a '53 DeSoto or a '48 Packard.

I'm sure you have lots of candidates for many more categories than I mentioned. Feel free to send them to me. We've got to get Michigan on top in State Things.

— March 6, 1969

From 2,000 feet up, you can't see Detroit's scars

Bob Hynes and I were traveling down Grand River at 135 miles per hour and 2,000 feet straight up. He dropped the Piper Cherokee 180's nose slightly and Detroit spread before us like a toy, mock-up, tabletop version of a city non-planner's sprawling metropolis.

"This should give you a brand-new view of our city," Hynes said, maneuvering the compact plane with the same deft touch with which he conducts his daily 90-minute "Morning Show" live on Channel 7.

I'm not a nervous flyer. None of that white-knuckle jazz for me. But before the flight, Hynes' staffers tried to have a little fun 'n' games with me about their boss' ability as a pilot. "Get him to show you his pilot's license," they said. "He got it out of one of those plastic balls you get from a 25-cent machine in shopping centers."

But Hynes is an exceptional pilot. In fact, if I had to call Central Casting for a pilot, I'd want one who looked like Bob Hynes. Handsome, just a little gray at the temples, steady eyes and hands, wide shoulders, the whole bit. And Hynes takes his flying seriously.

Don't give me one of those wisecracking gum-chewers on my

flight. Leave the joke-telling to me. It may bore my seatmate to tears, but an aviator dropping bon mots in cloud banks leaves me in tears. Better me than him, with the funny stuff.

Hynes is also serious about his city — Detroit. It's his city like it's my city — we adopted it. Or it adopted us, we're not sure which. Hynes, the proper Bostonian, me, the Carolina hillbilly.

Hynes' variety show every morning from 7 to 8:30 is a daily reflection of Detroit, a collection of the triumphs, tragedies, trivia and things that make up the country's fifth largest city. Hynes has caught Detroit's tempo beautifully since his show's inception, Labor Day 1966.

The Detroit below us had a different look to it than the Detroit whose streets and freeways I drive every day. Detroit is not symmetrical. It is vertical as well as horizontal, which creates a great number of squares in more ways than one.

Detroit's buildings seem to pile up downtown as if someone had shoved everything together to make room for something yet to come. There are other neat bunches of buildings like the New Center and ugly smoke-belching clumps like the Rouge.

The city is laced with transportation arteries and veins, all flowing full of multicolored corpuscles, produced in our automotive heart.

From 2,000 feet everything about Detroit looks closer. Grosse Pointe is right next door to Dearborn. Farmington looks like it could reach out and touch Ferndale. I was really shocked by how many freeways cut the area up into neat, easy-to-get-to chunks.

Landmarks look different from the air. Tiger Stadium is grand looking, not the creaky old has-been whose transplant is causing so much concern. Belle Isle is beautiful, not rotting, and much, much bigger than driving around it leads you to believe.

And the riverfront is almost naked. There are acres and acres of undeveloped riverfront, which is a civic shame. It should be put to use by public or private funds. But from 2,000 feet Detroit looks ready to blossom and bloom.

From 2,000 feet everything looks clean, washed by the melted snow. From 2,000 feet you can't see the pockets of crime and violence, the sections of intolerance and prejudice.

From 2,000 feet the activity, the movement, the energy doesn't indicate business is bad, or storefronts are boarded and burned out. From 2,000 feet you don't see the corporate shackles of sterile committees which meet and and meet and form newer committees which will meet and meet and so forth.

From 2,000 feet you wonder if you could ever look into all those houses and find out who all the people are, what they are like, how they feel about the city, what has thrown them together and kept them apart.

A city is an experience, an emotional thing. We are never very rational about emotional things. We either hate them or love them, with very few so-so's in-between. And the love or hate can't be based on any one given set of values. One man's charming old buildings are another's decrepit eyesores. The saddest thing is when people don't know this and can't accept another person's liking what they don't like.

This intolerance may be the worst disease of our city, any city. For a city to work, its heart has to beat happily. Its soul has to sing a bird's song. Its head has to lift and its hands have to work. Its back has to bow and its legs have to pump. Its feet have to make tracks. It has to move forward. It has to work and play and enjoy.

From 2,000 feet, Detroit looks ready for all this. From 2,000 feet Detroit appears primed for the challenge. I wish Bob Hynes could take each of you flying so you could see what I mean. It would make a believer out of you.

— March 11, 1970

Detroit's mass production keeps rumor mills humming

In a little over 2½ years in Detroit, I guess I've heard them all. In addition to manufacturing automobiles, Detroit is one of the world leaders in turning out rumors. They come in almost as many models, styles, colors and sizes as the cars, and have an equal number of accessories, before and after the fact.

I have collected these rumors — half-truths, unhalf-truths, shibboleths, prejudices, unexamined truisms, etc., and you can sort out the ones you believe and the ones you don't. Me? I don't believe any of them, except maybe two or three:

Van Patrick wears a toupee.

Van Patrick doesn't wear a toupee, but lets his hair grow long on the side and combs it over the bald top.

Van Patrick is really the coach of the Detroit Lions.

Grosse Pointe allows no blacks to buy homes and has a "point system" to let a few Jews in.

Without his producer, Hal Youngblood, J.P. McCarthy would be nothing.

Without his writers Bob Posch, Tommy Ryan and Tom DeLisle, Dick Purtan would be nothing.

Nobody comes downtown anymore because they're afraid of being mugged.

An oil company bought up a simple device that would allow cars to get 100 miles per gallon.

Ralph Nader owns 100,000 shares of Chrysler stock.

Jerry Cavanagh is going to run for Senate.

Dave Diles has a bigger ego than Bill Kennedy.

Bill Kennedy has a bigger ego than Lou Gordon.

Lou Gordon has a bigger ego than Dave Diles.

Bob Talbert steals all his material from Herb Caen.

Detroit's Common Council is a collection of clowns and clods.

General Motors is secretly moving out of the GM Building.

Dope pushers peddle their junk at the all-night doughnut shops.

The Mafia runs the building and construction industry.

Mafia dons hang out in Greektown all the time.

Blank blank, the TV personality, is getting a divorce. (Too many mentioned to single out any one person.)

Tiger Stadium is falling down.

William Clay Ford really has no plan to move his Lions to Pontiac but is using it as a threat to get a downtown stadium tailored for football.

Police in the middle ranks are paid off by dope pushers.

General Motors' brass have put the lid on outspoken John De Lorean.

The Detroit News is secretly planning to move its entire operation to the suburbs.

Michigan winters are fun.

People who drive Volkswagens have higher IQs than people who drive Detroit compacts.

Michigan spends more money each year repainting stripes down highways than it does on the entire state court system.

You can pick up girls at Jim's Garage and the Steering Wheel.

Dollie Cole has a feud running with other auto exec wives.

Police will arrest a long-haired youth quicker than a short-haired one.

Tobacco companies have already patented names for marijuana cigarets.

Marijuana is less harmful than drinking liquor.

Dearborn realtors will not sell to blacks.

All local restaurants use pre-prepared vegetables.

A lot of wife-swapping goes on among Detroit's Beautiful People.

All Wayne State students smoke pot.

The auto companies have kept Detroit from having a rapid transit system.

General Motors makes all the transmissions for the other auto companies.

The Free Press and the News automatically take opposite editorial stands on all issues.

Belle Isle is taken over by the blacks in the summer and it's not a safe place to go.

New Detroit Inc. is a do-nothing organization.

Detroit Renaissance is just New Detroit with a new name.

Roman Gribbs has no personality or style.

George Romney won't last another month in Nixon's cabinet.

Motown Record Company is moving everything to the West Coast.

Women like men who smoke pipes.

People who wear hard hats are exceptionally patriotic.

People who wear beards are exceptionally unpatriotic.

If Bach and Beethoven were alive today they'd be writing rock songs.

Dr. Spock is responsible for all the trouble with young people.

No one laughs at ethnic jokes anymore.

Gambling is a disease, like homosexuality.

Television commercials are better than the shows they sponsor.

Chuck Muer owns 83 restaurants.

The London Chop House is overpriced.

If Congress outlaws guns, only outlaws will have guns.

People buy Playboy to look at the pictures and the New Yorker to read the cartoons.

Only the very rich or very poor can live well in Detroit.

Canada is a much better place to live than the United States.

Canada is a much worse place to live than the United States.

There is DDT in everything we eat.

I will make half of Detroit angry with this column.

— Feb. 25, 1971

Eight Mile: Riding road to rebirth?

Streets are streets, but Eight Mile is more than just a road.

Beginning (for me) as Baseline in Northville at one end and becoming Vernier in Harper Woods on the other, Eight Mile is more Detroit to me than anything else I can think of.

It has everything.

Soon after coming to this city, I figured out that if one could tell where all the main freeways, expressways and four-lane highways crossed Eight Mile, the rest would come easy.

Once, many years ago, a fine gentleman drove me out Grand River and told me at one time it was one of the state's key roads because it was once the only direct road from Detroit to Lansing.

Grand River, from Brighton on into Woodward Avenue, is very representative of what this area is all about. Jefferson from Gibraltar to Metropolitan Beach is another remarkable look at the extremes in which some of us live.

Gratiot from downtown Detroit to downtown Mt. Clemens is still another slice through the Detroit cake. How about Michigan from Dearborn to Ann Arbor? Telegraph, from Flat Rock all the way up to Dixie Highway in Waterford, is perhaps the longest slice of Detroit one can find but it has become mile after mile of sameness.

And then there's Woodward. Good ol' Wood'urd that begins at the river and turns into Pontiac's Wide Track Drive. The great drag-racing strip of yesteryear, when skinning wheels was a bigger diversion than skin shows.

A lot of people will pick Woodward as the most typical of Detroit's streets. For one reason, it divides east and west for us so neatly and runs through a dozen different cities.

There are some other shorter stretches, of which I am very, very fond — Ford and Fort and Van Dyke and Groesbeck and Maple and Plymouth and Outer Drive and Michigan and Hines Drive — but the biggies are still my favorites.

From beginning to end they traverse the spectrum of this community, but the one that is the widest-ranging to me is Eight Mile Road. For one thing it connects the tri-county area. It is still the fastest east-west route we have. Some hold out for various expressway routes, but not me.

Eight Mile can't match others in beauty, 'cause mostly it's one little business, one little service, one little office cluster, one little and big shopping center after another.

I doubt if many drive these roads, all of them, as much as I do. More drive one road than I do, but your job is not one that takes you around to so many places unless you happen to be in sales. But even then, you probably have an area, a territory.

I've driven from one end to the other of Eight Mile many times, sometimes in bumper-to-anger traffic and sometimes late at night when the road is still awake. Eight Mile is 24 hours a day, 365 days a year. Only thing closes it is a wreck, but not for long.

I don't know what the statistics are, but I'd have to say the average Eight Mile driver is Detroit's finest. The freeways have become Indy prelims. Eight Milers drive the limit, but seldom over it.

And they are more courteous. They use more lane-switching signals, and are, in general, more aware of the traffic around them. Now you may be a regular driver on Eight Mile and say that I am full of soybeans, that Eight Mile is a jungle. OK, I will admit that during rush hours I try to shun all streets, roads, etc.

Rush hours angry up the blood and I remember Satchel Paige once said that "angry-ing" the blood is real bad for you. Because I have copied much of my life from Satchel Paige, Ozark Ike and Li'l Abner, I will say that un-angry blood is the best. Ozark Ike and Li'l Abner were two hillbillies who made good.

Course now, I was also influenced by Wimpy, Popeye, Pluto, Ted Williams, Gabby Hayes, Billy Batson, Smiley Burnette, Trigger and Lassie, so take that into consideration. I also wanted to be Johnny Sheffield (he played Boy to Johnny Weissmuller's Tarzan), but he didn't influence me.

But every time I drive Eight Mile I'm amazed at new places that have arisen and old places that have closed. The balance is even, thank goodness. Another thing that amazes me, make that dumb-founds me, is how they make it — all these little shops and stores and restaurants and what have you. I know of nothing you can't find on Eight Mile.

When Coleman Young took office as mayor of Detroit, he made that flip remark for all the crooks and bad guys to "hit Eight Mile." I was at a little affair recently, where a thousand folks gathered for the Central Business District Association's annual meeting. If all the good guys and women had, that day, stayed north of Eight Mile, Mayor Young, you'd have been speaking to half a house. I saw people there from Ann Arbor and Pontiac and Mt. Clemens. That's where they live, but they still work in Detroit.

And they also support Detroit when Detroit offers them something that makes it worth their while. Nobody, not even the indefatigable Diane Edgecomb of the CBDA, will support a city "just because." Nobody will hang in or on to something "just because" it's a good idea for it to remain. If there's to be a rebirth of Detroit, let's look at Eight Mile as the connecting line of this area, not the dividing line. If you ask me, it now looks more like the main drag than Woodward ever was.

— May 3, 1977

Lindell AC: The legend at Cass and Michigan

Edgar (Doc) Greene named it the Lindell Athletic Club years ago in his sports column at the News, to take a dig at the Detroit Athletic Club's richer, snootier crowd.

This was when it was the Lindell Hotel Bar, which Jimmy and Johnny Butsicaris had opened in 1950. When they moved to their present site at Michigan and Cass 15 years ago in May, the name stuck and was shortened to Lindell AC.

It is now an international dead-solid fact about Detroit. It's like the zoo, Belle Isle, the London Chop House, Greenfield Village, Greektown and the other institutions or legends we are proud of.

For 28 years the Butsicaris brothers — opposites if you ever met two in your life — have operated perhaps the single most successful bar operation in the city of Detroit.

They burned the mortgage on that expensive little piece of property a few years ago. They were going to have a burning party until I announced it in the paper and they found they could not accommodate all those hundreds and hundreds of athletes and entertainers who wanted to come in and help hold the match.

It is always my favorite way to start a night on the town. Hit the Lindell for still my favorite hamburger and fries in the world. Whether it's a concert, ball game, show — you name it — doesn't matter. The Lindell is always my starting place.

If I were a drinking man it probably would be my last stop because I'd know Jimmy would take care of me if my snoot was too full. It's a bar I've never been afraid to take my kids into — they love the burgers and fries.

It's also a lunch stop — over which Johnny presides — where I've taken and met some of the more famous folks of our time from art to athletics.

It has survived fires, freezes, floods, famines, fools, freaks and any other f-ing thing you can think of. It has survived and prospered because of the brothers Butsicaris. Its maddest, most thrilling moment was the night the Tigers arrived back home 10 summers ago after winning the World Series in St. Louis.

The Lindell became the center of that mania, that beautiful fever, that remarkable delirium that possessed this community. Someday I shall write a novel about that night. That's a promise to me.

And the promise the Butsicaris brothers made to each other 28 years ago is one that holds to this very day: We only will run a bar we are comfortable in — a bar where our customers will be our friends.

They are so different. John runs around at lunchtime like he's going crazy and Jimmy moves around at night like you are crazy. But they are alike in this respect: Professionally, they're the hardest of noses in business. Socially, they're the softest touch around.

They've saved the skins, noses and reputations of more names than would like to be mentioned. They've gone to bat for lost causes, hopeless cases and have turned them into productive contributors to our society.

They've wet-nursed more than their share of celebrity babies, boozing politicians, suicidal stars and who knows what else they surely didn't need. But maybe this, too, is part of what they both have enjoyed about the Lindell AC, their life for 28 years come this May.

The ups and downs, they'll tell you separately, they've enjoyed and learned from. They've loved what they've done, what they're doing and what they've created.

Men like this need to be applauded from time to time for hanging in there, keeping their oasis in downtown Detroit open and flourishing. One more time, maybe, a night like that unforgettable October night in 1968. That would be so nice with the Butsicaris brothers leading the cheers.

— March 23, 1978

In the Detroit game, the rules change a lot

I didn't catch the name of the game the TV commercial was talking about but it had something to do with Detroit. The slam-bang announcer was saying something about how it's played with real Detroit businesses and locations.

Sounded like some sort of take-off on Monopoly, the classic board game on which most such games have been based over the years.

I checked a few stores and could find nothing like what I heard described.

But it dawns on me that we really need a game about Detroit. A How-to-Win-in-Detroit game.

What I propose to do here is give you a few simple ways of scoring in the game. You'll have to make up your own board. Rules?

Well, if the game is true to life, the first rule is that the rules are changed daily.

Perhaps you can make up your own rules as you go along. That's what I plan to do here. Consider this a starter set. I'm sure you'll be able to come up with some advanced versions.

Give yourself 25 points if you've ever been put on by a Dick Purtan put-on telephone call. Subtract 15 if you happen to look like Dick.

Take away 10 points if the Anonymous Gourmet pans your favorite restaurant. Make it 50 if you own the restaurant. Collect 20 points for an AG rave of your favorite restaurant, 50 if you own it. Knowing who the AG is gets you a bonus of 100 points and a Status Card.

If you've ever attended a Tom and Diane Schoenith party, collect 12 points, but only if it was a charity affair. No points, but a Status Card, if you attend one of their private shindigs.

If J.P. McCarthy calls you in the morning for your comments, go directly to the In Crowd space and collect a bonus of 15 points. If you coach a Detroit sports team, deduct 25 points.

Collect a Get-Out-of-Jail card if you can name Brooks Patterson's latest caper. Go directly to jail, do not pass Go, if you are involved in the investigation.

If Al Ackerman knocks you once, lose 15 points. If he continually knocks you, go to the In Crowd space and collect a 25-point bonus.

Agreeing with film critic Mike Clark earns you two Intellect Cards. Disagree with him and immediately go stand in line to see the movie again.

If you were a Detroit Symphony fan before Antal Dorati, collect an old Status Card. If you are a DSO fan because of Dorati, draw from the Instant Status pile and follow the directions.

If you've taken a trip to Greenfield Village in the past six months, go directly to the With-It square. If you've never been to Greenfield Village, lose two turns.

Sitting directly behind Jim Fitzgerald at a show or next to him in a bar, draw from the In Crowd pile and add 20 points to your score. If Fitz has something to say about you in his column, forfeit 15 points.

Riding late at night with Bill Bonds in Bloomfield Hills, collect two Bravery Cards. These can be traded for a Get-Out-of-Jail Card.

If you can find your way around the RenCen, move directly to the With-It square. If you get lost, still move directly to the With-It crowd.

Knowing what Emily's is across the street from is worth 10 points.

If you have season tickets to the Lions, Red Wings, Tigers and Pistons games, forfeit two Intellect Cards.

Watching the Auction Movie on Channel 62 is worth two Bravery Cards.

Collect two Status Cards if you find yourself at a party attended by Jackie Gordon, Dollie Cole or Kathy DuRoss. If all three are there, move directly to the In Crowd space. Dropping their names the next day earns a 10-point bonus.

If Mayor Young comes to your party, collect 50 points south of Eight Mile, lose 50 points if it's north of Eight Mile.

Agreeing with Nickie McWhirter is worth 15 points. Disagreeing with her is also worth 15 points.

If William Cahalan knows you socially, collect 10 points. Professionally, lose 15.

If you've been to a vacation spot before Rick Sylvain, collect a bonus 25 points and an In Crowd pass.

If Frank Angelo writes about you, receive three Good Guy Cards.

Going to the Joe Louis Arena is worth Instant Status and Bravery Card bonuses.

Subtract 10 points if you think the Summit Restaurant is stationary and the Plaza Hotel revolves. Subtract 50 points if you think the hotel is stationary and the city revolves.

Being a guest on David Newman's show is worth four Intellect

Cards. Being a guest on the Ron Cameron show, lost 10 points and half your mind.

Getting stuck in a Silverdome traffic jam is worth three Stupid Cards.

Opening another Chinese restaurant in the northern suburbs, collect one Stupid Card.

Getting a Love Letter in a George Puscas column is worth five points. Getting slammed by Jim Hawkins is worth another five.

If you look at Guindon, collect an Intellect Card. If you understand it, collect a Stupid Card. (Or is it the other way around?)

If you understand Bill Kennedy, forfeit two Intellect Cards.

Pass Go and collect $200 if Action Line helps you. Lose 200 points if Action Line calls you with a complaint.

Collect two Bravery Cards if you go to the same bar Jeff Komlo goes to.

Move directly to the Out-of-It space if you watch Channel 4's news.

Lose two turns for owning Chrysler stock, but collect two Good Guy Cards.

Move forward 10 spaces if you have played the game so far. Collect 100 bonus points and three In-Crowd cards if you recognize all the names.

— Dec. 19, 1979

West coast beauty isn't half a continent away

Out of my mind up the west coast of Michigan . . .

I've been promising myself this trip for 12 years. A dozen years of looking at a map of the State of Michigan and wondering what that west coast along Lake Michigan is all about.

We slide off I-94 at St. Joseph-Benton Harbor and begin working our way north through Riverside, sort of a starting point on the south shore. It's like entering a foreign land, so removed from my Detroit mind-and-tempo set, yet so familiar.

South Haven, much bigger than I thought, but still not BIG big. Resorty and lovely, just like Saugatuck. Already I can tell it's going to be nice. Urban America seems a million miles away. One can feel the tension draining away.

Holland is just as Dutch as I imagined. Do all the names have double A's? Seems like it. Must come back here for a tulip-to-do. Love the name of the Warm Friend Motor Inn. Whole town seems like that — a warm friend.

Lunch at Point West, a lovely spot facing both Lake Michigan and Lake Macatawa. Its clam chowder is divine. Feel a little out of place in jeans. Fancy spot. Another place you'd like to spend more time to watch the boats tack and listen to the little old ladies at the next table talk.

To our left glimpses of Lake Michigan. To our right the loveliness of Ottawa County slides by in flash-frames of color made for framing as our western Michigan color tour shifts into high gear.

Grand Haven is aptly named. Work our way through Muskegon along Lake Muskegon into North Muskegon to pick up the scenic route, pulling over at all the scenic turnouts for an eyeful and a snapshot or two.

White Lake and Whitehall and Montague. What does the bumper sticker on that car say? "Never Re-Elect Anyone." Hmmm.

Silver Lake shimmers in the afternoon light as the two-lane highway begins to move up and down through hilly landscape and gets prettier with each mile as we approach Pentwater and Ludington. Reminds me of the Carolina Piedmont terrain.

Sunset at the beach in Ludington. Great picture with the lighthouse in the background. A mess of smelt at the Kuntry Kupboard and a good night's sleep before the next day's north shore leg of this excursion. Day 1, an enormous success. Whatever happened to Detroit?

Quite taken with the homes in Manistee. Would like to tarry longer and look some more some day. Seems like this section of the shore is just before buttoning up for a long winter.

Bowls of oatmeal at the Pepper Mill on Portage Lake at Onekama take the bite out of the fall's crisp air as we push on up the coast. Lynn's camera is busy recording the still beauty and the shouting reds and screaming yellows of the trees.

We know we're in Benzie County because to our left some hang-gliders are catching thermals above the famous Benzie bluffs — world-famous to hang-gliding buffs who know Elberta and Frankfort from above.

We feel we are in another world as we tunnel along 22 between Pilgrim and Crystal Strands as the trees meet overhead and the gold and green and red leaves of the changing trees allow a brilliant sun's rays to dapple the macadam, adding to that another world setting.

Stop for gas at Dave Taghon's service station in Empire. "Do yourself a favor," he says. "Take a couple minutes from your busy lives and drive down into Empire. Our own bluffs on one side, the Sleeping Bear Dune on the other." Great advice, Dave. Love to take a couple of days out of our busy lives and just sit there and soak in the sight.

Few lovelier spots in the world than the Sleeping Bear Sand Dune. God knew where to put the world's largest natural sand pile, didn't He? Someone has written in 25-foot letters, "I LUV-U," in one of the dunes. As we leave we are humming, "Don't change a hair for me, not if you care for me, stay, little Sleeping Bear Dune, stay just the way you are."

Glen Haven, Glen Arbor and Pyramid Point. Goodharbor Bay and Leland and the beauty of the Leelanau Peninsula unfolds before us and the mysterious Manitou Islands beckon from the distant left. Paradise found.

Down 22 from Northport and Grand Traverse Bay emerges on our left. Omena and Suttons Point and now our eyes are cameras for our memories. But we also snap off a roll of film in case the memory ever fails.

We arrive at our destination — Traverse City. What a state we live in, folks. What a state!

— Oct. 10, 1980

This is the time to love my city the most

My city was going through one of its changes, shifting seasonal gears — fall to winter.

You could taste it in streets. A taste of wet gray and metallic blue washed down with the crisp crackly to-the-bone pre-snow wind.

Better-bundle-up time. Well-it's-here time. The city turns its collar up and tries to remember where it left its gloves. Our cars grow snow tires and sprout ski racks.

You could feel it in the streets. Fall's goodby. Winterset nigh. The city's one big, steamy sigh, waiting for those emotional, economical and thermostatic signals to click it on.

Our collective wait is heavier this year. More to sigh about, I guess. More things making our heads shake than the coming cold.

You could sense it in the streets. Heavyweight worry. Major league concern. Mystery time. What's in store for us? What's going to happen? What is already happening and we don't even know it?

Is it too late? Can anything be done? Is anything being done? What can we do? What can I do? My city is probing its psyche, its soul, with a brow-lined intensity not seen in a while.

This is when I love my city the most, when many others love it least.

It's easy to love this place when it's looking good, when it's on a roll as it was before and during the Republican convention this summer, when the public's in a car-buying mood, or when one of our sports teams revs us up.

Tell me it wasn't exciting around here when Billy Sims and the Lions stepped off in the early season in championship form. We dreamed of a silver rush on a sea of blue but wound up with a drippy stadium, dippy traffic control and a team with a death wish, perhaps.

But we WERE pumped up for a while. Just like when the juices flowed as Lee Iacocca and the Chrysler bunch gave us the K-car and we felt competitive once again. And it sure felt good, didn't it?

And didn't we do well by and for the GOP and didn't the GOP do wonders for our spirit, our prestige? Hey, look at us, America, we are, after all, really something special, and we're glad you're getting to see and hear all about our positive side for a change. Preening's fun, isn't it?

It's easy to smile and puff with pride when these emotional bandwagons parade down our city's streets. Everyone knows it's easier to march in fair weather, not foul.

It's when you have to turn your collar up that counts. That's when our city needs our love the most. When the doom-peddlers and nay-sayers begin to leave their insidious calling cards on our conscience, inviting us to our own funeral.

That's when I love my city the best. When it struggles through doldrums and depressions. When it's on a knee for an eight count. When it slips easily into the underdog role.

My city is the classic, urban underdog. How's that line go? Been down so long, seems like up to me? We are a world-scale underdog. Oily religious wars and roboted assembly lines far away and outlandish interest rates and government regulations here are a hamstring of handicaps and obstacles to overcome.

My city wouldn't know how to act in the favorite's role. Can you imagine us spotting someone else points? We know coming from behind. It's rare when we get to sit on a lead. We are always racing the clock and the calendar.

It's a fast track — the fastest. A rested-on laurel turns quickly into a funeral wreath. A city can never live on yesterday's headlines because tomorrow's news is being written today.

A gusty, meaty, sinewy city. Tough, demanding — a hard-knuckle place. A raw-boned, calloused city — a counter-puncher. A city of grit and grease.

A battler when the bell rings. No glass jaw here. A stomach used to body blows and cramps. A heart used to aches. A back no stranger to a heavy load.

A contender, not a pretender. An honest-to-a-fault place. A city that never puts on airs or strikes a pose. A city that doesn't run, doesn't hide.

A city that makes no excuse, passes no buck. What you see is what you get. No more, no less. A city that knows you have to play the cards that are dealt and have the chips to back up all bets and raises.

It's a city I fell in love with 12 years ago, and the passion is still there, even if the romance has faded under reality's stern gaze. A city I identify with and a city that identifies with me.

How much do I like this place? I wish it were my hometown. Can you understand that? The fact that it isn't my hometown makes it even more special because it's a place adopted sons and daughters appreciate the most.

Natives may argue this, may express a deeper and more undying love for Detroit than those of us who weren't born here. But I ask you natives this: Of all the places in the world to live, did you and would you pick Detroit?

I did.

That's why I love Detroit the most when it's down, because I know it'll never be counted out. Black eyes and bloody nose, this old city — my city — is going to be standing at the final bell. I, for one, intend to be ringside.

— Dec. 10, 1980

Let's graze through the list of sacred cows

A front-page spread in a recent Sunday Boston Globe Living Section about that city's abundance of sacred cows got me to thinking about composing just such a list of Detroit's sacred cows.

I use Globe staffer Nathan Cobb's definition of sacred cow: "Any individual group or organization held in such popular esteem as to appear exempt from all, even justified, criticism."

The Globe broke it down into 24 current and living sacred cows, 10 dead 'uns, 10 up-and-coming "sacred calves," 10 sacred hopefuls-who-work-at-it-but-never-will-be, and 10 sitting ducks, about whom no one ever has anything nice to say.

Without getting into all the subcategories, I began my research on our own sacred cows. Who in this community is held in such esteem? Icons garnering such reverence not even justified criticism is hurled their way, even by media types trying to build a reputation.

Boston's Top 24 Sacred Cows included Julia Child, John Kenneth Galbraith, Carl Yastrzemski, Fenway Park, the 1941 Boston College Sugar Bowl team and Bill Rodgers. I wouldn't last a minute in Boston as I think Yaz is overrated, Child is an irritant, and I hate to say what I think about Fenway's cut-rate leftfield Green Monster.

My initial Detroit sacred cow list was short: Tiger broadcaster of 20 years, Hall-of-Fame-bound Ernie Harwell, everybody's favorite human being; the most lovable and revered ex-zoo director in the world, Robert (Doc) Willson and our marvelous jocks, Gordie Howe, Al Kaline and Dave Bing.

You don't last long around here knocking those folks. Are they the only ones? Free Press Managing Editor Neal Shine told me shortly after I arrived here 13 years ago that this paper had no sacred cows, including civic projects and friends of the paper's execs and owners. I had run into problems with this at another paper.

After hearing my short list of sacred cows and recalling what he told me, Detroit-born Shine agreed with my choices, but emphasized his previous position of no sacred cows.

"Doc Willson is a certified sacred cow, as you say, but if we found out he sold monkeys to Chinese restaurants we'd certainly nail him to the wall," says Shine, who would add Tiger Stadium and the United Fund to my sacred cow list. Consider 'em added.

Free Press Editor Joe Stroud, whose editorial page constantly draws and quarters the would-be and could-be-but sacred cows and cowards, also feels the Free Press is as free of sacred cows as any paper in the country.

Stroud's addition to the list were the tongue-in-media-chic Pontchartrain Wine Cellars and Polish weddings, reminding me of the punch-up and protest raised in this community several years ago when a Sunday Detroit magazine piece painted Polish weddings negatively. That episode proved that truth hurts, but not nearly as much as having to apologize for it.

Detroit's veteran sports columnist George Puscas warmed up to the sacred cow game in a hurry, as he has watched the herd change, come and go and grow bigger, sometimes, as the years go by.

Irascible George interjects some spice. "How about the biggest one going — Mark Fidrych!" snaps George, admitting that the Bird's in his last year as an instant sacred cow, a category we'll add.

Puscas nominates Bobby Layne (agreed) and George Kell (agreed) for the list, saying "Kell's sacred cow factor" may be higher even than Harwell's, which I will argue about till the sacred cows come home.

CKLW's Dick Purtan, who is almost one himself and makes a living milking sacred cows every morning and serving 'em up in funshakes, digs up a few dead ones for us, Van Patrick and George Pierrot. And add Jerry Cavanagh to the belated sacred cows category.

Tommy Hearns, Magic Johnson and Lily Tomlin are sacred calves, still in the celebrity feedlots. Takes time in the sacred cow business around here. Detroit also has some other sacred-cow idiosyncrasies.

Hudson's was until Dayton bought it. Cardinal Dearden was close till the current Poletown church-sale caper. Bob Lanier was until he got traded. The London Chop House is when Les Gruber is there, but is definitely not when he's not. How 'bout WJR radio, the '68 Tigers and U-M's sports program?

Fun subject. Who's on your list?

— March 5, 1981

Learning what's wacky will come easily

Should I introduce my weirdos, wastrels and wackos to Guindon? Every day is April Fool's Day to them.

Should I take him to some of my favorite places like Kooks' Corner, Loon Lane or Bozo Blvd.?

Picture these encounters:

Guindon meets Angelo the Philosopher at Lafayette Coney Island! Wouldn't that be a trip?

Guindon pogos with Coldcock at Bookie's! Funk meets punk. He may never recover. I still haven't.

Guindon discovers Blackjack Kelly at a City Council meeting! Can you imagine the field day Guindon is going to have in the City-County Building?

I'm a likely choice to introduce Guindon to his people for three reasons.

• One — I *always* understand Guindon, unlike our boss, Dave Lawrence Jr., who says he may sometimes need an explanation from the artist. But anyone who'll hire someone he doesn't understand half the time is a certifiable Guindon character. Half the time Guindon is just reading my mind.

• Two — I look like about three-fourths of the people Guindon draws, male and female, unfortunately. I act like the other fourth.

• Three — Bag ladies and one-man bands are my heroes.

Guindon really doesn't need me, of course. He seems to be right at home and already has a handle on what's funny around here.

He has skewed the alligator breasts of Grosse Pointe. He'll love the Pointes. To the rest of us anything said or mentioned or drawn about Grosse Pointe is funny. Pointe people think it's funny that we think they're funny.

Guindon immediately latched onto the fact that Channel 2 weatherman Sonny Eliot is funny. Sonny's name alone, like Zug Island, is a one-liner. He was when I arrived on these shores, another displaced person like Guindon, 13 years ago.

Guindon will discover that dour sportscaster Al Ackerman of Channel 4 is funny, but Channel 7 sportscaster Dave Diles, who really *is*, isn't. Channel 50's movie host Bill Kennedy is funny, but would never admit it, while Channel 7's talk host John Kelly, who has the most outrageous laugh in town, isn't.

Guindon will also discover that Channel 4's entire humorless newscast is funny, while Channel 7's and Channel 2's laugh-a-break casts aren't. Detroit's funny that way.

Guindon will discover his characters breed in our area's malls, or so it seems every stroll I take through them. And he'll find some malls like Somerset are funny, while Northland isn't.

Coney Islands are funny eating places, Big Boys aren't. Neighborhood bars are funny when the neighborhood isn't, but not funny when the neighborhood is. Without trying, CKLW's Dick Purtan is funny, but WNIC's Jim and Jer, who try too hard, aren't.

Mr. Belvedere is always funny, but not Ollie Fretter. The Lions and Tigers are funny, but jokes like the Wings and Pistons aren't. The Pontiac Silverdome is funny; Joe Louis Arena isn't. Olympia was.

Kennedy Square is funny; Hart Plaza isn't. Grand Circus Park is funny; Harmonie Park isn't. The Detroit River is funny; Lake St. Clair isn't. Woodward Avenue is funny; Grand River isn't. Eight Mile is funny; Telegraph isn't.

Antal Dorati and the DSO are funny, but Fred Cummings and the DIA aren't. Rocker Ted Nugent is funny; Bob Seger isn't. Pine Knob is funny; Meadow Brook isn't. Downtown Birmingham is funny; residential Birmingham isn't.

Bloomfield Hills is funny; West Bloomfield isn't. Dearborn is funny; Dearborn Heights isn't. Hamtramck is funny; Highland Park isn't. The Lodge Freeway is funny, but I-75 isn't.

Chrysler, which never has been, is funny, but Ford, which has been from its beginning, isn't. GM's bosses are; its workers aren't. Teamsters are funny; the UAW isn't.

Wayne State is funny; U-D isn't. MSU is funny; U-M isn't. Hazel Park Race Track is funny; the DRC isn't. Downriver is funny; western Wayne County isn't. Oakland County is funny; Macomb County isn't.

Neighboring Toledo is funny; across-the-river Windsor isn't. Cass Lake is funny; Orchard Lake isn't.

It won't take long for Guindon to discover all these things. Members of the Warp Patrol sort of naturally gravitate to them. I did. Welcome to our town, Richard Guindon.

— April 1, 1981

Out of my mind on a Monday moanin'

No one can give you street directions unless they use their hands.

The next woman you see talking to herself on the street will be carrying a paper bag.

All Ray Coniff albums sound alike and all Doris Day movies are the same.

Every time I hear "Moonlight in Vermont," "April in Paris" and "Chicago," I want to leave that very minute and go there.

Detroit's rock jocks all seem to have names made up of either two last names or two first names, but never a normal first and last.

You're no different from the rest of us: The first thing you do with a new telephone book is look up your own name.

Seems to me that the trouble with most politicians around here is that they have one-lane minds and six-lane egos.

The typical Detroiter is a graduate of a multiversity who lives in a megalopolis, works for a conglomerate, shops with the masses and still feels sort of lonely.

Can anybody really enjoy fishing alone, eating lunch at his desk, or waking up before the sunrises?

I always feel a little bit sorry for women who wear too much makeup and not enough clothes.

Honestly now: How many drum solos have you heard that you really cared enough about to applaud?

I don't care if I never dine in another little restaurant whose music is a radio tuned to an AM or FM station.

I never believe female politicians, entertainers or executives who tell interviewers that their husbands are the boss at home.

I've never seen a street-cleaner, floor-sweeper or dishwasher who seemed in a hurry to get his job finished.

Are you prepared to debate the subject of which is better: round or flat toothpicks?

Couples who have triplets and quadruplets always seem to live in one-bedroom homes and hardly seem able to afford one child.

How come nobody on television ever dials a busy signal, runs out of ice, turns on the hot water for cold, cuts his finger opening something, breaks a shoelace, or has trouble getting a package open?

PEOPLE

Rockwell's dilemma:
How to paint it like it is

Is homespun Americana dead?

Have the country's uptight anger and social problems killed it?

Will the corpse be put away in a plastic coffin, shrouded in vinyl and wash-and-wear, with a credit card picking up the tab?

As a nation of no-deposit, no-returns and dispose-alls everywhere, we are ironically disposing of some of the slices of Americana once held so dear to our hearts.

In a day when a pot isn't cooked in and grass isn't walked on, the old apple pie America is no more.

The man who knows this better than most is 75-year-old artist Norman Rockwell, himself a slice of Americana and a candidate for his own canvas.

Rockwell's search at the moment is for a glimpse of the "new" Americana, the scene that typifies a world in transition and turmoil.

A story about Rockwell's hopes of doing a painting "that would bring America back together" has brought hundreds of suggestions to the New England illustrator's home in Stockbridge, Mass.

"But none of them have hit that chord," Rockwell said as he prepared to leave the United States for a vacation in Denmark.

"I just hope that I can get away from things and sit and think about something I could draw which would really draw this nation together," he said. "It's the most challenging thing of my career."

That career began 53 years ago when he illustrated "something for a book of 'Tell Me Why' stories."

"For 47 years," says Rockwell, "I did Saturday Evening Post covers — over 300 of them — and they pictured the mood of the times we lived in.

"It is almost impossible to do this today because the disunity everywhere is so complete. You tell me: What is the typical American scene or mood?

"You can't draw a picture of 200 million people. Any picture you drew today would have to have something to do with the problems of race and campus and drugs and morals and all the other things churning us up.

"If I could create something like the 'Four Freedoms' I did during

World War II . . . it helped bring us together then and was certainly the most praised and most seen of my works."

Rockwell hesitates to call "Four Freedoms" his favorite work, much as he hesitates to name a favorite or unfavorite subject. "The next picture and subject will be my favorite," he says.

He calls himself an illustrator "who paints story-telling pictures. It's a form of artistic communication. It was a major form in the Renaissance. That's exactly the sort of work Raphael and Rembrandt did." Rembrandt is his favorite artist.

When Saturday Evening Post began to run Rockwell's freckled kids and mongrel pups, along with darling grandmoms and grandpops, his covers became collector's items.

So detailed, so lifelike, so warm and human, they seemed almost to speak.

Who can forget the great cafe dining room scene of the big truck drivers watching the little old lady and her grandchild giving thanks before they ate? Or his great Boy Scout calendar drawings?

With the death of the Saturday Evening Post, Rockwell switched to Look magazine, which gobbles up everything he will produce. He has finished a triple foldout section on Apollo 11, which features 25 men — astronauts, scientists, etc. — symbolic of the team linking men to the moon.

Rockwell has never drawn a nude for publication because no one has asked him and "because I'm 75 years old and sexy pictures aren't my thing."

He has done dramatic pictures about the racial situation in the country, and feels it is the major part "of the current scene. There is so much bitterness, misunderstanding and militancy today that finding the single theme and mood may be impossible.

"I asked to go to Vietnam, but Look said I was too old. Funny thing, though, I stay busy seven days a week. It takes me an average of four weeks a picture. I've worked as long as two months straight on one, and I once did a Post cover of Charles Lindbergh in less than a day."

His recent work with political figures has brought him much enjoyment, Rockwell says, but a few headaches. On a national television show he said Nixon's eyes were hard to paint and it came out in print as "Nixon has hard eyes." It has made the artist a little gun-shy about interviews. Of all the recent Presidents he has done, he says Eisenhower was "a cinch" and Johnson was the hardest.

His one big hope is that Norman Rockwell's America doesn't die.

It should also be America's biggest prayer, too.

— June 11, 1969

Facts, figures and trivia from a couple of wiseacres

If there's anything I hate more than a know-it-all, it's a wiseacre who always has the facts straight.

So picture my pique at meeting Norris and Ross McWhirter, the 43-year-old English twins who compile the famed Guinness Book of World Records and now the Dunlop Illustrated Encyclopedia of Facts for Doubleday.

They literally know everything there is to know and when they answer you in that bloody superior British accent you feel like a cotton-headed dum-dum.

Being a polite sort, I opened the conversation with my usual sparkling bon mot, "Whacha guys know?"

"Everything," they said in stereo.

They do. They do.

Since 1955, the McWhirters have been collecting the world's superlatives, facts, fancies, phenomenon, oddities and other trivia so that now their word is considered gospel for barroom arguments and other disagreements.

Nothing makes them madder than to have someone pose a question for which they have no immediate answer. Without referring to either of their books, they can rattle off heights, weights, ages, names, dates and places like two Limey computers stuffed with everything in and out of the British Museum.

What makes a conversation with them even more intriguing is that one of them will start a sentence and the other will finish it. You become a ping-pong earball, bouncing back and forth between them. The twins are extremely knowledgeable about twins, for example.

Norris: "The interesting thing about twins . . . "

Ross: " . . . is that the highest proportion of them . . .

Norris: " . . . occur in Belgium . . . "

Ross: " . . . while in the United States the . . . "

Norris: " . . . ratio is 1 in 18 births but . . . "

Ross: " . . . the country where twins are rarest . . . "

Norris: " . . . is Thailand because of a nasty habit . . . "

Ross: " . . . they had once upon a time of knocking them off . . . "

Norris: " . . . because twins were supposed to be bad luck."

The McWhirters point out that the United States seems to have the market cornered in "extremes," superlatives and records.

They also agree that the most perishable of records are sports and gastronomical marks. "Three or four swimming records fall every month," they say. "And we are always receiving word that someone has set a new record for eating and drinking something. But people may as well quit trying in the eating areas. Bozo Miller of San Francisco is undefeated in gastronomical contests since 1932. He eats and drinks anyone under any table. He's good for a snack of 400 ravioli, or a dozen spring chickens at a sitting."

The McWhirters say that sports records are the only ones from the Russians they tend to accept without great research into the verification. "Most of their national accomplishments and discoveries have been dismissed by most authorities," they say.

The McWhirters dismiss completely such record-keepers as circus advertisements and Ripley's Believe-It-Or-Not. "Ripley was so full of rubbish it's hard to believe that anyone could ever have believed him. Circuses never gave true figures of their freaks."

To compile and update their record and fact books, the McWhirters have established a worldwide network of "aficionados" and clipping services.

The most-asked question of all, they say with sly smiles, "is the one young girl's slap you for." They do say, seriously, that they are more often asked one of five things:

Tallest person — Robert Wadlow (1880-1940), born in Alton, Ill, died in Manistee, Mich. 8 feet 11 inches.

Oldest person — Pierre Joubert of Quebec, 113 years, 124 days at his death in 1814.

Fattest person — Robert Hughes of Fishhook, Ill., who weighed 1,069 pounds at his death in 1814.

Most births — Mrs. Vassilyev, a Russian peasant who had 69 children, including 16 sets of twins and never a single birth.

Smallest person — Pauline Masters, New York City, who was 23.6 inches when she died at the age of 19.

While most of their concern is of a humorous or trivia nature, the McWhirters show deep concern when asked what's the world's biggest problem. "Too many people," they say. "At the moment, the world's population given a square meter per person could all stand in one county in England. But the world increases by 60 million a year.

If the trend continues, the world has only 15 generations left before the human race breeds itself into overcrowded extinction. By 2600 A.D., there will be one person per square yard of habitable land surface."

And that, my friends, has to be the best reason I've heard of for us trying to get to the moon.

— June 13, 1969

It was a very good day after eight up-and-down years

The boat bent softly around Belle Isle's southern tip and headed into the sunset-washed Detroit skyline. Jerry Cavanagh forgot about the big city problems, the hassles, the critics, the hang-ups, the anger.

He was looking at a beautiful Detroit. His breath caught there between sigh and exclamation as the skyline swept by, rosy and warm in the river spray like a shimmering final scene from some movie.

It had been a good day. Happy people on the river to see brave men run the big boats. It had been almost a week since Jerry Cavanagh pulled out of the mayor's race. In that one move, Jerry Cavanagh had once again changed the course of the city, its people and himself.

He looked at the skyline — strengthened by handsome towers that weren't there when he took office eight years ago. The city he had given his indelible stamp. The city which in turn had branded and scarred him.

"It's been the eight greatest, most satisfying, most frustrating years of my life," Cavanagh said, leaning with the boat as it turned back up river. "Do I feel like crying? No. Not really. But I will miss it. More than I probably realize now."

It had been a good day with friends and companionship at the Manoogian Mansion. The people who came to see the race also came to see Cavanagh. "I think we're one of the attractions on the sightseeing tours every Sunday," he said, waving to people trying to catch a glimpse of their mayor.

Charm and charisma seem words made for describing Jerry Cavanagh. Critics and snipers would offer you a thousand other rawer phrases. It had not been nice the last few months.

But in that one move of withdrawing, everything changed. For the next week the people on the street went out of their way to say, "Hey, Jerry," and "Hi, Mayor." For some it was relief, sympathy, but others were glad to see a guy they like get out of the meat-grinder, the crunching, uncompromising thing that grabs cities and the individuals who try to govern the cities.

Even Cavanagh felt the relief. For a week, he had been looser, his wit wonderfully with him again. He could needle, without worrying. It had been his decision and now he planned to live with it in comfort.

In his eight years, Jerry Cavanagh brought a style to being mayor of a big city. He tried to change the city, and the city tried to change him. Both were successful.

For most cities and mayors, the relationship is a holding action: Keep your head above water and pray no one makes too many waves.

Jerry Cavanagh became adept, a damn good administrator of a billion-dollar corporation that would just as soon not be run by anyone and fights control every inch of the way. There may be tougher jobs, but you can bet their compensation is a hundred-fold more appealing.

No mayor of any city ever received more press. His every move, his every pound were duly recorded, raved over and roasted. Other phrases joined the charm-charisma list. One in particular, "presidential hopeful," had a heady, exhilarating ring to it.

Those who wanted to take credit for creating Cavanagh found him to be his own man and felt rejected. Those who saw Cavanagh becoming what they wanted to be, became jealous of this man who could move and change a city. Both groups became his bitter critics.

Cavanagh weathered the storms, the tempests, the tantrums. But even as he was changing the city, it was changing him.

A lot of people Jerry Cavanagh counted on, believed in, were somehow not around or available. The political animal reaches full maturity in eight years, he found. Cavanagh went from boy to man overnight.

There were crushing things outside of how to run a city. The assassination of Robert Kennedy is an example of the outside forces changing Jerry Cavanagh's life. This tore a nerve. Cavanagh had felt that in Bobby Kennedy, the nation had the one person to bring it all together — black and white, young and old, rich and poor.

The boat slowed as it neared the dock on the river and dusk was about to bring the good day to an end.

Jerry Cavanagh looked fondly at the skyline of the city he loved. Cavanagh, the mayor that every city in the country — except Detroit — wished it had.

Could it be that after eight years, the city has rejected its own heart?

— July 7, 1969

Superstar Gordie Howe also heads a super family

Every time I see Sonny Grandelius, he asks, "When are you going to write that Gordie Howe column?"

It has gotten to be a running joke between us for almost a year.

It started the week after Sonny and Marty Grandelius, Gordie and Colleen Howe, and Beryl and I had spent a relaxed, revealing evening together — one of those rare nights when the chemistries were right and the conversation was stimulating.

In the column-writing business, timing is very important. You don't want to write about the same subject everyone else is writing about. You don't want to overkill something or someone.

Every time I would plan to write the Howe column — things he had said that evening about his hockey life and personal philosophy — a major story would break, involving Gordie in some way. Gordie or Colleen or the kids.

There was his wrist operation. Then the shift from offense to defense. Then the super play of sons Marty and Mark with changes. All the trades. The Old-Timers game and the March of Dimes benefit which the whole Howe family — including young son Murray and only daughter Cathleen — took major parts. Now the current Howe retirement rumor.

Then it dawned on me. There is no right time to write about Gordie Howe because the Howe family is always in the limelight.

By tradition, the mayor of the community, his wife and children, are considered the First Family of any city. In Detroit, the Ford family — or families — often wear that title. This is a city where certain families have a way of dominating the social and business scenes.

But none of these families is accessible to you and me. None of these families represents the real Detroit personality, the true Detroit spirit and the honest Detroit image.

That's why, to me, the Gordie Howe family has been, is and will be the First Family of Detroit.

Detroit is not a flamboyant city, neither are the Howes.

Detroit is not a sophisticated city, neither are the Howes.

Detroit is not an egotistical city, neither are the Howes.

The Howes are plain, honest, respectful, mannerly, hardworking, appreciative, non-complaining, down-to-earth-and-ice, and thankful for everything they have received from the fans and community.

The family is a reflection of the father, naturally, but also goes Gordie one better in some areas. For example, Gordie is basically a shy, introversive person, while Colleen and the kids are outgoing and gregarious.

In times when the family unit is under such fire, it is remarkable to me that the Howe family is able to function with such ease and so smoothly. Just how much work they put into the March of Dimes benefit game which raised $30,000 will never be fully known. The Howes personally delivered large blocks of tickets to contributors all over the area.

The Howe family recognizes what Gordie Howe the hockey star means. They also know what Gordie Howe the father and Gordie Howe the husband mean, too. It is most difficult to be a member of a superstar's family.

But Gordie Howe has never known he was a superstar.

Gordie Howe is a person who would have admired a Gordie Howe. Think about that for a minute. Too many of your superstars have little or no feeling about other stars. Most barely acknowledge that other stars exist. They live in a supreme "I-me" world. Superstars are the world's worst fans.

Not Gordie Howe. He's a super-fan. I don't even know if Gordie has ever given much consideration to what an ego is. But Gordie Howe has his own heroes. How many other heroes admit to having heroes, past and present? Very few.

There's a lot of love and respect in the Howe family. Love and respect equate to a pride that's probably the secret to the Howe family success.

The Howes — from top to bottom — have never known failure. Sure, there have been defeats, losses, broken bones, painful injuries, but no failures. Not if a Howe has anything to do with it.

The Howe brand is the mark of excellence. The Howe name is a symbol of integrity. The Howe family is worthy of our praise and admiration. Of all Gordie Howe's achievements, his family is his finest.

— March 3, 1971

A TV era comes to an end: Thank you, Ed Sullivan

I think it's a cruel and dirty shame the way CBS-TV is treating Ed Sullivan. What they're doing to Ed, they're doing to me. Ed's my pal. I've spent more Sundays with him than I have preachers. You probably have, too.

CBS (Cold Business Sense) is not even going to tell us when Ed's last show will be. They don't seem to care that for 23 years he has been television for a lot of us. He has been the Met, Churchill Downs, Yankee Stadium and La Scala of videoland.

Being on the Ed Sullivan Show meant more to entertainers than CBS-TV ever really knew, it seems now. And more to us at home. I'm sure the network can give me rating facts, demographic figures, and cost-per-viewer statistics to prove that dropping Sullivan was the only thing it could possibly do in these video-type-tightening times.

I'll admit that I haven't watched Ed's Sunday night show very much in the past couple of years. The same guests he has I've been catching on the late-night talk shows or some of the other variety shows like Dean Martin's or Flip Wilson's.

I'm not sure what or even if I'm watching at 8 p.m. on Sunday nights, but it hasn't been Ed. I watched him this past Sunday and you know, that frozen-faced rascal hasn't changed a lock. Same dyed hair. Same words. Same sameness.

Maybe that's what CBS has been finding out too much lately, particularly on the profit line. The TV fan has two characteristics: a fierce loyalty and fickle heart. If you can figure 'em out, you can make yourself a cool one mil a year with no trouble, pal.

But there was ol' Ed, jerking around the stage, holding himself, heel-walking and acting sort of like a guy who needs to go to the bathroom. I think that's why I've always loved him. He's terrible. But so bad you feel for him. You're glad he's no better. If he were better, you wouldn't believe it when he tells you Rupert's Dancing Bears are the absolute most brilliant act "we've ever had right here on our stage."

He' has given me some of the greatest moments I've ever seen, TV or otherwise. I really saw the Beatles for the first time on Sullivan. And remember the Elvis Presley waist-up show? Any man who can give you Albert Schweitzer playing the organ on one hand and Jayne Mansfield playing the violin on the other has got to be a person you love.

I could identify with Sullivan because I always figured that's the way most of us would act if we were told we'd host a TV show in six minutes. We'd stumble through it. When Ed would try to cut up or kid around or take part in some tumbling act it was always the exact way my old man used to look when he was out of his element. But Dad was game and he tried and I loved him for it. It's the same with Sullivan.

I got my first dose of culture from Ed Sullivan, and I bet you did, too. I'm still not an opera buff, but I dug Jan Peerce and Roberta Peters every time they were on Sullivan, which seemed like every other week. But I'll admit I used to get the feeling every aria was "Un bel di vedremo," every ballet was "Swan Lake" and every dramatic reading was from the Bible.

But Ed tucked all that in between Flying Chimps on the stage and war heroes and sports stars sitting in the audience, plus film clips of movies I'd heard about being made. And sometimes one of these super-names would walk out and stand by Ed, who never seemed to know what to ask them. But I wouldn't have, either. You could tell Ed was really impressed by these greats and so was I. That's the point. Ed Sullivan really believed in the Ed Sullivan Show.

Ed also endeared himself to me over the years by goofing up, fluffing lines and malapropping all over the place. I think I knew for sure he was my man when he got all carried away once with his hosting-cheerleading and pleaded for applause by shouting "Let's HEAR it for the Lord's Prayer!" That was beautiful.

Ed made me appreciate juggling and balancing acts and water-skiing elephants (did you catch THAT really big shoe?)

I think the thing that bothers me the most about CBS-TV's coldness in this whole matter is the finality in which they are writing off 23 years of Americana — the 23 years in which I've grown up. I was 11 years old, that most impressionable age, when Sullivan began. He has been as big an influence on my tastes, my sense of talent, my judgment of culture and entertainment as any 10 other people.

Without fanfare, without tribute, CBS-TV is bringing down a

curtain on some of the best years of my life and the man who helped bring them to me. I'd at least like to thank Ed Sullivan. I bet you would, too.

— April 2, 1971

No one gives the words better than Frank Sinatra

You came and did it our way and we talked about you and us for a long time after. But you knew, Frank, that's exactly what we'd be doing.

Frank Sinatra's in town and you check out your memories.

For some it's a total review of the past — good and bad.

Fellow said, "Every middle-aged man in the world owes Frank one. A bundle, baby. I'd still be a virgin if it weren't for his records. One of his was always fifth. By the time I got the fifth record, we were flying to the moon. Started out with a bolero, then went to a . . . "

We all had our dreams, Frank. Couple folks even had a nightmare or two.

And all this time we've wanted to pay you back. You've been there a lot of times when we've needed you — your music and your image. Sometimes, pal, we've even gotten off on your good times and the bad ones, too.

We've had this vicarious thing with you. And cause you've been there with us — you were singing 'em in our ears, weren't you? — we figured you had a thing about us, too.

But how could we ever communicate this?

We're not in Palm Springs much.

When we were in Vegas, you weren't.

And you knew, Frank, that we wanted somehow to pay you back for all the good times you've brought us and shared with us and have been part of in our lives.

So you knew you would have to come back on the road just one more time — once! — as Mister Count Basie would say. Come back because the only way we could pay you back would be a little love feast, and you did this tour to let us.

Baby, it's good for all our egos. We like to know that we had whatever it took — money, influence, clout, etc. — to be there. And Frank, you had to have been flying while you were on that stage.

If you had just been doing it for the bread, we wouldn't have sold it out. You did it for us and for some of your favorite touches. We like that.

You did something I didn't think possible. You sold the Olympia clean, a record 17,500.

A 58-year-old grandfather-to-be does what rock stars Elton John and Neil Diamond do. It's not just amazing — it's unreal.

No one else in the world, Frank, could have gotten this crowd to come downtown to anything. They could have been giving away $10 bills and half this crowd wouldn't have bothered to drive across the street to get one.

But you got 'em here with no sweat. I heard one fellow offer an attendant $25 for a parking place. He didn't want to miss a thing.

Were they all shooters? No, but they all would like to be. There were no long-hairs and almost no blacks. Few of the rock-and-roll generation were there.

This is the lyric generation. The energy of the music isn't important. Our ears needed words, not vibrations.

And no one, Frank, gives those words better than you.

For the first time, I really understood some of those words I've been hearing you sing all my life. I think maybe it's because you're really understanding them yourself for the first time as you're mellowing into your legend.

The only other dude who can put this many fan-lovers into a place is Elvis Presley, but his is a crowd that would come down to get one of those free $10s. That's the difference.

But, Frank, you and Elvis share another thing. You're the only two superstars who are singing the songs other people write. But those people are writing 'em for you — Paul Anka wrote "My Way"and Jimmy Van Heusen even wrote "Nancy with the Laughing Face" for your daughter.

Today's superstars sing their own songs. It's some sort of honesty trip the kids demand of their heroes. I don't know if I buy that and I don't even think the artists buy it, either, but they DO make more royalty-writing-publishing money if they do their own songs.

When I say you did it our way, Frank, I mean you did it with class. Smooth. Clean. No hitches. You left New York City around 7 p.m., got here and did your 52 minutes of rhapsody on our nervous and love systems, were back in the air before most of us had gotten to our cars in the parking lot and you were eating a steak with your pals at your suite in the Waldorf before midnight.

Took less time than a nap. Yet you gave us all part of a lifetime once again. Each song was a trigger. Each motion you made was a smile for us. We'll sort out those memories for a long time.

You did it all alone, standing out there with no huge banks of equipment nor amps nor backup people. Just you, a mike, a great orchestra, the best of sound systems and — oh, yes, — us!

We had worried about how you would look and sound.

We shouldn't have worried. You aren't worrying about those things, and that made us more comfortable. Thirty minutes into your show, almost 30 of my years had passed by. Like everyone else, a couple of times I felt you were looking right at me. We've been through it together, Frank, and we've survived this far. You're saying to us, "I'm doing OK, how about you?" OK, too, Frank, OK. And thanks a lot. We're even.

— April 23, 1974

Van Patrick, a dream maker who painted hero pictures

The Dream Maker is dead.

And a part of me died with him.

Van Patrick painted hero pictures I will never forget.

He had a magic mouth.

He wove my boyhood dreams together.

Van and the rest of the Dream Makers.

Voices like Harry Wismer and Ted Husing and Red Barber and Bill Stern.

They gave me my heroes in wonderful locations. The giant arenas of physical combat. The stadiums and the square gardens.

Van made 'em 10 feet tall, seemingly able to leap buildings with a bound.

Growing up, I didn't dream of just scoring the winning touchdowns or striking out the side.

I dreamed of Van Patrick describing it from coast to coast. I dreamed of those great Dream Makers making my dream come true.

When the TV announcer broke in during the Lions-Packers game to tell us that Van Patrick had died Sunday afternoon in South Bend, I turned off the TV sound and turned on WJR radio.

I used to do this before the game, but lately it had been tough to listen to my friend who was dying. No one wanted to say that, but he was dying. You could hear it.

So I hadn't been listening to Van's radio broadcast. It hurt too much. Hurt when he wasn't on the broadcast and you wondered how bad he was suffering somewhere.

Sunday I could hear Bob Reynolds weeping inside. We all were.

It was a strange day. George Cantor, who grew up with this Dream Maker, too, extended the sadness by noting that Patrick's death, coupled with Al Kaline's announced retirement, brought an era to an end.

A pre-TV era. An era where the Dream Makers talked ball games to us. They made us feel and smell and taste the excitement. They made us become part of the thing they were part of.

They also make it official.

The Dream Makers gave sports to the world. Eventually it will be recorded that they made sports what it is today. Without them our dreams had no flesh, no blood, no crunch.

Sure, the Dream Makers exaggerated. But for the moment the winning home run did, indeed, set the world straight. There was total joy in Mudville. Nothing else seemed to matter except whatever they — the Dream Makers — said next. They sealed the victory. They ennobled the feat. They made it all 10 feet tall.

I would get angry when I first came to town and heard our sophisticated journalists and broadcasters make fun of Van and Van's style. Man, they were making fun of me.

I guess meeting Van Patrick caused me as much pre-meeting excitement as anything I had experienced.I came out of a jock background, having played ball and then spent the beginning of my career writing about sports.

Van Patrick was as much a hero to me as the heroes he had told me about over the years. He lived up to my imagination and went beyond that.

Van Patrick was human, very human . . . Joe Falls said it so well Monday. Joe wrote: "As time passed, I found that he was a generous man. He would give you anything, do anything for you. He needed love. He had to be loved."

I had felt the same thing the first time I met the Dream Maker. What was mistaken for an enormous ego was an insecure overcompensation. There was his constant need to know he was a champion.

"The Ole Announcer" was what he liked to be called. It gave him the ultimate status. It was better than calling him the Dean of

Sportscasters. It was better than calling him No. 1.

Van Patrick, the Dream Maker, lived out his own dreams. His world centered around Van Patrick, coast to coast. And sometimes the reality of it bothered him deeply.

"That's right, Van" was the way we all talked when we were around him. He had a way of making this happen as he broadcast his life and feelings about everything. I think he wondered if we really meant it. I know he always wondered if we loved him.

We did, Van, we really did.

— Oct. 1, 1974

Bertha Gordy gave her all to make the most out of life

She'd been "Mama" to a lot of the boys.

Bertha Ida Gordy — a Detroit institution who gave birth to a legend.

So it was sort of natural that some of the Motown boys like the Temptations and David Ruffin were a little tense as they waited in a holding room at the Bethel Afro Methodist Episcopal Church on a snowy Wednesday in Detroit.

Bertha Ida Gordy was 75.

As a street wise and socially attuned observer said as he looked around at the heavyweights from the black community attending the funeral: "She was a S-T-R-O-N-G woman. She was as heavy as any of these people here. They loved her and respected her."

That's why the Tempts were nervous. They almost couldn't get in because of weather-fouled airports.

But they made it with few moments to spare so they could sing "The Lord's Prayer" at Big Sister Sunshine's funeral.

When they were through basso profundo, Melvin Franklin said, "Man, it was warm in there and quiet. I mean quiet."

Later, David Ruffin echoed this after he concluded "The Impossible Dream." There was great dignity connected with the funeral as there was great dignity connected with Bertha Ida Gordy's life.

Some who didn't know this lady could say, "Sure, it was easy for her to be a leader, a political power because of her son's enormous influence as head of Motown Records. Having Berry Gordy Jr. as a son is pretty good clout."

But they didn't know Bertha Ida Gordy.

In her own right she had might.

She had the ability to lead and she had the wisdom to follow when it was necessary. She knew the streets, but she also knew the churches. She knew the problems of being black in a white-oriented society, but she also knew the true beauty of being black and proud.

She lived a full, rich life that brought her great rewards and great honors. Just this past December she won the Spirit of Detroit Award.

But the white community didn't know about this lady, because she did her work in the black community. She didn't move in that part of the community where blacks and whites meet together, rap together and then go back to their respective groups and talk about co-operation.

That part of the community deals in words mainly. Bertha Ida Gordy dealt in deeds. She was a mover who made the black world, the black community work. She asked blacks to help blacks.

Bertha Ida Gordy didn't play games with her blackness and this was a valuable lesson she passed on to her children, relatives and friends. "We can do anything anyone else can do if we'll only just do it," was a credo she observed.

At her funeral Wednesday, the Rev. Jesse Jackson, the charismatic founder and organizer of Operation PUSH, said it all. In part, he said:

"Death is a natural thing to Christians. They do not see it as final. They do not see it as a period, but a comma. Death is certain, life is by chance.

"We do not determine who will be our parents, we cannot determine our race, our sex nor where we will be born — an extremity of life. We can seldom determine death dates, when or how.

"Thus, we cannot be judged by our birth dates, our race or our sex. Rather it is how we live life between the two extremities.

"We will see some tombstones today and on every one we will see a birth date and a death date. Most of us will concentrate our sight on these two dates.

"I'm here to tell you there is a dash in between! We cannot make a decision on those two numbers, but on that dash. There is something suggestive about that dash, because on tombstones it's always a straight line.

"But in life it's on that dash we know the mountains high and the valleys low and every day is not a day of sunshine but nights and years and days of hell.

"But we are measured by our ability to function on that dash. On that dash came forth from this life new hope and new possibilities. From that dash comes an inspiration for others."

Life is a dash. A sprint, really.

Looking back can only slow you down. Looking too soon toward the finish line can fool you. But putting your all into your own dash is what the human race is all about. It was what Bertha Ida Gordy was all about.

— Feb. 7, 1975

Rocky Colavito looked like a major leaguer

It has taken me a good hour to get this column started.

My body has been locked in front of my typewriter but my mind has been drifting back to a summer 25 years ago when I guess I was just about the most excited 13-year-old in the world.

My world at that time, you must remember, was the small Southern textile town of Spartanburg, S.C.

R.E. Littlejohn had asked my dad if "little Bobby would like to be the batboy for the Spartanburg Peaches."

Do you have any idea what this meant?

While the rest of my friends would be picking peaches for a summer job, I was going to be the batboy for the hometown Class B Tri-State Peaches.

Excited? For the only time in my post-diaper life, I wet my pants. And I've never told anyone this before. But I got so excited when they introduced the teams for opening night, I just couldn't control myself.

I just hoped everyone thought I was sweating, but just in case they didn't, I kept holding a pair of big Louisville Sluggers in front of me all night.

Funny how that comes back to me after all these years.

I had three great summers as batboy for the farm club of the Cleveland Indians. By the time my third season rolled around I was a seasoned veteran and even showered with the players. The first two seasons I was too embarrassed.

The reason all this has come up was a lunch I had the other day with Rocky Colavito, who was in town to film some television commercials for his old pal, Eddie Robinson of Star Furniture and a loving godfather to more than a few professional athletes who have drifted through Detroit at one time or the other.

The first thing I said to the Rock was "Ann and Betty Jo Cannon."

Colavito nearly fell out of his chair. "Spartanburg, summer of '52! Right?" Absolutely right.

The Cannon sisters were without question the choicest of the choice when it came to high school beauties. They were head-turners and mind-warpers and Rocky was the Peach of their beautiful blue eyes.

The Rock came to Spartanburg in mid-season for a little more seasoning. When the handsome slugger hit Spartanburg, the girls went gah-gah. I can't quite say the same for the Tri-State pitchers, who managed to hold the Rock to only 11 home runs and 55 RBIs in 66 games.

Rock was only 18, just three years older than me, but he was a professional baseball player and it made him seem older. But the minute Rock stepped into the batter's box you could tell he was a major leaguer.

You could always tell. The minor leagues were filled with hundreds of players who had reached their levels, but only a handful who were leap-frogging up the line. They had that look in their eyes, plus a certain energy reserve stars seem to have.

"You could look around any of the leagues," Rocky recalls, "and know which players would make it and which wouldn't, but it's a different ball game today."

This was in the early '50s before television exploded the sports world into a super-business where players almost have to start out as stars.

Back then, baseball was still the singular route to stardom for most young athletes. Rock was no different and knew from his New York sandlot days that he was in baseball for good. Momentarily out of baseball and tending to his in-laws' mushroom business in Pennsylvania, Rocky will eventually be back in baseball, hopefully as a colorcaster in the TV booth — something he likes and does well.

Looking at it today, the Rock says a young athlete picks his sport from a business angle first. "Baseball and football players are stars today before they ever set foot in the big leagues. They become national names while in college. Financially, some of these players are set for life before they ever play their first game.

"But what notoriety does a college baseball player get? How many can you name? When's the last time Sports Illustrated had one on its cover?

"It's no wonder the premier athletes in high school today go into basketball and football. It's only in baseball that you become a star after you prove yourself in the big leagues. That's one of the things that still makes it an exciting game for me."

And for me, too. And it is one of the reaons I'm really getting excited about the season opening next Tuesday. Not quite as excited as 25 years ago, but excited for a lot of young Tiger superstars-to-be.

— April 4, 1975

J.P. McCarthy makes it a new day every morning

Quite frankly, I was shocked. I didn't want to quit doing J.P. McCarthy's "Morning Music Hall" on WJR radio Wednesday. The little hand was moving up toward 10 and I wanted to lean over to Hal Youngblood and say, "Tell Jimmy Launce, Marc Avery, Warren Pierce, Karl Haas, Mike Whorf, Gene Elzy, Fat Bob Taylor, Jay Roberts and the rest to take the day off. I'm just getting started. I'll do the whole day and night for you."

But Youngblood has been around this neophyte's first-ride trip before and he was reading my mind. He's also the best I've ever seen at reading what's on your mind. You don't even have to ask questions around him. Producers have those powers.

Youngblood is the best. Everything about that place reeks of the best and I guess this is why — with a giant-size lock on the audience and a jam-packed lineup of advertisers, plus awards and honors like you wouldn't believe — WJR can call itself, without fear of contradiction, "America's great radio station."

I've been in a few radio stations in my time. Rather, I just thought I had. But it all changes when you look out from high atop — and it really is high — the Fisher Building and know that you have 50,000 clear-channel watts pumping out what you are saying. You begin to float.

Honest. It's like a dream. All of these pros — Jack Hood, Frank

Beckman, Bill Nordstrom, Jim Garrett, Gene Healy, Tom Camp-
bell, John McMurray and Dave White — doing all those things that
have to be done. News, weather, sports, breaks, commercials, etc.

And mind-reader Youngblood. These people could do a "Morning Music Hall" show with an Airedale barking out the musical
intros and telling you the time and such. I mean, they are that good.

But the man they are revolving around most of the time, J.P.
McCarthy, is the glue, the force and the energy that makes this one
of the most successful radio shows ever on the air.

American Indians were so right about so many things, but they
were never so right as when they said that to know another man you
have to walk a mile in his moccasins. I've known J.P. McCarthy since
the day I arrived in Detroit. I've known him on the radio and off.

We've shared a few times, stories and opinions. But now I can
share one more thing with him, and respect him even more. I had a
healthy amount of that before because I respect figures like ratings
and salaries. And above all, I respect professionalism.

Joe's a pro's pro. He doesn't even know how hard it is to do what
he does every morning. Because this "Morning Music Hall" is him.
All these people circling around doing their things so well and so
easily because of J.P. and a format he never quite got around to
establishing.

It was a new day for me Wednesday. Was it ever! Who wouldn't
jump at a chance to sit there in that high perch and talk to all those
people? A totally new experience. For one day, I'm sure it would be
new to all of you.

But J.P. McCarthy makes a new day of it every morning, whether
or not he, the news events, the listeners, the callers, the staff or the
engineers care if it's a new day. That's one of J.P.'s secrets.

Wait a minute. That's wrong. There are no secrets to J.P.'s and
WJR's success. All you have to do is listen. But if you and I tried to
do what they do in the morning we'd fall right on our ARBs.

J.P. McCarthy has no secrets, just enthusiasm and respect for
what he does. These are the handmaidens of success for anyone I've
ever met who attains it in the abundance of a J.P. McCarthy. They
have an enthusiasm for what they are doing that is contagious to all
those around them and all those who are affected by them. And they
respect this control they have over these people.

They never abuse their audience. I'm afraid I probably would
have a tendency to let all of that instant communication run away
with me. I was again shocked at what a jolt of power it was sitting

there, much different from the print side of the communication business.

I can stop and pause here and try to get it right before I write the next sentence. I control it. But on the radio it's different. Nothing controls it. It just keeps rolling on like some monstrous, legendary surfer's ninth wave.

That's the very power you feel. This show keeps rolling and the J.P. McCarthys of the world can gracefully keep their board right on the crest of this huge shelf of water, dipping in and out, but always emerging ahead of everyone as they give that ol' wave the ride of its life.

But you have to ride over things. You can't worry that this caller was cut off and that break was missed. You tighten up the toes and loosen the tonsils and skim right along.

One drawback about this job is that you have to do it right there, not that a regular gig in studios like WJR's wouldn't be good duty. But every morning at 6:15 you have to be there and do your thing. Personally, I'd rather roll over, close one eye and listen to J.P. Hurry back.

— *May 7, 1976*

With Zero's memory, I don't dare cross him up

When Zero Mostel puts on his fierce face and his angry words rumble up out of his baritone to the end of his stubby, pointed finger, you listen and you obey.

"Bob Talbert, if you write about this place while I'm still in town with 'Fiddler,' I will personally strangle you with both these hands!"

It took great restraint. If a columnist sees a celebrity's performance and likes it, the writer wants the performer to read about it. Columnists who deny this are lying through their press cards. Some writers even take particular delight in hoping performers get to see the reviewer or columnist pan them. There are jerks in every trade.

I wanted to write it while he was here so I could tie in the fact that I thought his Tevye in "Fiddler on the Roof" that just finished a record run at the Fisher was an international performance and so good I wanted to hug him all night long.

But what does he care what anyone writes about him? He has

done the role some 1,200 times by now and he ought to have it down. He knows he does it perfectly because Zero Mostel is painfully honest with any and every one, including himself.

This isn't a story about how well he can sing a song that has made him become the rich man he asks to be. After a nice lunch at Topinka's on the Boulevard — and it was a pleasant and wonderful surprise to see former owner Ken Nicholson stroll in and join us — Joe Nederlander suggested I'd like to tag along with Zero, who was looking for a certain valuable painting at a good price. Anyway, the painting wasn't where it was supposed to be and time was running out.

Zero looks at me and says, "Why don't we go to the Claes bookstore?" Joe and I got these blank looks on our face. Joe's lived here all his life. I'm supposed to be one of the know-where-it-all-is-ers around here. "The what?" we said.

Zero played Detroit in 1946 and remembered being taken there. "A great place," he said. "Filled with great and sometimes rare book finds." Thirty years ago and he expects it to be there. It's probably torn down and is a parking lot or freeway.

Zero, laying a finger aside his nose, thought a moment. "It's on something like Eleventh and Leverette," he recalled a 30-year-old address. We checked the Yellow Pages and sure enough the B.C. Claes Book Shop is located (since (1932) at 1670 Leverette at Eleventh, just south of Michigan. Book collectors never forget.

We pulled up to this clean old two-story house with a simple sign saying "BOOKS" in the window. When we went inside, my, what a wonderful new world Zero Mostel turned Joe and me on to — and we live here. Hilda Claes, old as half the books at least, and her daughter, Ethel, needless to say, were a little overwhelmed by these two bear-like creatures — Zero and me — and this handsome, short fellow grabbing every book they saw.

We must have spent a couple hundred dollars in there. I went cra-zy over their copies of old National Geographics and the American Heritage history series. Joe bought a set of 16 books on how to be a better speechmaker. I thought it was just brother Robert who was in politics.

It was impulse-buying time. Rare, old, out-of-print books. And Zero is a first-edition freak about a few authors, some of which he found "at literal steals," he whispered.

That's the reason Zero made me promise not to write about the place, which is ceiling to floor, wall-to-wall, desk-to-desk and shelf-to-shelf books, until he had left town. He planned to return several more times and didn't want you beating him to any first editions.

As we were leaving, he did a wonderful thing. He and Joe arranged for the two ladies to be chauffeured to the Saturday matinee of "Fiddler." That was so nice.

But it was Zero's amazing memory that got me. Not only had he remembered a bookstore from 30 years ago, he did something else that absolutely floored me. With my accent, he naturally asked where I was from. With his,I should have asked the same, but forgot. I said Spartanburg, S.C.

"I was in the Army there in World War II. We did shows," he said.

"Sure," I said. "I used to go to war bond drives out at Camp Croft all the time . . . "

Zero interrupted with "1943. Some girl singers. Movie stars. A wrestling match . . . "

I added, " . . . between Man Mountain Dean and Cowboy Lutrell."

Zero's face beamed as if God had made him a rich man and said, "Exactly. Remember the number with the comic who fell into the drum?"

"Sure," I said. "How could I forget? Stole the whole show. They laughed for 10 minutes."

"I was that comic," Zero smiled again.

So that's why I waited until now to write this. With a memory like that he'd strangle me for sure the next time we see each other.

— Nov. 9, 1976

Mark (The Bird) Fidrych is the new American hero

It all started last summer and we didn't even notice. Maybe you could call it the renaissance of the great American hero.

He died, you know. Oh, yes. Back there in the late '60s and early '70s the old-fashioned American hero just keeled over dead from overexposure on television and an overdose of bucks. A victim of superstaritis.

Superstars replaced heroes. But you spelled it $uper$tar$. TV became the big dealer of this dollar drug and various marketers and agencies became the pushers, along with personal agents, worst of the lot. Endorsements. Just give us your name and your mug on camera.

No longer could the crew cut in a white hat mount a charger. Too many hair styles, too many types of hats and the chargers themselves like Secretariat became $uper$tar$.

America has been re-examining what it wants from a hero. I think it started when Joe DiMaggio started selling coffee makers. Say it ain't so, Joe, many of us said who grew up with Joltin' Joe as our untarnished hero. A fellow who still loved another great American hero — a tragic one — the late Marilyn Monroe, once his wife.

We went through and are coming out of that period when we liked our heroes a bit tarnished — the Denny McLains and the Joe Namaths — or what some sports journalists described as honest reporting. But those heroes of yesteryear such as the Bobby Laynes and Babe Ruths and Ty Cobbs weren't goody two-shoes.

Even our political heroes died, not from assassin's bullets but from their own tapes and indiscretions and strange bedmates. Musical heroes were expected to have wild orgies and espouse radical causes.

There was a glorification of the punk in both films and in a new hype for music. The punk is dying and may even be dead. But it takes America a long time to plant the corpse.

O.J. Simpson had to become a $uper$tar before he could become the hero most American boys said they looked up to in a poll that had Farrah Fawcett-Majors as the girls' top pick. But I'm afraid Farrah is far from the sex symbol hero of a Marilyn Monroe.

The new American hero and model for heroes to come is growing right here in our own backyard, Mark (The Bird) Fidrych. Perhaps our refocusing on new heroes began with those young foreign gymnasts who astonished us with perfection. Maybe it helped us appreciate perfection of talent once more.

Then along came last summer and Jimmy Carter went from Jimmy Who? to President Carter and he still maintains a high personal popularity with his seeming openness and frankness. If he gets this country going again and doesn't try to be a hero, he may well become one.

But not in the John Kennedy crowd-jumping sense. Carter is becoming a new kind of political hero even as the Bird is carving out a new kind of hero for sports heroes of the future. No longer is the question, "Is he for real?" It is now, "Long may he fly!" And he will.

The Bird is the genuine article. A talent and a temperament in perfect synch. And unique in an uncontrived and unmarketed manner. He came to us a perfect stranger last summer and became a part of this nation's tapestries. They know him all over.

Mention Detroit and they'll mention the Bird, no matter where you travel in this country, and, I'm now told, abroad, too. Sorry, Marvin and Smokey and Diana and all you Motowners they used to mention. And no longer do they say, "Detroit? Murder City" or something equally as damaging and wrong.

Detroit. The Bird. Even the controversial RenCen takes second place to this curly-locked young man who has locks on the strike zone. Whatever it is that gives him his control, let's not tamper with it. Let's hope his national agency and representatives let him tend to his business, which has ignited this nation with his talent and do-it-in-unique ways.

He is not a flaky phenom, but a phenomenal talent — perhaps a little flaky around the edges, but who isn't these days? — and someone who won't be changed by his success and fame.

The Bird's appeal crosses all social, racial, age and economic boundaries. In a world of phonies a real person has arrived. It's what some folks have said about California Gov. Jerry Brown, who has to prove himself. It's what the Georgia Cracker Corps in the White House would have us believe about President Carter, and most of us still do, but are waiting for less soft talk and more use of that big stick. Hope he senses this.

When the Bird's at home and is ahead in the top of the ninth every Tiger in the place is 10 feet tall and playing that much over normal capacity, and the fans are going absolutely starkers. A crazed goodness. A delirious insanity takes over the ball park.

It's the Bird's favorite moment in the world. For my money and a lot of baseball experts' money they compare the Bird to former Yankee pitcher Whitey Ford in this situation, maybe even better. Those crowds' roars and chants pump up the Bird, and he bears down in the top of the ninth like no one else in the game. He loves it.

The crowd knows it, and it is one of those experiences we all must share — being in the presence of a hero doing his or her thing. Not your $uper$tar$. But your authentic new American hero like Mark (The Bird) Fidrych, who doesn't even realize he is only just beginning and is only just THE beginning of a whole new era of unaffected heroes.

— July 9, 1977

Elvis Presley's death
helped some of us grow up

Memphis was less than four hours away and we were tempted. We had just been through one of the natural wonders of the world — Mammoth Cave. The newspaper racks outside our Bowling Green, Ky., motel tolled in gigantic type the death knell of another natural wonder — Elvis Presley.

South on I-65 to Nashville, pick up I-40 to Graceland and we'd be there with thousands of others. You could already see the start of the pilgrimage. Fellow at a service station said he couldn't remember when he had seen so much out-of-state business.

"Ever'body's heading fo' Memphis, I guessh," he sighed. "Yawl going?" Lynn and I looked at each other. "Maybe," I said, signing the gas ticket. We were tempted until we turned on the radio and heard the beginning of the overkill.

We tried over 20 stations. All Elvis. Some doing live broadcasts from Graceland. All playing the golden hits Elvis used to turn out with the regularity of a well-oiled and perfectly programmed computer.

I turned north on I-65 and headed for the beautiful Cumberland Parkway and on into the heart of Kentucky's famed Bluegrass country. One of the biggest stories of my time ending facedown on a stained rug in his bathroom, but I couldn't bring myself to go and cover it.

It would have been a lie for me to do this. I wouldn't even drive out to Silverdome to see Elvis the last time he was in town. So I just could not, in good conscience, go to Memphis and become part of the carnival these things become.

I decided that I wasn't even going to write about Elvis' death when I got back from vacation. By then — now — what could I say that hadn't already been said and re-said? I was going to stick by my guns until I read Mike Royko's piece on Elvis' con-artistry in this space last Saturday.

I happen to think Royko, a Chicago-based columnist, is one of the nation's best, an adroit writer who has made a profession of contrived cynicism. But I think Royko was a little heavy-handed in his assessment of Elvis' talent or lack of talent.

Elvis was the wrong metaphor for Royko to use for the inequities in the music business of the '50s, which saw white artists "cover" the records of black artists. Top 40 was white. Pat Boone's "Ain't That a Shame" was a big hit, but Fats Domino's original was better even if most of the country never heard it.

I know enough about the music business to know that if someone writes a song that someone else records, the writer of the song gets royalties forever from recording sales and air play. Elvis rarely wrote a song, but made a lot of songwriters, both black and white, rich because he recorded their material.

Ask Mac Davis. Elvis' recordings of Davis' songs helped sustain Davis through his early lean years. Davis will be the first to tell you this. And many others will do the same.

The thing that bothered me the most was the attitude Royko copped in his piece. It had those same resentful overtones that first greeted Elvis, when he was our nation's first example of the Generation Gap in communication.

Elvis, with his sideburns and ducktail all slicked back, his pelvic gyrations, his curling lip sneer and his clothes, turned off adult America, even as the Beatles were to do the same thing a decade later.

It was crew cut and white buck thinking that rejected Elvis, made fun of him, held him up to ridicule in the beginning. How many times did I hear adults listen to "Hound Dog"and "Heartbreak Hotel" in the mid-'50s and say, "He'll never last." Well, Elvis did last. More than that, he became a part of the American tapestry.

No other American entertainer has ever spawned a full-time circuit of imitators, who make a good living of parodying Elvis' every move, twitch and hitch. Unfortunately, Elvis himself seemed to be doing this in the last few years.

I was never an Elvis Presley freak. I liked some of his music, watched few of his films, and was never really even a fan. But I know why. I was jealous of Elvis when he first started, and found myself rejecting him even as the adults around me were rejecting him, too.

I was jealous of Elvis 'cause all the girls — well, practically all of them in my high school, anyway — were in love with him. The same sort of jealousy maybe some women have for Farrah Fawcett-Majors today. They'll say they don't like her, but then wear their hair like her.

I did the same thing. Let my 'burns and DA grow. Practiced sneering in front of the mirror. Could even do a passable Elvis imitation on "W-e-l-l-l-l, since mah baby left me, found a new place to dwell . . . "

But would I admit it then? No way, Jose! In fact, this is the first time I've ever admitted it. Maybe that's what Royko was admitting, too, if one could read between the lines. For years, fans of Elvis have been telling Elvis' critics this. "You're jealous of him!" is the fan's first cry. Defensively, the critic says, "Don't be ridiculous."

I think the fans are probably right and Elvis' critics are ridiculous. Maybe we envied all the fun and freedom and fame we thought Elvis had. And until he died, we never appreciated the problems that being Elvis created for Elvis.

I find frightening parallels between Elvis and Howard Hughes. Hughes was another many of us envied and were even jealous of. But look at his final years and days. Look at Elvis. The life of a recluse is one helluva price to pay for all that fame — a fame that I was jealous of once upon a time.

Elvis' death helped some of us grow up.

— Aug. 24, 1977

'Ray Charles just plays what's inside him'

I was so nervous I would have stood on my head or turned inside out if someone had asked me. Nervous and eager.

My first hero. The lady who ran the Columbia, S.C., Township Auditorium came from backstage in a fluster. "He wants some vegetable soup. Where am I going to find hot soup this time of the night?"

"I'll go get it!" I shouted. "I know where!" I was out the stage entrance as fast as my fat legs would carry me and ran two blocks to an all-night eatery. If I'd had to, I'd have made it myself.

My man wanted soup and he was going to get it.

This was Nov. 9, 1960. A cold wave had hit the South and the band bus had been late. I'd been there since 6, waiting. The people started arriving at 8 and by the time the band arrived on stage it was after 9:30.

That band put some jazz on that audience they would never forget, particularly those solos from Texan David (Fathead) Newman and a young trumpeter from Detroit named Marcus Belgrave.

But that's not why those people had braved the cold and jammed the auditorium to its rafters, although they dug that band. Those people, me included, were there for one reason: Ray Charles was in town!

And there I was — a link between my hero and that night — I felt as I raced back with two cardboard cartons of hot vegetable soup. It was like a gift offering to a god.

After all, when his "I Got a Woman" hit my high school senior year in 1954, didn't our quartet make it our showpiece number? We even had the Raelettes' parts down cold. I can still do my part. Wonder if Duck, Trigger and Con can do theirs.

As I raced down the street with Ray Charles' soup I remember wishing Duck, Trigger and Con could have seen me then. I was in a young reporter's heaven. Not only was I going to meet him, I was going to give him some soup — and maybe he'd give me an interview.

Charles' road manager was nervous. There wouldn't be time for an interview. "Some of those people been waitin' out there two hours," he told me. "I understand," I said.

"But you can meet him — take him that soup," the manager said, trying to make up for a clock's hour hand that was nearing 11. As we walked backstage behind the curtain, Newman and Belgrave were dueling musically out front and I broke out in alternating cold sweats and chills.

"Here's a guy from the paper who found you some soup," I was introduced. Ray Charles was silently rocking back and forth on a bench in a borrowed overcoat two sizes too large for him.

He looked very small and cold and gratefully accepted the soup. As he smelled it, the soup steamed his extra large, wide dark glasses. He took a sip and a canoe-smile broke his face and the chill. "Ahhhhhh!" he said and offered his hand.

It was smooth and soft and warm from the soup cup. I stumbled through a thank-you-sir-glad-to-meet-you-sir-you're-my-hero-I-love-you tongue fluster and Charles laughed. "Relax, son," he said.

"Whatcha want to know about Ray Charles?" he said. He kept referring to himself as Ray Charles. "There's not much new 'bout him. It has all been written. Some of it truth, some of it lies. Depends where you read it.

"Take this soup. By the way, it is very good. Betcha a sister made it," he said and everyone laughed. I assured him a sister HAD made it and had made it special because she knew who it was going to.

Finishing up the first carton, he said, "What she did with this soup is what Ray Charles does with music. Think she'd make it the same way twice? She makes it how she's feeling. She was feeling good tonight."

Everyone laughed again and he continued, "People always asking me what Ray Charles means by this and what Ray Charles means by that when I play. They say, 'That's the gospel influence.' Or, 'Aren't those basic classical chords you bring at that point?'

"These cats aren't satisfied with sitting and listening. They all the time gotta be thinking and working up their brains over something. When I get out there on the stage, I play and sing like I feel at the moment. I just sit there and play. Something pops in my head, I sing it.

"People always talking about Ray Charles is a genius. I never planned on being one and never intend to be one. Ray Charles just plays what's inside him. What feels like coming out at that particular moment.

"Man gets to know some good times and bad times if he bumps around this world long enough. And all of this will come out if he lets it. People always talking to Ray Charles about art forms and things like that. What's an art form, man? You know? To me, art is telling someone something you feel without them having to think about it to understand. Art is crying and laughing without thinking about it.

"Music should laugh and cry, because music is people.

"Speaking of people," Charles said to his manager, "how long those folks been waitin' out there? We gotta go. You tell that sister she makes great soup."

Spotting him being led to the piano, the band went into that unmistakable vamp to close the number they were playing. Charles stood by the piano until it finished, slid onto the bench and shouted into the microphone, "Tell me, what'd I say now . . . "

The place went crazy. Eighteen years later Ray Charles is in town at the Music Hall. Wonder if he remembers that soup? I'll never forget it or that night.

— Dec. 29, 1978

The music was hot, but the musicians were so cool

I was 14, big for my age, and one helluva liar. I somehow talked my way into the dressing room-rehearsal area at the 3,000-seat Memorial Auditorium in Spartanburg, S.C.

I used the oldest groupie story in musical history: I was a jazz columnist for the high school newspaper. And the road manager for Stan Kenton bought it. I was in! You can't believe the joy for this becoming-a-teenager, whose biggest passion in life was jazz and the Stan Kenton Orchestra in particular.

Bags Bagley on upright bass. Shelly Manne — the Main Man — on drums. Bob Gioga — Kenton loved saying his name — on baritone sax. Trumpet action? How about Maynard Ferguson and Shorty Rogers for starters? The Candoli brothers — Pete and Conte — had just joined the band which featured one of the greatest unheralded trumpet players of all time, Buddy Childers, first chair against all that competition.

At the time in the jazz business the "cutting contest" was the rage of the day, when two masters of their instruments would square off against each other to see just who could outplay whom.

Those famous Flip Philips-Illinois Jacquet sax battles at Norman Granz's Jazz at the Philharmonic concert series in the mid-'40s helped fire up these musical duels. Remember those "axe contests"?

Only the terminology dates them. Duels in jazz started with the music and continued as an unstated, but ever-present theme woven throughout the music's historical fabric. '

I was thrilled just to have snaked in to watch these musicians warm up, unlimber, get their lips and timing right. Stan Kenton always had a penchant for giving the best young jazz talent available a showcase for their solo talents, as long as they would play his ensemble riffs, too.

Off in one corner, Bagley's taped fingers were tearing up that bass, down in its deep rich guts. Young Maynard Ferguson caught Bags' thing and took it for a flutter or two. Then Ferguson started up the scale, climbing into those rarified decibel levels reached by birds and dog whistles.

Everything sort of stopped as Ferguson topped it off in a near-screech. Which one of the trumpet players would accept the challenge? Childers, who had just unpacked his horn, saw everyone watching him. He took a deep breath, then blew one screech of a note that topped Ferguson's, then collapsed in a heap, laughing and gasping.

Everyone laughed, and it was only then that everyone noticed Bud Shank and Art Pepper over in a corner. These two great saxophonists were going at it softly, but head-to-head with the intensity increasing.

Upstairs, over 3,000 had packed the auditorium — mostly college students, ex-GIs and every musician within 200 miles who could get there. The Kenton Cult was enormous.

But down below in the basement I was witness to a once-in-a-life-time experience. Shank and Pepper went after it and each other. One would play a run, which the other would duplicate and add further frills in a flurry of fingering impossible to believe.

Chorus after chorus of "How High the Moon," a big Les Paul and Mary Ford jazz-pop hit of the time. Shank. Pepper. Shank. Pepper. The rest of the musicians had picked up on it and were doing this soft vamp behind them.

It's now hard for me to finish describing that amazing moment. The man standing there beside me those many years ago died this past Saturday night. Stan Kenton had seen right through my high school journalist dodge, but admired my brass — he loved brass in all forms — and offered to introduce me around.

Trombonist Bill Russo laughed with Kenton over my scam. Then the incredible music started. I'll never forget Kenton's great huge hand and fingers gripping my shoulder.

Stan the man seemed to tower above me by a couple of yards, and at least a yard over the rest of the room. Shank's and Pepper's bursts became more brilliant and briefer until Kenton, with his other hand, gave the hand a signal and all of a sudden the whole basement became one huge unison riff.

His hand left my shoulder and his arms spread like a blond-headed eagle's wings, then together, back apart, together — the band in perfect synch — back apart, together, building toward the final note, which they all cut off like a halved lightning bolt.

"Gentlemen," Kenton's deep and distinct baritone rolled across the silence like thunder, "this is jazz!"

I shared that long-ago moment with Stan Kenton, and we re-shared it in every conversation and communication we had. His death takes from me deeply.

I subsequently had many moments with Stan Kenton. Cherished memories. From a kid groupie to an adult writer-for-real arguing philosophy with a man he idolized. I shared many of his ups and downs, his rebounds, his hurts and some of his depressions.

I'm having a hard time seeing what I type. Those are tears, Stan. I feel your hand gripping my shoulder again . . . .

— Aug. 29, 1979

A racing legend born on a sultry July night

It was 10 days after his 21st birthday and his father had given him the family convertible for the night.

Some of the older guys were kidding him. The irrepressible Little Joe Weatherly scolded, "Boy, you so much as put one dent in that car and your Daddy'll have your fanny."

The gangly kid just grinned. He had been waiting for this night for years. Dreaming about it since he learned to drive a car.

He always loved the joking around that goes on before a race. He had his own pre-race line when anyone asked him what kind of advice his father gave him that night. "Well, Pop let me have the car and said make sure I put gas in her," he'd joke nonchalantly.

We were all hanging around the kid's blue Olds convertible, No. 42, that sultry Southern night in West Columbia, S.C. It was July 12, 1958, at the Columbia Speedway, a big hunk of my life in the late '50s.

From February's Speed Week at Daytona Beach, Fla., to the Southern 500 at Darlinton, S.C., on Labor Day, I covered the NASCAR late-model stock car racing circuit, then divided into two divisions: hardtops and convertibles.

It will probably shock some of you that back then they actually raced convertibles, the cockpits fully open except for a roll bar. They also used to race on Daytona's sandy beaches before that high-banked super speedway was built, which is another story.

But that 90-degree Saturday night in July was chapter one in what would eventually become the biggest story in stock car racing history: Richard Petty's first race.

Lee Petty, the patriarch of the Level Cross, N.C., racing clan, was a couple hundred miles away in Ashville, N.C., running that night against Cotton Owens, Jim Paschal and Rex White in a hardtop race. Lee had sent nephew Dale Inman, 19, and son Maurice, 16, to Columbia as son Richard's pit crew.

Normally, Richard was the pit boss for his father and considered invaluable in that department. But Richard had long been pestering his old man for a ride.

The Pettys were the first to run their stock car operation like a business. A family business, closely knit, almost secretive. And Lee was the best, most consistent driver of the time. One of the few to make big money.

Lee would've loved to have kept Richard in his pit but it made financial sense to have two cars running every weekend, so Richard had been promised a ride when he was 21. He had been practicing turning left and floor-boarding it on a dirt track behind their Level Cross garage.

Shortly before track announcer Johnny Evans said, "Gentlemen, start your engines," for the 100-mile race, I asked Richard if he was going to make stock car driving his career.

"I guess it'll depend on how I do tonight," he said. "I've never driven in any race before, not even the sportsman or modified type. The only experience I've had has been to take a couple of laps warming up Pop's car before he races."

It wasn't the easiest race to break into the business. These 200-lap convertible races on half-mile dirt tracks were slam-bang affairs. Seven times that night the caution flag went out as drivers crashed through fences and rammed into one another.

Although he finished only a distant sixth behind Bob Welborn, Fireball Roberts, Larry Frank, Doug Cox and George Dunn, the pits were buzzing after the race about how well Richard could handle a car and how he wasn't afraid to mix it up.

Richard's patented grin filled his pit. You'd have thought he had won the race. "Nervous? Naw, but I was scared a-plenty. I think maybe I should've done better. You know, that racing really gets you."

The following day I wrote a column about how the kid had been bitten by the racing bug and concluded:

"Lee Petty doesn't have a 'little boy' any more. Instead another Petty has begun his climb in the 'left-turn' business and from the gleam in his eye. the Petty name will be in the racing game for many years to come."

And in the history books forever. His $4 million-plus career winnings are a million bucks ahead of second place. No one comes close to his 193 career victories. His dramatic seventh Daytona 500 victory Sunday doubles the next best and is one of sport's most awesome victory records.

As I watched Richard win the big one on TV Sunday, all I could think about was that July 12, 1958, Saturday night when Lee gave his son the convertible to drive.

— February 18, 1981

Their love story overshadows any game

I read a book Sunday.

All because of a love story I ran into Sunday morning.

I know, I know, the big game is in our own backyard and pay attention to the TV, Talbert, see who else dumps on us.

My attention wouldn't stay on the tube. What else could they say, anyway? Dump ahead, cheap shots. At least you'll be gone soon and forgotten.

The game itself didn't hold my attention because it was a bore, frankly, but we all knew it would be, didn't we? These things always are. A bore and a letdown.

It's funny how the Super Bowl reminded me a lot of the made-up-for-TV Superstars show that was on earlier. Television, the voyeur for us all, showing off its trained athletes/celebrities, putting them through their teletronic paces.

Only scene I'll remember came at the end when the cameras showed Cincinnati's losing quarterback Ken Anderson carrying his son off the field. One Sweet XVI moment out of six hours.

But this game of games had little meaning for me Sunday, except as a centerpiece in the love story of Ginny and Erskine Caldwell.

Ginny Caldwell is one of the ol' Kezar Stadium bunch. She remembers when San Francisco was a city worth remembering. She's a Niner to the bone. And Erskine Caldwell, the 78-year-old living legend, is madly in love with his wife Ginny, who wasn't even a teenager when Erskine's "Tobacco Road" was published 50 years ago.

When the Niners won their way into the Super Bowl in the Silverdome, Ginny just had to come. So the Caldwells called their best friends — the voice of the Detroit Tigers, Baseball Hall of Famer Ernie Harwell and his "Miss Lula." This friendship developed when they all lived on the same block in Dunedin, Fla.

Ernie and Miss Lula are another love story I'll tell you about one day. But one love story per column, and today's is about Erskine's love for Ginny, his bride and traveling companion for 25 years.

The last place the painfully shy Erskine Caldwell wanted to be was in a strange city in the frozen north in the dead-cold of winter, with slippery freeways to drive in a stick-shift rent-a-car he wasn't used to. And all those crowds!

But it was the only place Ginny wanted to be and so there we all were having breakfast at Denny's next to the Red Roof Inn in Farmington Hills on Super Bowl Sunday morning. I was with 'em because Ernie had a correct hunch I'd like to meet Erskine.

Ernie got the Caldwells tickets for the game and they had flown up from Scottsdale, Ariz., the night before, bearing lemons they had picked from a tree on their front porch. Ernie kidded them about bringing lemons to Detroit. Ginny kidded the Harwells about leaving Florida after six years for a winter like this.

Erskine was nervous, edgy about getting to the game as early as possible. He is fiercely independent and rejected any notion that we arrange for them to ride with people more familiar with getting to the Silverdome. Anyway, you could sense, this was Ginny-the-fan's trip-of-a-lifetime and it was Erskine's mission to conduct it all himself.

"It's really for her, this trip," he whispered to me. His eyes caught Ginny out of the corner with that look of devotion that said: "Doing it for her is enough for me."

Then he looked back at me and said, "And maybe I'll write about it. It would fit in the book."

He had been talking about his latest writing project — a series of 18 or 20 travel sketches, episodes of their recent adventures all over the world. Caldwell's "50 books in 50 years" have sold over 80 million copies internationally and the only way he can collect the royalties in some countries like the Soviet Union is to visit those countries and buy goods and works of art with the money. Ginny, an artist who illustrates her husband's books, is good at this, Erskine says.

It was departure time and as soon as the goodbys were over I headed for a bookstore and bought the only Caldwell book on the shelf, "God's Little Acre."

Once I started re-reading it Ty Walden and Pluto Squint and Darling Jill became utterly more fascinating than Hacksaw Reynolds and Joe Montana. For Ginny's sake I'm glad the Niners won. For my sake, I'm glad she brought Erskine with her.

— January 27, 1982

THINGS THAT
MAKE ME MAD

The uptight game: People, things I've had it with

Free Press Editor Mark Ethridge and I were comparing mail the other day and we came to the frightening conclusion that the whole world is uptight.

Practically every letter contains a slice of vented spleen or an angry word. Encouraging words are rare as buffalo herds.

The whole world is irritated, angry, rude and impatient.

And frankly, so am I.

I've had it . . .

With knee-jerk jerks on the right who see a communist conspiracy in everything.

With bleeding-heart intellectuals who see every rapped knuckle and new establishment rule as an encroachment on someone's freedom.

With black militants.

With white militants.

With hawks and doves.

With those ladies who put all those straight pins in new shirts.

With those people who seal ham and cheese in cellophane packages that can't be opened with anything except a blow torch.

I've had it . . .

With campus dropouts, dissidents and dissenters who demand control but have no plan of operation to control with.

With magazine editors who can't decide whether to number their pages on the top, bottom — or at all.

With sportswriters who write stories about the "last time I saw Mickey Mantle play" or the "the first time I saw Ted Williams play."

With bountiful actresses like Raquel Welch who wear high-necked, cover-up evening gowns on TV shows.

I've had it . . .

With restaurant menus larger than the table you sit at.

With people who say "I'll be honest with you" and then aren't.

With executives who hide behind the phrase, "It's company policy."

With all the talk about pot-smoking.

With high school principals who make such big issues over

student clothing, but fail to realize the more basic shortcomings of their schools.

With airline hijacking jokes.

With hard-to-cut hunks of tomato in tossed salads, especially in salad bowls that are overflowing.

With everything that adds in small print "optional at extra cost."

I've had it . . .

With secretaries who say "Just a moment, sir, and I'll see if he's in," when they know all along he isn't.

With swingers who ridicule squares.

With squares who detest swingers.

With sex for sex's sake movie scenes for box-office's sake.

With people who insist you taste whatever they're eating.

With taxi drivers, ball-park vendors and parking lot attendants who take forever making change.

I've had it . . .

With garages that don't tell you they're full until you get halfway into the entrance.

With people who respond to your questions with "Whatever you think's best" or "Whatever's right."

With plastic spoons, forks and knives.

With double-parked delivery trucks.

With public restrooms that require keys.

I've had it . . .

With memos headed "From the desk of — "

With people who surreptitiously run a finger over your business card to see if it's engraved.

With people who make it a point to read the labels in your coat and jacket.

With waiters and waitresses who fill your coffee cup to the brim, making it impossible to drink without spilling some.

With older women who talk and act like teenagers.

With teenagers who talk and act like older women.

I've had it . . .

With those who insist that the revolutionary young people wouldn't be so successful if the news media would quit covering their antics because all they want is their picture on television and names in the headlines.

With young people who claim they're alienated and misunderstood but won't even try to understand the establishment, their parents, police or realities of living in society.

With people who "rap" instead of talk, who insist we "overreact" when we just react, who ask me what my "bag" is, who "cop out," take "bum trips" and have "confrontations."

— March 12, 1969

Some of many things that can turn me off, click!

It's one of those days when . . .

Michael Brody's utter stupidity and the sheer greed of those begging for the money turn me off.

The constant reportage and alarm over the Pill, drugs and unwed mothers turn me off.

Mel Ravitz and the Common Council's sneaky closed meetings turn me off.

The New Detroit Committee, with its money-lined nipple, serving nothing more than a pacifier to the black community turns me off.

Sam Wagstaff's promoting of sculptor Robert Morris' junk and garbage at the Museum of Arts turns me off and makes me realize that some sculptors are really nothing but chiselers.

Advertisers in their phony graphics and wording obviously pandering to the youth market turns me off.

Over-30 reporters and writers like Nicholas Von Hoffman sucking up to the militants and alienated youth turn me off.

No-talent rock groups like the MC-5 having reputations far beyond their talent and ability turn me off.

William F. Buckley and other innuendo and half-truth princes of the right turn me off.

Top Ten Best or Worst lists of anything and anybody turn me off.

People who criticize long hair, beards and mode of dress before they find out what's under the hair, beard and funny clothes turn me off.

The pseudo-shock of the affluent suburbs like Grosse Pointe when it's discovered that their kids turn on turns me off.

Minorities demanding something before they earn it turns me off.

Unqualified athletes and celebrities like Denny McLain sounding off on issues such as Vietnam and drugs turn me off.

All this snow on top of snow on top of snow turns me off.

Jane Hart's trial and Lenore Romney's possible political candidacy turn me off.

The automotive industry's utter failure to take the leading role in creating a healthy core city with new housing and a new Detroit domed stadium turns me off.

Just looking at George Wallace turns me off and listening to him doubles it.

People who moan and groan over smoking or stopping smoking turn me off.

Malcolm Boyd and most "hip" priests turn me off.

Black and White Panthers. Minutemen and Birchers all representing twisted people turn me off.

Airline commercials that make it look so glamorous when air travel is really long waits, so-what service and assorted discomfort turn me off.

The self-righteous news media's failure and inability to accept or generate criticism of itself turns me off.

The sudden discovery by everyone of Middle America's Silent Majority and the heavy-handed courtship of it turns me off.

Eldridge Cleaver and Strom Thurmond turn each other off and me, too.

Frank Ditto and John Sinclair and the public attention paid to them turn me off.

For lots of reasons, Rodney Dangerfield, Doris Day, Jackie Mason, Rex Reed, London Lee, Joyce Brothers, Al Capp, Lester Maddox, Peter Lawford, John Lennon and Gloria Steinem turn me off.

Ed Sullivan putting on such show biz freaks as Tiny Tim writhing on the floor and Michael Brody mouthing on the floor turn me off.

Richard Nixon has never turned me on.

J. Edgar Hoover for not retiring long ago turns me off.

Spiro Agnew turns me off and do I have to have a reason?

Poor-mouthing for Alex Karras not making the Pro Bowl game turns me off.

The utter lack of black leadership in this community at the street level turns me off.

Suburban politicians, mayors and governments gloating over every blemish and scar on Detroit's face turn me off and where would they be if Detroit turned them off?

The failure of any positive programs to emerge yet from Roman Gribbs' administration turns me off.

All the busybodies trying to mind the business of privately owned
Detroit Lions turn me off.

— Jan. 20, 1970

I've gotta get this wide load off my chest pronto or bust

This is one of those days when I've had it up to here with all your
angriness, rudeness, impatience, bitterness and discontent. To hell
with it.

I've had it with being "with it" and hip and groovy, and being "in"
and all that jive.

I've had it with all the now talk and mod fashions and freaky
things and hot places and chic chicks.

I've had it with sucking up to important people and politicians
and policymakers. To hell with them, too.

I've had it . . .

With publicity seekers who show up the night the photographers
come, but are never there when work's to be done.

With campus dissenters and dissidents who demand they get
control of courses and dorms and have no plan to operate or control
them.

With people who think I'm a racist because I'm for law and order.

With rising highway deaths and mollycoddling judges who're
light on sentencing drunk drivers and the Ralph Naders who blame
everyone but the rotten drivers.

With clergymen and politicians who make careers of integration
causes and send their own children to private schools.

I've had it . . .

With filth peddlers who're in some sort of obscenity race to see
how dirty our movies can get, how trashy our books can be, and how
vulgar our plays can become — then cry that this is culture.

With the bad-mouthing of extremist groups, trying to polarize
our nation, unfortunately more susceptible to polarization now than
any time in its history.

With rude and bored sales persons who act like they're doing me a
favor to wait on me and take my money.

With too much bleeding-heartache over criminals in prison, when
it clouds over the fact that those convicts didn't get in there by being

good or being very considerate of other people.

I've had it . . .

With people who still get bugged by the length or style one wears his hair and on the other hand by people who insist I campaign against all dress and hair codes.

With out-and-out criminals and hoods being kid-gloved by courts and jails when they shout they're "political prisoners" and disrupt communities and destroy property in the name of "freedom for the people."

With slack-jawed bigots who wrap themselves in sheets or flags and commie-bait anyone who doesn't agree with them 100 percent.

With feeling guilty when I watch a lot of television, the good shows and the bad.

I've had it . . .

With sour-faced, unmannered, unwashed youths who claim they represent a "new wave" in America and sneer at "old-fashioned" virtues of honesty, integrity and morality.

With revolutionary "political radicals" who say they have the right to determine what laws of the land they're willing to obey, and openly disobey and flaunt the laws they feel are wrong.

With thin-skinned, rabbit-eared members of ethnic and minority groups who can see nothing funny in ethnic humor.

With people who get uptight with me because I don't drink booze or smoke cigarets or pot.

With Democrats who label every move by Richard Nixon as "political."

I've had it . . .

With politicians who have yet to come up with a long-range realistic plan for this country, but have plenty of vote-getting emotional plans ready.

With advocacy attorneys who make a mockery of our courts, our judges and our entire judicial system.

With ships from foreign countries unloading millions of tons of goods on our shores when millions of productive Americans are out of work.

With certain self-annointed demagogues "speaking for" vast groups of people when I know damn well they're only speaking for a small, select, self-serving group.

I've had it . . .

With media overkill of such things as Howard Hughes and women's lib and drug stories and movie violence and rock music and pro football and busing.

With busing kids any great distance for any purpose.

With paying my taxes to support people who haven't the gumption, the desire or the least bit of intention of trying to help themselves when they are perfectly capable of doing so.

With government telling private business how it should run its business, when government has made a helluva mess out of its own business.

I've had it . . .

With the Republicans' phony economy and political doubletalk and Alice-in-Wonderland federal control.

With labor strikes for higher wages and fantastic fringes which lead to higher prices.

With parents getting all the blame for the Communication Gap.

With people who vote AGAINST things instead of FOR them.

With phony standing ovations and applauding anything that doesn't really merit it.

With segregationists and separatists who try to hide their true colors behind cliches and dishonest brotherhood.

With people who get upset with me when I write this type of column.

— *March 24, 1972*

At least voicing gripes can clear the air

I'm not exactly jumping up and down about the prospects, pal, of who's going to get this old world straightened out and how. If you don't recognize we've got a mess on our hands, I'm talking to the wrong person. We've got to admit this country just isn't working. Just look around and listen. Uptight is our middle name. Short-fuse is our nickname and To-Hell-With-It is our catch phrase.

I'm so damn tired of all the angriness about, I feel like packing it in, too, and striking out for Canada or Australia or the South Pole. But those places have problems, too. They've got problems if they've got people. And they'll have more problems 'cause people always manage to have more people.

Try to cope with one problem, and a new crisis arises. The 1970s are fast becoming known as the Decade of Crises. There's crime in the streets and in the corporate towers. How much more do you want to hear about that? There's racial injustice — just as much against the white man today as the black man, and don't kid yourself that the blacks catch all the hell. Vietnam is still with us. But I'm going to tell you something. Us getting out of Vietnam is not going to bring peace in this old world. It's not going to end those two dozen or so wars now raging.

Environmental pollution has had it as a chic cause. Someone told 'em what it's going to cost to clean up. And all of us "someones" found out we're going to have to pay for it. Let's see how chic it will be to be for clean air and water when it costs you $1,000 a year. Things are right on until you have to put your check where your chatter is.

Another fashionable concern is do-something-about-the-drug thing. What's to do except take the profits and glamor out of it? Simple as that, but you think these things will happen? The President's Commission on Drug Abuse is a classic example of the doublethink that goes on in the drug area. The report said smoking marijuana in the privacy of your own home should be perfectly legal as long as no one gave it to you, sold it to you and you didn't grow it yourself. Just how the hell else can you get it?

This doublethink and doubletalk style is also shot through the entire busing crisis. It's an easy place to hide our prejudices. I can tell you right now I don't see how busing can possibly work because no generation of parents is going to martyr its own kids, black and white. I'm not. I'm too selfish.

I'm tired of people expecting me to apologize for being white, affluent and middle-aged. I pay my dues and I pay my taxes and take my turn in line like everyone else. If things do seem bigoted and prejudiced, then they'll just have to seem that way. I'm sorry as I can be, but I'm tired of paying it out and out and getting damn little in return. And don't blame me for what my parents did, OK. I don't blame you for yours.

I'm not exactly jumping up and down about the prospects of who's going to finance the straightening out of this old world. Why should I have to work harder and harder to pay more and more taxes so everyone is guaranteed getting $6,000 a year just for being here? It's also irritating the fizz out of me that I'm going to have to pay more Social Security tax. Why not get some Social Security relief that'll help even more? Let Social Security recipients earn more money outside, instead of limiting their outside earnings to under

$2,000 as it is today. Many are earning more, anyway, and just aren't declaring it.

I'm also beginning to wonder just what the word rights means. They're now telling you where you have to live if you're going to work in certain jobs in certain places. That's a crock, pal. They get away with that and they'll tell you what stores you can shop in and what you can put in your sandwiches and which way you have to brush your teeth. Don't laugh.

Young people are screaming at us that they didn't ask to be brought into a world like this. Who the hell did? You can bet I didn't. But the counterculture display of egotism and arrogance substitutes idealism for insight. I hear 'em holler, "I just want to do my own thing!" Why not say, "Let's do our thing?"

I've had it, too, with the victimless crime talk. There ain't no such animal. Society itself is the biggest victim from the mere fact that it causes callouses on society's psyche. All crime makes our world a bit coarser, not exactly the sort of handicap you want your kids to have for life starters.

Our courts seem clogged with headline-grabbing and tax-burdening social cases, concerned with what to do about dissent, violent or non-violent. Our heads are equally as clogged with methods and plans and ideal situations and statistical balances. But no one seems able to unclog society's sewers. No one, yet, has stood up and said, "There is no ideal America, no united United States, so let's figure out how to make what we have operable in its various fragments and segments. America is no longer "everything to everybody." An admission like this is the first and most important step this nation will have to take.

— July 14, 1972

Name your rudies of the year

Rudeness knows no barriers of age, sex or ethnic background.

Rudeness crosses all economic, philosophical and educational lines.

Rudeness, today, knows no bounds or boundaries.

It is everywhere.

An American way of life. More fearsome, THE American way of

strife.

A lot of times I'll get these feelings and think it's only me. More and more as I talk to others I find I'm not Jay Silverheels' running mate in some of these matters.

I am not alone. I'm certainly not alone in noting the rise in rudeness. I better believe it, right? You betcha, Red Ryder.

For all the great things the Watergate era did for this nation, I think it helped turn us into a bunch of greedy, insensitive, discourteous and downright rude people.

Me, too. I'm no different than the rest. I try not to be a rude person. Make an effort to be non-rude, if there is such a thing. There should be, if there isn't.

But the Rudies of the world take advantage of you when you try to be non-rude. Rudies are everywhere. I've met them all over lately.

Airports, this time of the year, is where they hold conventions. It's Rude Central, U.S.A. Splinter factions can be found in all your shopping malls, parking lots, supermarkets and freeways.

I waited patiently at the airport to get a bag that made three revolutions on the luggage ramp. Every time I'd try to get it, Little Old Ladies and Big Old Boys would shoulder me out of the way. So we just stood back and watched good old American rudeness at its finest. It's enough to make you swear off everything but carry-on luggage.

I don't even think we have to discuss the major battleground, when Surly Service runs head-on into Surly Consumer. It's a two-edged sword of nastiness that has taken the fun out of retailing. We could spend a week talking about this area alone.

How do you know when you're rude? You don't three-quarters of the time, and that's part of the problem. Usually, your friends and loved ones will finally tell you, probably after it's too late and the rude trait is ingrained in your personality.

Unless you can take hints like I got recently from my wife. Esquire's December issue devoted a section to the New Etiquette, whatever that means.

Under a section titled "Enough of:" Lynn wrote "Pay Attention!" and circled this item: "Free-lance nutritionists ('Do you know how many calories units there are in that order of French fries?')"

I'm going to clean up that part of my act by eliminating it. Who needs it? And I'm only pulling a tsk-tsk stunt, showing off and putting you down when I do these things.

I've done a lot of rude and gross things by design. Shock value is dynamite — dangerous, but dy-no-mite when it works. I also sort of worship at the Shrine of Irreverence.

It's my nature. But it creates rude traits (unless you know me, which is a weak copout we all use) and bad manners. I'm also a 4.0 motor mouth. That's even got to bother people who do know me.

While on vacation I discovered other rude traits. You find this out about yourself when you are where you don't know a soul and not a soul knows you. Where you live they may know you, so you watch it.

I wish Good Manners were a communicable disease. This nation is in need of a major epidemic of it.

Then we could zero in on some of the Rudies We Hate the Most:

People who leave the television on when you are visiting them.

People who play their car radios at the loudness they want.

Compulsive interrupters (I confess, I'm guilty).

People who think the express lines are expressly for them, regardless of whether they have 12 items or 24.

Any stranger who calls you "honey" or "dear."

People who keep talking on the phone when you've already said 10 times that you have to go.

Tailgaters with their brights on.

People who double-park or take up two spaces and leave the fanny of their big gas-guzzlers sticking out half a car length.

People who ask why you have or why you don't have children.

Waiters and waitresses who bring you one course, then disappear completely.

People who smoke in public.

Reformed smokers who lecture.

People who push at counters, into and out of elevators, and in stores and restaurants.

People who talk through movies, plays, concerts, speeches, etc. (Another spawn of the TV era.)

People who are constant hummers.

People who talk to you but won't look at you when they do it.

People who go through the Rituals of False Intimacy with people they've just met and play kissy-face and huggy-wuggy with strangers.

Now I've had a say. These are just some of the Rudies that will have to be reckoned with. Now it's your turn. Nominations for Rudies of the Year are now open.

— Dec. 28, 1977

And now for what we don't need

People and things I can do without:

Fun couples.

Discussions about meaningful relationships.

Sportscasters who use real as an adverb.

Dried-up apple pie.

People who say "Have a nice day" with the emotion of a tape player.

Listening to the Bee Gees everywhere you turn.

Jokes about Bert Lance, Larry Flynt, Dolly Parton, Billy Carter and short people.

Bell-bottom pants on people without belle bottoms.

Soft-boiled or poached eggs.

Not being able to sleep late on mornings when I can.

That black-water slush at every curbside.

Anonymous letters and telephone calls.

Unpacking after a trip.

Ultra-small type which shrinks more every year.

Having a pimple right in the middle of my face when I'm 41 years old and have to go out and make a speech in front of a lot of people.

Licking the untasty glue on postage stamps.

Shoelaces that are too long.

Magazines without all the pages numbered consecutively.

People who say "Let's face it" and never do.

People who expect miracles from people who promised miracles to get elected.

Vacationers to sunny isles who spend the rest of the winter telling us about it.

Actors, actresses and guests on TV shows who smoke.

The Sammy Davis Jr. syndrome, where everything is "the greatest."

Anyone who has fooled himself or herself that a college education has made them educated.

People who can eat onions without upsetting their stomachs.

People who can't wait to tell you what an interesting weekend they had.

Dogs that sit up and beg on command.

Kids who do the same without being commanded.

Any new government bureau.

Snow stories.

People who confuse appearance with character.

Award shows on television.

Restaurants in stained glass, old wood and potted plants.

Sports fans who live and die with the home team.

People with fingernails bitten to the quick.

People who don't know when to stop shaking your hand.

Commercials that tell me I'll have a richer, fuller life if only I'd change my deodorant or toothpaste.

People who won't take no for an answer and people who won't give no for an answer, preferring the dreadful maybe.

Plastic bags in supermarkets that are hard to tear and get open.

Ten best and 10-worst lists.

Action Line's "Sound Off" results when they don't agree with mine.

White bread, salt and sugar.

Worrying about the lives of others who never really heed anyone's advice.

Directionless people.

People going in too many directions at once.

The vulgarity of punk rock.

Those inane situation comedies built around black or white stereotypes.

Crossword puzzles that don't tell you whether it's more than just one word.

Having to go to the bathroom after getting all layered and bundled up to go outside and shovel snow.

People who sucker me into playing their best video game with the ol' hustle line from my pool days.

Starting my day without my morning Free Press.

"The Tonight Show" when some nerdnik is guest-hosting.

Sincere people with causes but without a sense of humor.

Short hair coming in fashion.

Anything coming into fashion.

Natural disasters becoming political issues before any relief is given.

— *Feb. 7, 1978*

I've become scared to death of crowds

Know what scares me more than the Iranian situation?
More than the lack of leadership across the board?
More than the rising double-digit inflation?
More than our daily diet of carcinogens?
More than crime on our mean streets?
More than greedy corporate suites?
More than anything else?
Crowds.
I didn't always feel this way.
Once upon a time I loved crowds.
I looked forward to going to a crowded event.
But that was once upon a time when people knew how to behave in crowds.
Now, I'm sad to say, people in crowds have become one of our biggest national turn-offs.
Frankly, I've become scared to death of crowds.
I just returned from an attempt at some Christmas shopping.
I'm still shaking in anger.
My stomach is a backlash of gnawing knots.
When we get into crowds we become an intolerable group of rude and crude people.
We seem to lose our respect for the other person.
We become a grabby, me-first, to-hell-with-you bunch of animals.
That's right, animals.
I know of no other way to describe us.
Insensitive and loathesome animals.
Crowds have become life's most sickening spectacle.
And it looks like it is just getting worse.
The phrase, "It's a jungle out there," fits as no other phrase in our language fits.
We are jamming, jostling, jousting jerks.
A mob of creeps and cretins. Rowdy, unruly and pushy.
I just watched an elderly woman get knocked to her knees in a crowded mall. I went over to help her up and help collect her packages.

"Please don't take my things," this tearful gray-haired lady said, trying to reach her scattered packages. Fear and tears filled her face.

"I just want to help you," I explained and introduced myself.

She recognized me and grabbed me, sobbing and shuddering.

"Oh, Lord," she moaned, "can you help me get out of here?"

I turned to the nearby couple at a crowded counter who had walked right over this woman in their thoughtless haste.

"The least you could do is help this lady pick up the things you knocked out of her hands," I told them.

"Mind your own f------ business!" the man said.

"She was in our way," the youngish, fashionably dressed woman said. "And you can go to hell."

The sales personnel behind the counter looked away, trying to avoid the shameful scene that was taking place. A scene, unfortunately, I had become a part of.

A security guard standing not four feet away quickly moved in the opposite direction. I shouted after him to come back. I could see shame redden the back of his neck and ears, but he never turned around.

I turned back to the couple. By then I was in an almost blind rage. I wanted to tear off their heads. I, too, had become an animal.

"Please, Mr. Talbert," the old woman said, "just help me get away from here." She had those frightened shakes and was clutching her packages tightly to a sob-wracked chest.

"Something should be done about those people!" I shouted.

By now other people were sheepishly watching us. The old woman was near hysterics. "Just help me find my car," the old woman sobbed. "My daughter's there and I just want to go home."

I helped her gather all her things and walked her to her car. On the way, two impatient motorists, jockeying for parking spots, almost ran into us.

I couldn't believe all this.

I was shaking now. I waited with the old woman at her car, which was locked, until her daughter returned. The daughter eyed me suspiciously until the old woman explained.

"You could have gotten my mother hurt," the daughter accused me, slammed the car door and they drove away.

I went to my car and shook for about 30 minutes.

My heart was crying for all of us. It was crying for those 11 people who died in the Cincinnati rock crowd stomping. It was crying because of the totally helpless feeling one has today in crowds.

What has caused us to become so uncaring in public places? What is wrong with us? Did I do wrong? In trying to help the old woman I think I frightened her as much as that disgusting couple did.

In the department store I had reverted to that animalistic urge, too, when I wanted to do bodily harm to that unbelievably rude couple. I still do. I can't help it.

Somewhere in the past decade, it seems, we have lost our politeness and manners. I pride myself on my patience. But I had lost it. Totally.

Even putting this down on paper hasn't helped.

Because it won't change anything. I don't think anything will any more. That's why crowds scare me so. My jaw muscles are permanently cramped. We can grit our teeth and bear it. But for how long? You tell me.

— December 12, 1979

Will you stop repeating my every word?

I've had it with . . .

People who repeat every word you say a millisecond after you say it. Or those who hit the last word of each phrase.

People who pick things off my clothes — they're my strings and lint, leave 'em alone.

Couples who argue in front of me, which embarrasses me. Why should their grief cause me such trauma?

Stores that advertise storewide half-off sales and when you get there the items half-off are on two racks of tables right in the front of the store.

Feeling guilty when I watch some piece of garbage on TV.

Drivers who turn their heads toward the passengers to carry on a conversation while you are in heavy traffic.

People who have to use "you know" to get through a sentence.

The excess packaging of the products in the fast-food-to-go business. That's what's littering up America.

People who plop themselves down in a group discussion, without being asked, and try to dominate the conversation.

Parents who let their small children kick the back of your seat in movies, arenas, ball parks, stadiums, etc.

People who leave their television on when you visit, or worse yet, those who come to visit you and automatically turn on your TV set.

People who seem to enjoy being called "Big Guy."

Bicycle riders who bunch up three abreast on roads used mainly by auto traffic.

People who notice you are fatter.

People who don't notice you are thinner.

People who pretend to be gee-golly-whiz humble when you praise 'em. Inwardly, they're the first to know they deserve it.

People who sit in movie theaters and talk only a couple decibels below a scream — as if they were sitting at home, watching the TV.

People with 20 items to be rung up not letting someone with one or two items take cuts in the cashier's line.

People who tell you only what they think you want to hear, or the reverse — those who always try to antagonize or irritate you.

People and companies who don't update their mailing lists, wasting millions and millions of dollars a year in postage, materials, etc.

Parents who let their toddling children wander into your space in a public place.

Sick, deformed humor in any guise — public and private.

Over-promising politicians.

Parents who treat their children as possessions, forcing children into uncomfortable roles.

People who are strictly fair-weather people.

People who abuse the public privacy of recognizable people.

Sales people who won't leave you alone while you're just looking but are nowhere to be found when you're ready to be waited on.

People in the broadcasting business who are in love with their own voices.

All this intrigue in every layer, strata and area of our lives. Whatever happened to direct confrontation?

People who insist you taste whatever it is they are having.

People trying to pass off surliness as cool.

People who deliver every line as if it were a complaint.

People who push at counters, in stores, in restaurants, in bars, etc.

People who try to get on elevators before others have even begun to get off.

Those little advertising and subscription cards some magazines are filled with.

Public nose-pickers, spitters and uncovered coughers and sneezers.

Restaurants who overload one section — and one waitress — and let other areas and waitresses stand idly by.

People who vote against, but never for.

Disc jockeys who fail to tell you the name of a song and who performed it.

People who talk loudly just so others will hear their thought-to-be witty comments.

— July 9, 1980

Out of my mind on a Monday moanin'

Baseball will be a lot better off when the players start reading the Sporting News again instead of the Wall Street Journal.

When the AAA truck breaks down, who tows it away?

You see so much about "living color," can anyone tell me what dead color is?

I suspect that Marlo Thomas, Phyllis Kirk, Barbara Feldon, Phyllis Newman and Mary Tyler Moore are all the same girl.

I'm beginning to believe the Generation Gap is located between the ears.

If Orson Welles' "War of the Worlds" shocker were broadcast today the kids would just think it was another newscast.

They ought to put all paper towel dispensers at waist level so when you wash your hands the water doesn't trickle down your wrists as you reach up for the towels.

Murder is a crime, but describing or depicting it isn't; sex is not a crime, but describing it or depicting it is.

Today's biggest bore may well be the guy who tells you about when he could have purchased such-and-such expensive property for a song but didn't.

The two greatest perils to pro sports these days aren't knee injuries and inconsistent officiating, but the agent and the union leader.

Somehow it seems strange that we have over 500,000 laws to enforce just Ten Commandments.

THE U.S.A.

Non-heroes may be the only reality

In case you haven't looked lately, Jack Armstrong is down 45 points.

Paul Bunyan is a size 37-short.

Horatio Alger is on welfare.

Superman's pants need pressing.

Tarzan is scared of cats.

Captain Marvel is a corporal.

Hopalong Cassidy limps.

Sir Galahad is a woman-chaser.

Prince Valiant uses a rubber lance.

Frank Merriwell fumbled.

Tom Mix got hung by the rustlers.

Samson couldn't open a jelly jar.

Even Uncle Sam wears a false beard, King Kong works for an organ grinder, and Dagwood is a wife-swapper.

The great American hero is dead.

It will probably be recorded one day in the 21st Century that "an embryonic communication system known as 'television' killed the great American hero."

And the public sat in silence as he died, twitching and whimpering.

Television has manufactured dime-a-dozen heroes. These discount demigods are not taller by a head, swifter by a foot, stronger by an arm, or smarter by a thought than their contemporaries. They are merely our reflections.

Through the ages heroes have been created by the young scholars, the collegians, the campus poets and their peers. Young Greek students wrote the epic poetry of Achilles and Ulysses. Brilliant young Roman scholars recounted the antics of that great bridge-defender, Horatius.

Today we watch Joe Namath's tearful farewell to football one month and then his gridiron heroics the next.

We watch political heroes crumble and crack.

We watch mouthy militants like Rap Brown and George Wallace become stenciled symbols of society's misfits.

We watch John Lennon and Timothy Leary do their strange things and we don't flinch, or even blink.

Dustin Hoffman, cast as the world's biggest nothing, becomes bigger box office than John Wayne, who even plays a pot-bellied old ne'er-do-well his last time out. Next thing you know Wayne will be playing Tojo.

It is a strange age of put-on and put-down, where the Beautiful People are ugly and have had breath.

An age where warts and scars are pluses.

An age where humility is a handicap but arrogance and ego are assets. Modesty is a mental block. Vanity is a virtue. Manners get you only a backhand.

Clean-cut is corny, a clinker. Only losers love dogs and small children. Starting each day with a good breakfast is a laugher.

To be notorious is money in the bank. Every time Jim Brown socks it to a girlfriend or policeman they line up for blocks to see his flicks.

Were they suited up today, Ty Cobb and Bobby Layne would be considered choir boys.

Layne, the lumpy legend, always argued that he was no better nor worse than anyone else, but he believed in being honest about it. He always entered and left through the front door in a time when we wanted our heroes to sneak if they had to do those things.

Today's heroes could care less about what we, who make them, want them to do and be.

Today's heroes figure that the idealism we wish for them is, in truth, unreality. That honor is nothing more than blind rigidity. That integrity leads to self-destruction. That the rules of the game are outdated and unneeded.

We want our heroes to be what we aren't and the heroes say to hell with that.

Because of modern communication, the essential ingredient in hero-development — mythmaking — is impossible. Heroes in the classical sense were unflawed by human frailties — uncomplicated, unswerving and totally unreal. They were ideals personified, and righteousness in a white hat.

Today's hero can't hide and doesn't want to. He is humanized to a fault perhaps, until heroism is sissy, innocence is stupidity, and gallantry pays off in a pratfall.

When these new heroes visit places like Vietnam to see our troops they are asked what it's like back in the real world. They can't answer. In a wildly unreal world, the heroes themselves may be the only real and honest things left. Their feet and feats are made of clay and they know it.

Whether we like it or not, that's the way it is. Our once-upon-a-time worshipping eyes may fill with tears because of this, but the heroes have let us know that they are their own men. We no longer own them.

— Sept. 18, 1969

Mr. Average gets caught in the middle of the fray

I don't blame him one bit.

He's confused, bewildered, saddened and now he's mad. Boiling. But, for the first time, he doesn't really know who to be mad at.

He's witnessing maybe the most painful moment in American history, and he doesn't even know where to put the Band-Aid.

If it weren't so tragic, it would make him laugh.

Now he's even confused about his own name.

For years and years and years he's been Mr. Average American. His lifestyle has been one of trying to get along and play by the rules.

It's all been fairly simple. He didn't come in contact that much with the new computerized complexities and social upheavals. Mr. and Mrs. Average American getting up every day and going about the business of being Mr. and Mrs. Average America.

But not now. No longer is he average. He has become Mr. Silent Majority. But he's not really silent. He is majority, all right, but not that conservative, to-the-right majority the media have painted him.

No longer is he Average, because every minority and ethnic group asks, "Where's my fraction of that average?" Even the women's liberation crowd claims he shouldn't even be a male.

He's wondering now about why he has come to all this. Where did the wheel run off? When did the explosion occur?

Then he couldn't even get his mail!

The mailmen, they are his people, his neighbors, his brothers, his father, him. They, too, have always played by the rules and obeyed the laws.

But even they've said to hell with the System and the Establishment — whatever those things are — and have told the rest of the world they won't take it any longer.

So Mr. Average American is taking a look around, taking stock, and suddenly he feels very stupid, like a jerk, a sucker, a dum-dum for trying to cope with life's problems in an orderly by-the-rules fashion. Maybe the mailmen are right.

He's dismayed that his country can't find one qualified judge to fill a Supreme Court vacancy. He's sick that his athletic heroes make more front-page headlines and spend more time in court than they do on the sports pages.

He's heartsick that violence and blowing up buildings and people are accepted so matter-of-factly — cruel obscene acts far more dangerous than all the pornography preachers cry about.

He's utterly amazed that we can stand by and watch our country get involved in still another unpopular tangled war in Laos when we still haven't solved that senseless one in Vietnam.

He's bewildered by the recession that's done everything but drive down the prices and cost of living. He's astonished that the public blindly and silently accepts so much garbage, nonsense and vulgarity for its entertainment.

He has tried to understand the way of these things. He can understand the Black Panthers when they say law without justice is tyranny and knows that if someone — his own forefathers probably — hadn't broken laws once upon a time we'd all still be Catholic or British or both.

He has backed the aroused students of the left and the flag-wavers of the right — but he sees them both shout down speakers who don't suit their views and he wonders what they really mean by free speech.

He has watched with disgust as pandering government officials play politics with the lives and futures of children because they are blackjacked and whitewashed by vote-mongers and power merchants.

He has confronted all the gaps — communication, credibility, generation — and found that instant anger only freezes men's minds into rigid stupidity.

He's being frightened to death by alarming talk of an environmental collapse and has been shocked with hard charges that all his children are or will be on hard stuff.

He has been pulled at and pummeled by extremists on the right and left. He's damned if he does, and damned if he doesn't. He has found that even the mainstream is polluted and the safe middle-of-the-road is a street of crime now.

He has looked for but can't find a common standard for decency and manners. He has searched everywhere for respect and pride and tolerance and found they've vanished. And he can't find very many people who are happy anymore. The only thing he does find in abundance is the finger of blame pointed at him for all these ills, and this he doesn't understand. This is the most frustrating thing of all.

— March 25, 1970

For my children, a song to rekindle patriotism

For Dafna and Jason:

Song dedications over the radio are pretty corny, and probably the same in newspapers, but your Daddy's a pretty corny fellow. Anyway, "Where Have All Our Heroes Gone" is dedicated to you, Dafna, soon-to-be a blush-beautiful 11-year-old, and to you Jason, soon-to-be four and rarin' to have a go at the world.

"Where Have All Our Heroes Gone" is a song your Daddy wrote with a friend, Bill Anderson, a first-class Nashville country music singer and songwriter. To me, Bill is to pure country music what Andy Williams is to pure pop music.

It all started a few years ago in Columbia, S.C., when Anderson and I got to reminiscing about heroes we had when we were growing up. We realized that today's youngsters don't have the Joe DiMaggios and Joe Louises and Jesse Owenses and Stan Musials we had.

A few months ago, Anderson came to Detroit for a big country show at Cobo and we talked again about our heroes and where have they all gone. Anderson said for me to write it all down and he'd do a song about it. Me, a songwriter? Why, I'm so non-musical I don't know which end of the guitar to blow.

When I got home, I sat down and started to think about the media-made heroes today's youth have as idols. It wasn't pleasant. Idols like Jerry Rubin, John Lennon, Abbie Hoffman, Che Guevara, Cassius Clay, Denny McLain, Angela Davis, John Sinclair, Joe Namath, Jim Brown, Huey Newton and a host of other extremist types — from freaks to fascists who flout the rules of society and advocate disruption and me-firstism.

Well, kids, those just aren't the sort of heroes I want you to have. I searched the world of athletics, politics, entertainment, science, etc., and came up with only a handful of the Gordie Howes, Al Kalines and Arnold Palmers.

Television and a general media-overkill have created an instant-hero who isn't prepared to be a hero, and has absolutely no feeling for what a hero should be. He would rather sign deals than autographs. He'd rather endorse things than inspire kids. The old clean-cut hero, All-American boy type — where has he gone?

Well, Dafna and Jason, your song has created quite a bit of talk and controversy. Bill Anderson's inspiring recitation of it on Decca Records is getting played on all sorts of stations all over the nation even though it's a country music-type song.

Since you two are the ones who inspired the song, I thought you should know the truth about it. "Where Have All Our Heroes Gone" is not a political song. It's a gut reaction of a 34-year-old middle-class, middle-of-the-road, middle-American parent who worries about the type of heroes his kids will have to look up to one day. That's all there is to it.

There are people who put it down because they say hero-worshipping is passe. I don't believe these people know what children are all about if they can say this and believe it. I wonder about the type of childhood they must have had. There will always be a need for heroes. Whether we have heroes to meet the need is my point.

I'm told some spiteful people, with weak minds, have tried to read extreme right-wing philosophy into this song and make it out as pro-Vietnam and anti-youth. Your Daddy, as well you know, is not a flag-wrapped patriot who says "Love It Or Leave It" or a radiclib who says "Change It Or Lose It."

You better believe I love my country, the United States of America, spelled with a "c" not a "k," thank you. I love my country as one loves a good wife, which I have in your mother, Beryl. She's not a perfect wife and this is not a perfect country. It would be unbearable if she were or the country were. Average people like me can't live in perfection or with it.

Pro-Vietnam? I think you children know your Daddy's against war and aggression in foreign countries and in our own streets. Anti-youth? Your Daddy's a great admirer of today's young people but not the frauds, fools and ego-crazed self-styled leaders and spokesmen who have complete disregard for our country's laws and both private and public property.

I'm told that one of the underground rock stations plays "Where Have All Our Heroes Gone" and follows it up with the National Anthem as a put-on. When playing the National Anthem is considered a joke, then I know it was time for a song like "Where Have All Our Heroes Gone" to have been written.

America to me, Dafna and Jason, is a collection of all our crises, quarrels, chronic ills, points of view, passions, problems, paradoxes, persuasions and is a bullheaded, alive, shy, cruel, contradictory, sympathetic, loudmouth, tender, very dear and beautiful place.

A place I'm not ashamed for you to grow up in, to become a part of. I just hope when it's yours, it will be a place of peace and smiles. I think if we can find some heroes who respect children and feel children are important once again, we'll have that place. I hope so for your sakes.

Love,
Daddy

— Sept. 25, 1970

Reluctant heroes:
Just what we needed

Heroes. We've been needing them for a long, long time.

A patriotic celebration. We've been needing that for a long, long time.

This hungering nation needed a reason to salute, and the American hostages' flight to freedom gave it to us.

An unabashed America with tears in its eyes and pride in its heart. America's red, white and blue on a rampant field of yellow ribbons.

An America full of love and compassion, overflowing with flag-waving emotion and oneness. An America swelling in song — a "God Bless America" chorus from sea to shining sea.

A goose-bumped America discovering once again the power of patriotism and the flush-rush feeling of national unity. A proud and celebrating America, feeling good about itself.

"What an afternoon!" exclaimed CBS-TV's Dan Rather, normally the paragon of blase restraint. "What a memorable afternoon!" Indeed, it was. And how about that week?

Who will ever forget the week of Jan. 20-27, 1981? Or the 444 days preceding it?

A week that turned a long-soured national psyche into a soaring spirit. A week that turned hostages into heroes.

A week that just happened. A week that took on a life of its own. A roller-coaster week, climaxing in a stirring caravan of emotions in the nation's capital Tuesday.

There are some who haven't seen it this way at all.

Did you read Mike Royko's piece in Sunday's Free Press? The Chicago scold and American cynic wrote, "I just haven't been caught up in the TV-induced euphoria and hysteria about the return of the hostages. I just don't understand all the talk about their being heroes, or about their release being one of the great moments in our history."

In his column, Royko blamed television for this orgy of patriotism. It was Royko at his backlash best, punching out "TV pretty faces" and quoting a Vietnam combat veteran who said, "I went through a lot worse" than the hostages did.

It's hard to argue with that. Part of me agreed with the Royko bias, but a bigger and better part of me said what Royko wrote was really beside the point. In fact, it missed the point entirely.

The point is America once again has some heroes.

We've gone a long, long time without them.

And regardless of what Royko and his ilk say, Americans, not television, picked our new heroes. A nation that didn't know how hungry it has been for heroes. And the heroes we picked had no choice in the matter.

We are emerging from the most narcissistic decade in our history, ushered in by the Me Generation. No one had time for heroes. They have been out of fashion. Superstars replaced our heroes. Good guys in white hats were ridiculed.

Some will even say the notion of patriotic heroes began to wane three decades ago as this country was recovering from World War II and stumbled into the Korean war.

Do you remember any heroes, individually or collectively, from Korea? How about Vietnam? Our servicemen in these wars were in the right place, but at the wrong time, to become heroes. Sad, but true.

The American hostages in Iran were in the wrong place, but at the right time, and this historical glitch has given us our new American heroes.

Why didn't the Korean and Vietnam vets catch on as heroes? Simple. The wars they fought never caught on. Few losing causes create heroes. And what happened in Korea and Vietnam has never been placed in the U.S. win column.

But the return of the American hostages held in Iran for 444 days was perhaps the first international U.S. victory fit for rejoicing and saluting since the V-E and V-J days in '45.

There was a young student from Princeton on one of the networks Tuesday. He said he was in the Washington crowd because it was "the biggest moment in history" in his young lifetime.

He said the return of all the hostages alive was a symbol of the great respect this nation has for life. And for the first time in his life that young student said he felt moved by and overcome with patriotism. And it felt wonderful.

It was an American triumph, something we haven't had lo these many years. It was this sense of victory that spread warmly and honestly throughout the nation Tuesday, a sense of strength symbolically reborn in these hostages-turned-heroes.

Heroes who didn't seek the role. That's the difference.

Reluctant heroes who have made a difference, who touched this nation. Bruce Laingen, an eloquent professional diplomat and spokesman for the hostages, told of signs the bus caravan saw along the way to the Washington celebration.

He said a rather hastily made sign they saw as they left West Point touched them the most. A sign that explained it all, said it all, for the hostages as well as America.

Laingen said the sign read:

"And the world will be better for this."

Amen.

— *Jan. 30, 1980*

An Updated phony American Credo

Back in 1920 satirists H.L. Mencken and George John Nathan compiled a book of myths, shibboleths, prejudices, rumors, common beliefs and unexamined truisms which they called "The American Credo."

Periodically, someone comes along to update this. Time magazine did in 1970 and now Oui magazine has done so in its March issue.

Since Oui is a sexually oriented magazine, some of the new findings can't be reprinted in a family newspaper.

But anyway, from all these sources, plus listening to the people in the streets, here is my version of the American Credo.

You can always get a first-rate meal at a place patronized by truck drivers.

You can catch a venereal disease from a toilet seat.

A woman is not truly fulfilled until she has children.

The Mafia controls everything in the entertainment business.

Gerald Ford is a stand-in for Nelson Rockefeller's incipient presidency.

The Air Force has captured a spaceship and its occupants, which are being held at Wright-Patterson Air Force Base in Dayton, Ohio.

Five hundred million people will starve to death in the next six months.

Richard Nixon was pardoned because he was fixing to tell all he knew about Watergate.

Teddy Kennedy doesn't want to be president of the United States because of the threat to the Kennedys from the weirdos of the world.

J. Edgar Hoover did not die of natural causes.

John and Bobby Kennedy were killed by the right-wing-controlled CIA.

You are safer flying in a jet then driving in your own car.

The children of psychoanalysts are the most neurotic kids of all.

Cracking your knuckles as a child will make them swollen and ugly when you become adult.

Rattlesnake meat tastes just like chicken.

You can't freeze cheese.

Tight pants make you sterile.

If you talk on the telephone while sitting in a bathtub you will be electrocuted.

The inside of golf balls is poisonous.

You can survive a plane crash by sitting in the tail section.

Eating well-done charcoal-broiled steaks will give you cancer.

Homosexuality and gambling are diseases like malaria.

If you remove the DO NOT REMOVE UNDER PENALTY OF LAW tag from a pillow or mattress you may be arrested.

Children trained in new math can't add or subtracted.

All women subconsciously want to be raped.

A hairy chest is a sign of virility.

An icy tray filled with hot water freezes faster than one filled with cold water.

All prostitutes are lesbians.

If you are dreaming about falling and complete the fall before you wake up, you will die.

Blacks have harder heads and weaker shins than whites.

— February 11, 1975

Out of my mind on a Monday moanin'

Fat women eating gooey desserts always try to be so elegantly dainty.

You've got will power when you spot a friend with a black eye and don't ask how he got it.

In every group photograph, there's at least one person who looks as if he would have given anything to have been able to stay home.

Not many countries in this world would fight for their own freedom like we fight for theirs.

Three things you eventually learn not to judge: an eating place by the size of its neon sign; an organization by the beauty of its letterhead; and a man by how fancy his calling card is.

Today's home needs five garages — two for the cars, one for the junk, one for the workshop, and the fifth for garage sales.

It is interesting to note that statements which begin "it is interesting to note" are seldom interesting to note.

Women in their 40s dress like their 20-year-old daughters so that people will think them in their 30s.

If the safety pin were invented today it would have seven moving parts, two transistors, an on-and-off switch, and require a service check every six months.

While some pupils seem to get no grammar in grammar school many of them certainly get high in high school.

So many of our problems could be solved if only the rich man could find out how the poor man lives, and the poor man could find out how hard the rich man works.

Appearances are deceiving. A dollar bill looks exactly like it did

10 years ago.

No wonder our kids are cool. Any generation that can look at the polar ice from below, the moon from behind and Raquel Welch from the side is not likely to be surprised at anything.

Since the most comfortable chairs are the ones worn out the fastest and discarded it makes me wonder what our ancestors thought of those mint-condition antiques sold today.

The reason that so many women have aches and pains at 40 is because most of them are 50.

There's nothing funnier than the look on the face of the person on one end of a dog leash pretending not to know what's going on at the other end.

Nowadays a lot of people commute farther to work than their grandparents went on their honeymoon.

Wouldn't you like to see a fat mannequin in a store window just once?

Women will wear anything new no matter how uncomfortable, and men will wear anything comfortable no matter how old.

Have you ever had your car or TV set repaired and thought the bill was a fair one?

I figure it's more of a knock on the daughter than praise for the mother when the two are told they look like sisters.

When Tuesday Weld travels incognito, does she go under an assumed day?

The trouble with history repeating itself is that the price is always higher and the government always taxes it the second time around.

Parents who worked their way through college are now working their children's way through college.

A big city is one whose main street is never named Main Street.

Which has made the biggest liars: Golf, age, weight, sex, fishing or income tax?

Old-fashioned mothers who can remember their husband's first kiss now have daughters who can't remember their first husband's name.

Life is so fast-paced and programmed these days it is now possible to take a two-week vacation in four days.

I'll never understand how a dress that cost $200 can be described as a "simple frock."

I intensely dislike people who try to flatter you by putting other people down.

HUMOR

Daddy's girl takes over, cuz daddy has a cold

Good morning.

This is Dafna Talbert and I am goin to write the colum today as my Daddy is sick in bed with a cold and hot water bottle and he feels turribul and Momma says, "for hevvins sake dont disturb him or you will think the hole worl has come to an end."

It all started when Daddy got us up brite and early and says, "All rite, we are goin to the Detroit Zoo and have a good time."

He says, "This is an important zoo in the worl and has ever kind of animal there is and it is edukashunal."

This is what happens when me and Momma been begging Daddy to take us somewhere on Sunday stead of sitting round watchin him go to sleep watchin the football game. That is not very much fun for us, I think you will agree.

Anyway, we load up the car with me and Momma and my baby brother Jason who is 19 months old and halfway toilet trained, which Momma says is worst than being all the way or none of the way.

Daddy says he knows exactly how to get to the zoo and Momma says, "Uh oh, we are in truble already. Unless someone draws your Daddy pitchurs he can never get directions rite."

We drive along for about an hour and Momma tells Daddy, "Don't you think you orter ask somebody where we are."

Daddy got all red in the face and said, "I am not goin to let anything upset me this trip, not even your smart mouth. I know where I am."

Momma says, "Okay Marco Polo, then why have I seen that same shopping center over there six different times?"

Daddy stops the car and says, "Okay what if we are lost — it happens to lots of people every day."

"Sure thing," said Momma, "Christofur Clumbus thot he was in India."

Daddy then started to holler, "Jimmy Clark was the world's greatest driver becuz he didn't have a dam wife givin him instructions and they don't have zoos at no Injunapolis."

Anyway, we finally ask somebody where were we and find out we have been only two blocks from the zoo for the last half hour. Momma just laff and laff and Daddy turned redder and redder.

We finally find a parking place about three blocks from the zoo, and Momma says, "We were closer when we were lost." Daddy says, "Ha ha."

Momma suggested that we rent one of those little push carts for Jason and Daddy says, "The day hasnt come that I cant carry my son on my shoulders." Momma says, "You will eat those words dear."

"Dont dear me," says Daddy. "You girls just try to keep up with us boys."

When we got to the giraft place, Daddy tells everybody round us that the girafts front legs look two or three times longer than the rear ones but they are really the same size as it is all an optickle lussion.

"Dont talk so loud or people will think you are some kind of Frank Buck nut," Momma says.

We got to the monkey island and Daddy says to everybody standing around, "I could stay here all day and watch them monkeys."

"It's no wonder," Momma says, "for you it is a family reunion." Everybody there laff and laff and Daddy made us hurry and leave.

At the polar bear place, Daddy said how they looked like humans and Momma said, "They look at you and think they watching a mirror." Everybody laff at this too.

Everybody but Daddy.

Momma ask Daddy, "What are you sweating for? It isn't a hot day."

Daddy is riding Jason on his neck and shoulders and says, "I am not sweating. What makes you thing I'm sweating?"

"Well," says Momma, "that day has finally come."

"What day?" asks Daddy.

"That toilet-training day, when your son cant be carried round your neck," says Momma.

This cause Daddy to step back sudden and trip over a chain. He stumbled around and fell rite into this little duck pond with Jason still sittin on his shoulders all the time, laffing and laffing. Jason thot it was funnier than the mokeys.

Daddy didn't say much the rest of the day. He did coff and sneeze a lot and when we got home he went strate to bed.

So thats why I had to rite the colum today. Momma says we need the money and my Daddy is in no mood to be funny. Daddy says for

you not to believe a word of it. This makes everybody laff.
Everybody but Daddy.

— *Sept. 27, 1968*

Here's a horoscope
that might be the real you

ARIES (Mar. 20-April 19): You are a ram, but a ram aren't a ewe.
You are a pioneer, making it difficult when job-hunting, since
Pioneers are needed about as much as shepherds and court jesters.
Men are greatly attracted to you, which can be a hang-up if being a
super-ram is also your hang-up. Your sign rules the head and face,
which in your case would help considerably: A great month for you to
buy a midget.

TAURUS (April 20-May 20): Your sun is in Taurus, the Bull, a
feminine sign. Your son is in jail, the drunk tank, a masculine sign.
People born under the Bull have to dodge a lot. You like money and
cooking. Good month to rob a short-order cook. Your timing must be
perfect. You are a moneymaker, but be careful and make yours look
as much as possible like the U.S. Treasury's. Start a garbage
collection.

GEMINI (May 21-June 20): Both of you are impulsive. Sign of
Twins. Are you pregnant? You just think you aren't. One of you is.
Your sign controls your hands, arms and shoulders and if you don't
keep your hands off your neighbor's spouse you're going to be
controlled all right. You are restless and extravagant. Lavish
spending can be disastrous. Don't buy lavishes, even 10 percent
under wholesale. Hail a cab, then snow it.

CANCER (June 21-July 21): You are the Crab, a movable sign
that controls the chest and breast, a problem if you live next to one of
those handy Gemini people. You appreciate the home life and love
your mate, but your mate usually hates you. You have many friends,
but your mate has more. Water your mate's drink this month, eat
cottage cheese on Wednesday and save 1937 dimes. Beware of kids
with popsicles.

LEO (July 22-Aug. 22): You are a leader, and all Leos are, except
Leo Schwartz who has a hard enough time following. You are Lion,
kiss Alex Karras. (That's what's wrong with Leo Schwartz, if you
want to know the truth.) You will win a Lee Trevino look-alike

contest this month, and your husband will win a divorce. Leo Schwartz will be named correspondent. The second Saturday of the month is a great day for friends, terrible for you. Fold all bedspreads back.

VIRGO (Aug. 23-Sept. 22): Your Son is in Virgo, the Virgin, a cold, variable sign that rules the bowels. You are industrious, intelligent and a builder. Monday is your lucky day, green is your lucky color, and the bathroom is your lucky room. An exciting member of the opposite sex will enter your life this month. The person will be exceptionally constructed, most willing and 24. Which is not a very high IQ, but you can't have everything. Have your nerves restrung.

LIBRA (Sept. 23-Oct. 22): You are a compulsive ashtray emptier, which raises eyebrows since no one in your family smokes (except maybe your oldest son who has a joint or two on Saturday nights). You are an idealist. Your favorite color is orange. Your name is Carl. Bruce? Susan? Anyway, Libras are Balance, scales always even. You are a lousy tipper, too. You are strangely attracted. Stay six miles from all strangers. Fall in with bad companions this month. Broaden horizons; mingle with weirdos. Sin a little.

SCORPIO (Oct. 23-Nov. 21): You are dark and devious, Scorpio. The Scorpion, a silent, feminine sign that rules the secret parts. You could never work in the Pentagon. You are very magnetic, extremely attractive to the opposite sex this month, particularly if the opposite sex is a magnet. You enjoy life, but can't stand Time or Look. Your favorite color is battleship gray, which means you are either a Confederate spy or a crafty rhinoceros.

SAGITTARIUS (Nov. 22-Dec. 20): Sagittarians are the Archer, a sports fan and athletically inclined. You hang around locker rooms a lot, which can get you arrested or lots of friends, depending on your sex. A small, dark cloud will follow you all month long, raining, hailing and intermittently snowing on you. Pay no attention to it, or it will come back next week. You have a tendency toward halitosis. Keep your mouth shut, or suck Airwicks. Eat green salad bowls.

CAPRICORN (Dec. 21-Jan. 19): You are a goat (I'm sorry if you don't like your sign, speak to your parents about it, not me). Yours is a nocturnal sign that rules the knee. Beware of people born under the water signs, and also bosses who ask you to sit on their knee. You have a high moral standards and have a tendency to be a bit shy about undressing outdoors in public. You are sensitive to the feeling and desires of others, so you undress anyway. This month you will get sunburned, and a football knee — uunnnhhhh!

AQUARIUS (Jan. 20-Feb. 17): You are unpredictable, change-able and probably wet your diapers a lot as a child. Maybe as an adult, too. We never know about you Aquarians. You have strong ankles and bad left index fingers. Keep your hands closed this month. You are an individualist and still wear Nehru jackets, crinolines and white socks. Other people don't think you're playing with a full deck. The joke is on them — you aren't, because of your hang-up with one-eyed jacks and split-whiskered kings.

PISCES (Feb. 18-Mar. 19): You are a fish, but so fun-loving nobody has the heart to tell you. You have a great smile. Stay away from funerals and famines. You should drive a Marquis so we could finally have some fish in a Mercury! I thought you were fun-loving? I didn't expect you to go to Pisces over it but at least you could smile. If you don't watch out, you're going to make a liar out of this star and sign stuff.

— Aug. 2, 1971

Playing Ann Landers
is tricky question

The first big-time syndicated newspaper columnist I ever met was Ann Landers. She was the best-read newspaper columnist in the world even back then, which was more years ago than Eppie Lederer (her real name) and I care to remember.

She is a ball of fire in her real life, just like her answers to readers' questions. (No, she does not make those questions up, but she suspects some of her readers do.) I've always admired her talent with the one-line answers and ability to speak her mind about what she feels even if it may fly in the face of form and the norm.

And I'll have to tell you this, many's the time someone has asked her a question I've also wanted an answer to and Ann Landers' advice or answer hits the nail on the head, without mincing or manufacturing words.

I'll also have to admit I've always wanted to write a "Dear Ann Landers" column. And since I have just declared this National Secret Desire Day, I will do that little ol' thing right now.

DEAR BOB: My husband paid $145 for a rowing machine, saying he needed the exercise. And yet in the summer months I can't even get him to mow the grass! What's the matter with a guy like that anyway? — Wondering.

DEAR WON: In the first place, you can't cut grass with a rowing machine. Whoever heard of such a thing? Are you sure you're thinking this thing through?

DEAR BOB: What causes dandruff? — Embarrassed.

DEAR EM: Itchy white flakes in the hair causes dandruff, silly.

DEAR BOB: Monday night my husband plays poker. Wednesday he has a lodge meeting. Friday he bowls. Saturday it's softball. Yet every time I leave the house he hits the ceiling. Do you think this is fair? If my husband has four nights out with the boys, don't you think I'm entitled to at least one? — Tied Down.

DEAR TIED: Husbands are funny about their wives having a night out with the boys.

DEAR BOB: My parents will soon celebrate their 45th anniversary. And they have fought tooth and nail every day of every year. How can anyone fight like that and stay married? What's wrong? — Worried.

DEAR WO: If you ask me you ought to find out who this Tooth and Nail are. That seems where the problem is. They must be a real pain.

DEAR BOB: How many grandparents can a dog have? — Curious.

DEAR CUR: Since it was domesticated 10,000 years ago, the dog has gone through 4,000 generations, as contrasted to 400 for man. You figure it out. I never was good at math.

DEAR BOB: Is it legal for a man to marry his widow's sister? — Perplexed.

DEAR PER: Is that a trick question? Yes it is. You figure out why.

DEAR BOB: What is the significance of the round ball on top of a flagpole? — Patriotic.

DEAR PAT: Besides being the place where the flagpole stops, nothing.

DEAR BOB: How much water is there on earth? — Thirsty.

DEAR THIR: Hydrologists estimate there are 326 million cubic miles of water in existence on this planet. But 99 percent of this is brine and ice in oceans and island seas, so it's no wonder it's so hard to get a glass of water sometimes.

DEAR BOB: What is the life expectancy of a dollar bill? — Taxpayer.

DEAR TAXED: In circulation, a dollar bill will last around 18 months. If you are married and have children, the dollar bill in your pocket will last about a half hour after you get home.

DEAR BOB: My wife and I are having an argument about wigs. Personally, I think these fashion wigs do a great deal for a person, and she says they don't. We've decided to let you decide — Puzzled Pair.

DEAR PAIR: Look, why don't you just wear your fashion wig when your wife isn't around and that'll solve everything.

DEAR BOB: Why can't a person living in Detroit be buried west of the Rockies? — Anxious.

DEAR ANX: Is that another trick question?

DEAR BOB: My husband and I haven't slept together in 10 years. We have 12 children, and one or more is always sick and keeps one of us up all the time. — Tired.

DEAR TI: But what's the question?

DEAR BOB: What does a male chauvinist give his women's liberation wife for her birthday? — Piggy.

DEAR PIG: A divorce.

DEAR BOB: Do you think a young girl should learn about life before 18? — Soon-to-Be.

DEAR SOON: No. I think 18 is entirely too large an audience.

— *July 8, 1976*

It's one neat Talbert against the slobs

BY LYNN TALBERT

I now know how my dad must have felt living in a home where he was outnumbered three to one by the opposite sex. Living with one male like Bob was strange enough, but now I am in the minority for the first time in my life.

Since we last spoke — read? — I have inherited 14-year-old Jason, 11-year-old Smokey, the castrated dog who is still a male even if only in memory, a 10-room house and all the marvelous things that go along with living in a YMCA.

First of all, my only experiences with animals were several goldfish who died and a parakeet I couldn't stand. Smokey is an adorable cockapoo, but probably one of the five dumbest dogs in

America.

Whatever you say to Smokey, his response is the same: a doleful stare with his big brown eyes. I really have grown to love him, but occasionally want to rip his little face off when he leaves his favorite bone in the middle of the floor where guess who always steps on it, particularly when guess who's arms are filled with groceries and other spillables.

Another face-ripping time is the trip to the vet. The last time I took him — Bob and I draw straws, loser takes him — I asked the receptionist for a tranquilizer. For me, not him!

My only experience being around anyone younger then myself was when I was baby-sitting in high school. Particularly when they are younger than you and bigger. Jason and I are good friends. I have watched him grow from a little seven-year-old into a healthy teenager who towers over me. I haven't beat him in arm wrestling in four years. And he still likes to humiliate me — using one arm to my two and still beating me.

Owning my own home allows me now to sit in my backyard without 20 million people walking by. I also have to — one pays the price! — rake the leaves and weed the garden.

I revel in the security of owning our own home, but I am also aware of being fussier about housekeeping, which, as you know from my first column, was a point of contention with Bob. Now it is definitely three male Slobs against one female Neat!

I love all the conveniences of a home, but hate it when something goes wrong with the appliances. Bob and Jason think they are electricians, plumbers and carpenters. I think they are a scream — literally! — when they try to fix something together.

When I want to call in a professional, they look at me as if to say, "Just because you're unable to understand complex repairs doesn't mean we are!" I'm still cleaning up their messes and have waited 14 months for the toilet-paper holder to be put up.

It's amazing how big this house seemed at first. All those rooms and closets. We didn't think we had enough furniture to fill it. Our old townhouse must have been unbelievably crowded because not only did we fill up every room, the basement is half full of half-full boxes: Bob's half-finished projects.

When we moved in, Bob was in seventh heaven because he thought I wouldn't throw away his boxes, whose contents are mostly unknown and useless. Wrong, packrat breath!

Last Wednesday I arose at 5 a.m. to carry out every unpacked box for the garbage pickup. Think he noticed? Two years from now, he'll notice and ask me, "What did you do with that cardboard box labeled 'Immediate Action'?"

About the yard. My mother loved to garden — I did not. I do now. Not because I've become some earth mother, but it's either that or pay several hundred dollars for someone to pull weeds and trim bushes.

We decided to invest the money in simple equipment, like an electric weed-trimmer, hedge shears and mulching lawn mower. Bob, of course, wanted to get a riding/four-speed/fertilizer spreader/snowblower/tractor/loader/backhoe for our enormous vegetable garden (three feet by two feet by three feet) but I squelched it, explaining our subdivision would have to be rezoned to farm land, which it was not all that long ago. We compromised and got three heavy-duty shovels and a rake.

It has been two years since my last column, so I was amazed the other day when a Canadian border customs officer recognized me from the picture in that column. It really gave me the impetus to write another.

My ego and urge to mouth off had absolutely, definitely nothing to do with it. The last year has been a real trip. I'm now laughing longer and harder at Erma Bombeck. She doesn't make any of that up, does she?

— Nov. 4, 1981

Out of my mind
on a Monday moanin'

Children are a a great comfort in your old age and they help you reach it faster, too.

Men drive as if they own the road; women as if no one else were using it.

For $20 you can be tested to find out your IQ — and if you're willing to pay that price I can tell you your IQ for free.

"Bore," I feel, is the worst of all the four-letter words.

I never believe the man who says "I'm charging you exactly what it cost me."

A backward nation is one which doesn't have a pollution problem.

Dying for some cause doesn't necessarily impress me, but living totally for one against all obstacles does.

I love telling new people my wrong astrology sign because they will invariably say, "I knew it!" to any sign I claim to be.

Man's best epitaph is written on the hearts of his friends.

Is there a cure for wheat germ?

You can kiss it goodby when someone says, 'I'll pay you as soon as I get my check cashed."

Happiness is having a brother-in-law who makes less than you do.

The poor call 'em kinfolk, the middle class call 'em relatives, and the rich call 'em heirs.

Whenever someone tells you the time and says, "It can't be," you automatically feel like you've had a good time.

Fruit cups never taste as good as they look.

Thank goodness there are enough people who like dark meat and enough people who like white meat to make chickens come out even.

You can live without seat belts, but why die trying?

Furs look better on their original owners.

Wealthy people who say, "I was happier when I had nothing," either have poor memories or are rotten liars.

Doctors and dentists, for some reasons, have a notion your time isn't as valuable as theirs.

It takes the world's most special young person to get up in the morning and deliver the newspaper to you and no way is this person ever fully appreciated by publishers and subscribers.

People with low blood pressure never talk about it.

All in favor of conserving gas, raise your right foot.

Howard Cosell and Norman Mailer are legends in their own minds.

Sign on a closed east side bar: "Friends and relatives said it couldn't be done and they were right because they never paid their bills."

World politics is like a square dance, the minute everyone gets the hang of it and it is going smoothly, they change partners.

Your real friends believe in you even when you don't.

Fish may be dumb, but did you ever see one spend $300 on equipment to catch a man?

There's nothing sadder than watching a good movie in an almost empty movie theater.

If you fool around with Mother Nature long enough, Father Time will get you.

MY SOUTHERN ACCENT

Rye cheer is some hep to know what Tabbert's sane

Take typewriters. You really can't tell one from another.

A typewriter in Florida writes just like a typewriter in Michigan or the Carolinas or Texas or New York or California.

I've never met a typewriter with a Southern drawl, a Yankee accent, a New England brogue or a Midwestern twang. Drawls, accents, brogues and twangs are exclusive properties of the human tongue. And the one in my mouth must be a sho'nuff dandy.

I'm Carolina grown and I'll be talking to someone and they'll start smiling by the second sentence. By the fourth, they look like a mule eating briars.

Southern accents, for some strange reason, make people from other regions grin like an actor at a toothpaste tryout.

Brooklyn accents do the same thing to some people, but not necessarily Southerners. There's something about a "youse guys" that makes a Southerner see carpetbagger red.

I've been making a lot of after-dinner speeches lately and just opening mah ol' magnolia mouth causes 'em to break up.

I don't sound a bit Southern to me. I'll admit I don't sound Yankee or twangy or broguey, either. But people look at me as if I've got a five-pound bag of grits in mah mouf.

I don't like grits. Or molasses, hawg jowl or cornbread. And believe me, Southern fried chicken is exactly like Northern fried. There's not a finger-lick of difference.

There are scholars and comedians who make a living out of regional dialects. I'm not worried about making a living with mine, but I am worried about it being understood. So I've prepared a handy guide so you can understand Southerners when you hear them.

JEVVER — Jevver mail that letter?

WHIRL — Whirl we spend our vacation this year?

HARD — Ford hard 4,600 new workers.

WADDER — What the hard workers drink when they get thirsty.

ARSH — People who come from Arland.

HIZZEN — Opposit of hern.

ADAM — The adam bum is gonna blow us all to hell.

AIRS — The shortstop made two airs; also, what you hear with.

TOM — What tom he say he'd meet us?

YEAR — Yawl come see us, year?

NODE — If I'd node you was coming.

YORTER — Yorter node that I was coming.

CISTERN — My cistern me are going to see grammaw.

BUBS — The porch light bubs are burned out.

BOBBER — The man who cuts your hair.

BUBBIN — What hard hands mix with their wadder for serious drinkin'.

ATOLL — Atoll boy's a worker!

HOD — How good hard hands work.

NOME — Nome, I ain't seen 'im today.

SUMMERS — I ask him where he was headed and he said, "Summers."

THOW — Thow me the ball.

TOAD — The fullback ran toad the line.

AHMONA — Ahmona tote the ball this time.

SHURF — All criminals are frayed of the shurf.

CLOSE — My wife says she hasn't got any close to wear.

FAR — It burns; it's what you put the arn in to git it hot.

FOE — The number between three and five.

HIGH YOUNG — What you do with the coat you take off when you enter a house; you high young it up.

DRY INK — What you do with bubbin and wadder.

TARRED — What a hard-working hard hand is after a day's work is done; he is tarred, also woe out.

ABODE — A wooden plank.

RYE CHEER — Put it down rye cheer, please.

SANE — Speak up, we can hardly hear what you are sane.

AX — Would you ax me that question again?

CANE CHEW — Cane chew understand me?

FLOW — What you put rugs and carpets on in a house.

POKE — Hog meat; when sliced and fried, it becomes beckon, usually served with aigs.

POET — Transfer liquid from one container to another.

BERF — When's your berf day? The day you was borned.

SPECK — I speck she'll be home any minute; also, have a little speck for the dead.

CRINE — Wonder what she's crine about this time?

Think yawl got it? Yorter. But chew need enny hep, jest cowl me, year?

— *Feb. 10, 1969*

Here's a guide
to dulcet Dixie diction

I once had a fresh-from-Boston history professor friend who thought he would get on the good side of his class of Southern freshmen with this little joking question: "Do they let your brothers and sisters out of school for cotton picking?"

My friend decided to forego the humor when someone asked in return, "Cotton-pickin' WHAT?"

And a delightful Southern belle in all innocence heard her Midwestern college roommate exclaim, "Men are all alike!" Miss Mason Dixie replied, "Men are all Ah like, too."

There is a definite Nawth-Souf communication gap. "It" (in the Nawth) and "hit" (Southern style) is a problem.

Understanding that language of languages, "Sho'nuffyawl," requires a keen ear, sharp eye and a steady hand, plus a heart that's pure. It's knowing, for example, that "toreckly" means soon, "sho" means sure, and "chirren" are children.

One of the things ("thangs") that amuse me about Sho'nuffyawl is how Yankees "git a'holt of hit" and mush-mouth it so.

Yankees swear Southerners say, "Cane chew high-young yo' high-ut up?" for "Can't you hang your hat up?"

Yankees have a way of really laying it on thicker'n grits and 'lasses. Not only in our "lang-wedge" but Yankees think all hillbillies love corn pone and fried chicken and will serve it to you every chance they get.

Most Southerners, I know, would not know a chitt'lun if they met a chitterling walking down the street.

Yankees mess up Sho'nuffyawl "sump hen tar-bull," or something terrible.

Maybe the following list will clear up some of the problem areas in closing the Nawth-Souf Communication Gap. My advice to you is to read these out loud and s-l-o-w-l-y:

MINE EYES — salad dressing.

SAM ITCH — two pieces of bread with "sump hen" 'tween 'um.

HINES — what you have at the end of your arms.

BECKON — usually eaten with eggs at "brake fuss."

TONE — ripped as in "Yo' drass is tone."

HEP — to help, or assist; sometimes "a hep-her will hope you out of a jam."

CAD — to carry as in "He cad allus to town in his cah."

HITKIN — It can.

KANG — king, as in "I helt a kang-high straight poker hine."

SNOWIN' — what a lot of people wind up doing when they sleep with thier mouths open.

A BOOT — about, as in "Hit's a boot tom you got cheer."

TAR — what makes your "cah" roll.

WHYWALLS — what some "tars" come in.

SHAR — as in "He took hisself a shar bath."

WEENS — as in "Weens'll go this way and yoons go that way."

GRANITE — to concede as in "The judge granite her divorce."

LACK — to enjoy something as in "Ah lack bubbin and wad her."

MALLER — the last half of a snack treat as in "Let me toast them marsh mallers."

FUR PIECE — distance as in "He lived a fur piece from Fote Wuff, Taxes."

MINNERS — small fish bait.

RAIL — an adverb of degree as in "He got hurt rail bad."

YET? — an interrogative meaning "Have you eaten yet?"; often shortened to "Yet yet?"

STUD — to stand as in 'He shouldn't have stud unner that open winner."

— June 7, 1974

Jevver wonder what Tabbert's sane

A recent trip South refreshed my ears to the nuances within that great broad thing we call the Southern accent. There are differences as big as between New England and New York accents, but for some reason most Northerners have always grouped all folks from below the Mason-Dixon line as all talking one sort of semi-literate way.

When Jimmy Carter and his brother Billy arrived on the scene, everybody started to come out with their versions of the way

Southerners talk. I just want you to know that I was eight years ahead of them all.

Shortly after coming to this city, I realized right away that people expected me to sound in person exactly the way I sounded in print. If I were to read these things to you out loud, you'd probably get every third word I exaggerate.

(Editor's note: He does?)

I do have a Southern accent. No getting around that. But on Feb. 10, 1969, yours truly trotted out a column entitled "Rye Cheer is Some Hep to Know What Tabbert's Sane," which hepped spell out some true-'nuff S'uthern 'soresshuns.

Over the years from a variety of Southern sources, they have been collected and it might be sort of fun to recall and add to that list. Jist hep yo'seff:

ATTAIR — Attair lady you is looking at, son, is mah wye-uff.

BONE — I was bone in Sow Ca'lina.

BEEYUN — That's how many dollars we thought How'ud Hughes had.

STOW — Place where you shop and buy thangs.

BIGOTRY — Look at all them birds up in that bigotry.

COUSIN — I won't go cousin I don't want to.

COORS — She was a dancer in a coors line.

HUN-ID — Loan me just a hun-id 'til Sattiddy.

MARE — He's the head man in any city, as in Mare Young.

COWL — I been way-teen hall day for yo' fone cowl.

OFFEN — Git offen that car's fender, boy.

A PAWN — The way fairy tales start, "Once a pawn a tom."

SOD — There are two sods to every story.

TUTHER — Hits one or tuther.

VIOLINS — They's too much violins on telluhvision.

WUKKIN — Don't mess with hard hands when they're wukkin hod.

ZACKLEY — Zackley where were you when you lost hit?

LILAC — Nixon lilac he did before.

— May 17, 1977

Speak up, I can hodly hear what you sane

According to an article in the Wall Street Journal on American speech habits, the editors of an upcoming six-volume atlas on regional dialects say that American speech can be divided into four basic categories:

Eastern — New England and environs; Midland/Pennsylvania — the border states and the southern Midwest; Southern — the old plantation states; Northern — the upper Midwest.

The compilers of this atlas contend that the speech of the Eastern United States is the most varied. There are 18 identifiable regional dialects on the East Coast alone, they say.

You Midwesterners are always bragging about your lack of a dialect. Big deal. Everyone sounds just like everyone else. How dull, really.

Now yawl take the Souf. Witches whar lotsa you-uns take to this tom of yeh-ear. I now off her yawl a kleckshun of mah fave rights from all oh-vuh the Soufland:

FRAYED — In some areas it means you are skert-to-deaf.

MEER — Something that reflects an image.

CANADAS — People running for public office, as in "He's a canada for mare."

CIZZEN — People who vote on canadas if they are reg-stirred to vote.

FORRID — The area just above yo' eyes.

PAUL — In some regions this means "father will."

BUM — A means of destructions, as in a new clear bum.

GRANITE — To concede, as in "The judge granite her a divorce."

LIE BERRY — Place that keeps books.

CHALK-LET — A flavor.

DES MOINES — They belong to me.

FEEL — An open space.

GARNER — Someone who tends to flowers and yards.

ICE COOL — What some '80 grads just got out of.

JELL — What the shurf puts crim nails.

HIGHER — A shortened four-word greeting ("How do you do?")

GROAN — Increasing in size, as in "My, haven't yo' chirren groan."

PRE SHADE — To be grateful, as in "I pre shade what you did for me."

HOMINY — What number, as in "Hominy staying for supper?"

NUFF — Of this for now. Year?

— *Aug. 27, 1980*

Out of my mind on a Monday moanin'

The greatest gift you can give a child is a dream, and the greatest help is showing him how to make that dream possible.

Is there a happier moment than when you compose a hopefully funny telegram and read it over the phone to the Western Union girl and she laughs?

When people tell me, "I just don't understand today's young people," I wonder if I'm supposed to believe they understand everything else.

Taxing streetwalkers and criminals would be one way the city could get money by hooker by crook.

I've come to the conclusion that to get a green lawn it would be just as cheap to chop up money and sprinkle it all over the yard.

If someone would pay you a dollar for every kind word you spoke and collect 50 cents for every unkind word, would you be rich or poor?

Some women are attractive in tight pants, but that doesn't go for the bulk of them.

I'm always baffled and slightly irritated by a happy marriage between two people I dislike.

Why do birds hop instead of walk?

The two worst years in a women's life are when she's 11 and when her daughter's 11.

Disc jockeys who work at being funny never are as funny as they think they are.

Key words for historians recording this era will be "instant" and "portable."

Young people are so much younger today than when I was their age but people my own age always seem so much older than me.

Where did the middle initial "H" come from when people swear "Jesus H. Christ"?

If I understand doctors correctly, we could all live longer if we quit everything that makes us want to live longer.

Think back: In any Western movie you've ever seen on the screen or tube has a bartender ever given anyone change?

Three things that are virtually impossible: putting toothpaste back in the tube, pushing a chain, and getting off magazine subscription lists.

A bowler's affection for his bowling ball aproaches a pipe-smoker's love for his pipes.

The time I feel most like an idiot is when I wait for an intersection traffic light to change and there's not another car in sight.

You can bet that the fellow who says, "Now you can do me a favor," has never done one for you.

I wonder if waiters who toss Caesar salads with such magnificent flourishes do the same thing in their own homes?

Cat and dog food commercials rank right in there with deodorant commercials as the silliest on TV.

It's time for a diet when you push yourself away from the table and it's the table that moves.

At any given cocktail party 10 percent of the people eat 90 percent of the hors d'oeuvres.

I always have to look up how to spell hors d'oeuvres.

This is the era of the second car, the second job, the second mortgage, the second TV and the second marriage.

When a man helps his wife into the car and no one is watching it's either a new wife or a new car.

The same guy who asks the waiter "What's the damage" at the end of a meal will stand beside his home bar and tell you "Name your poison."

Have you ever noticed they play the same song in all the movies to indicate a character has amnesia?

Tell me, please, whatever happens in the WORST of families?

Some smart person will one day open up a "What did you bring me, Daddy?" gift shop in airports and hotels stocked with just that type of item.

CLOWNING AROUND

Ladies, I salute your fortitude in enduring panty hose misery

Ladies, you have my admiration and sympathy. How you can possibly cope with panty hose day after day is beyond me. Panty hose are next to impossible in addition to being next to you.

I got involved in this Great Panty Hose Put-On when I chided Bonwit-Teller's Bob Poore that if he would make me a pair of hot pants, I'd wear 'em. I said it right there on camera in front of all Sherry Kaye's "Woman's World" Channel 9 audience.

Poore is no slouch when it comes to promotion. And he was also looking for a way to get even with me. Poore and I had gone 'round and 'round over that abortive women's fashion — the midi. He was for 'em and you know how I stood on the midi. Poore, I must admit, is a good loser, but a sneaky devil.

He said he'd outfit me in the very latest hot pants and had Margo Czuckerman, BT's ace fitter, design a special pair of hot pants for me. Poore swears, "To fit you we just sewed two size 20s together." Smart-mouth store managers are a pain in the hot pants.

Let's be honest. Hot pants are nothing more than gym or tennis shorts. So to jazz up my outfit, Poore had "Sam" Harrington, a beautiful lady, make me a "manbag" out of mohair. Larry Sherman, who has a shoe store in Somerset Mall, fitted me out in a pair of Peter Max-looking, red-white-and-blue-stars-and-stripes sneakers. The final touch, Poore insisted, was a bright red pair of panty hose. Beautiful.

What better day to wear all this than April's Fool Day, right? After all, if I met someone important, I wanted to have an excuse. And it just so happened that I was the commentator at the Cystic Fibrosis Fashion Show Shirley Buterakos was putting on in Grand Blanc April 1.

I forgot that a lot of the Detroit Lions would be sharing the same dressing room with me, putting on great-looking clothes from Roberts David Alan in Flint. And there I am in my hot pants and panty hose.

"What's the matter with you," All-Pro Charlie Sanders wanted to know, "you got some sort of rash?"

"Those are panty hose," I sort of mumbled, trying to hide the fact that I could only get them halfway up my legs.

"Panty hose!" came a choral shout from Lem Barney, Mel Farr and Paul Naumoff.

"We always heard you writers were funny," said Farr, slipping into an all-leather ensemble complete with whip.

"I wouldn't talk," I mumbled, still trying to get the panty hose up.

Minnesota Viking Paul Krause said, "Don't let 'em kid you, I think you look just darling." Sure must get awful lonely in Vikingland, I thought.

But it was at this point my admiration for you ladies began to grow. There ain't no way with panty hose.

Virginia Knauer, President Nixon's consumer complaint screener, says the fit of panty hose is one of the biggest headaches women seem to have today. Well, the head wasn't exactly where my problem was. My problem with panty hose sort of centered around the crotch. Actually, my panty hose's crotch sort of centered around my knees. How the blazes do you get the bloomin' bloomers up tight?

Understand "Drooping Crotch" is just one of several problems you gals have with panty hose. The "Ankle Wrinkle" is another, as is "Baggy Knee" and the "Sliding Waist." My wife, Beryl, had the Sliding Waist hit her once at the worst of all possible times. We were in New York for the Broadway opening of "Applause" and arrived by limousine at the searchlighted Palace Theatre. Beryl's silver panty hose started the "Sliding Waist" bit as we were walking up the red carpet into the theater. Beryl's elbows searched desperately for the waistband, her legs kept striding wider and wider and somehow, smiling all the while, she made it giving one of the truly great but overlooked performances of the evening. I never really appreciated her problem until I wrestled with my own red panty hose.

First of all I tried putting 'em on standing up. Then I tried tugging them. No way. You have to inch your way into them. My legs are so big inching could take all day. Somehow I got them up enough to pull on my hot pants. I stood up proudly and sighed. Then I screamed. So help me, I thought a spider had gotten into those panty hose and was climbing up the back of my leg. You ladies know what it was — a run! My first run, and hopefully, my last. It's the most horrible, frustrating feeling in the world.

— April 5, 1971

Take my advice:
Don't fight a chimp

I used to do a lot of crazy physical things and write about them. Now I find it less trying and a lot safer to just think crazed thoughts and write about them.

During my salad years at this trade I had no responsibilities like wives and children. There was also a rage within me to experience it all.

I've plunged Rocky Mountain rapids in a truck tire inner tube. Cracked a couple of bones, damn near drowned, but got one pretty fair column out of it.

When go-carts were first popular, I rode a hot-rodder's souped-up cart (it had eight little engines) 100 miles per hour. Rather, I bounced a quarter of a mile in it, trying to keep it from flying.

I once ate 78 fried catfish, washing 'em down with over two cases of beer at one five-hour sitting. If Guinness had a record for indigestion, that little caper would have earned it for me.

Taking full leave of my senses, I once climbed into the ring with a professional wrestler name of Gypsy Joe, who didn't take kindly to some comments I'd written about wrestlers not being athletes. Before I was carried out, Gypsy Joe made a believer out of me.

To help promote a polio-vaccine campaign, I lived in an iron lung for a couple of days — letting it take over my breathing — and I've had claustrophobia ever since, plus a great deal of empathy for the handicapped.

George Plimpton isn't the only writer who scrimmaged with a football team. Ol' Bob Plumpton once did the same thing. As a sportswriter I had written something to the effect that even I, overweight and slow afoot, could gain consistent yardage against the University of South Carolina defensive line.

"Put up or shut up," I was challenged. I put up, was murderously put down, and forevermore shut up about that line. On cold mornings my bursitis twinge reminds me oh-so-painfully of the bottom of that pileup.

I once put on a rubber suit and headgear and let a 427-horsepower dragboat pull me through the water at 80 miles per hour. It was like being pulled through loose concrete. I was black and blue for months.

Since arriving on this scene, I've done far less physical craziness. I got into Michigan winter sports by letting Peggy Fleming give me the most embarrassing skating lesson anyone has ever had. I'm not exactly your most coordinated individual and her eyes were so unbelievably beautiful I just wound up melting in heaps all over the ice.

When the Red Wings had that great scoring line of Howe, Delvecchio and Mahovlich, I again took leave of my senses. I padded up and got in the goalie's position and tried to see how many of their shots I could clock.

They scored several hundred goals in a few minutes. The goal looked like a puck bin. They were using me as a carom post. They had promised not to lift 'em. Don't believe a professional hockey player's promise. Not only did they lift 'em, they aimed 'em.

I stopped two. Gordie Howe laced one so hard that it lodged in my belly and pads. A save's save. The other was more embarrassing. Howe again. Grinning, he told me this one was coming right at my face.

Well, I watched that puck from the ice as it rose straight for me. I watched it right into my glove, then I watched the force carry the glove right into my eyes, knocking me half-crazy. No, I was half-crazy to begin with for even getting on the ice. That made me all crazy.

But two things recently reminded me of the craziest thing I ever did. As I look back on it now, it was also the most dangerous.

In the Sept. 26 issue of Sports Illustrated, an article on Ringling Bros. circus star and animal trainer Gunter Gebel-Williams says that the chimpanzee is the most dangerous of all animals.

And over the summer I received several dozen clippings from a Florida newspaper telling of the death of Joe, the boxing chimp and star of the Noells' Ark Gorilla Show, out of Tarpon Springs.

I fought Joe twice. Once, on a lark, at the South Carolina State Fair, when the hairy little rascal wanted me within a minute. If you've ever run into a big tree at night you know how I felt when that chimp crawled me.

I was prepared for a one-two boxer combination, but Joe had a one-two-three-four — and the four was a conga kick to the kidney.

I weighed about 275, half suet and the other half crazy, as I've said. Joe weighed 95 pounds, stood four feet and his arms drug the ground when they weren't dragging me around the cage.

The second time I fought Joe was for Argosy magazine, back in '64. It gained some national limelight for this little battler who had fought over 25,000 men and never lost a match.

In hand-to-hand battle, a chimpanzee will beat a human every time. For a man to beat a chimp in a fight he'd have to kill it. For one thing, chimps know no pain in a fight. You can't hurt 'em. If you do, they never let on. They fight over it and to the death.

As Curry Kirkpatrick wrote in his excellent SI article: "Contrary to popular opinion, the most fearsome creature in the circus may be the darling little chimpanzee that rides a motorcycle and bangs the cymbals . . . If dressing-room gossip can be relied upon, the roaring Bengals are caged beauties incapable of doing harm, the huge elephants gentle souls. Chimps? Chimps would just as soon tear your face apart."

And I fought one. Twice. Craziness.

— Oct. 4, 1977

Exposing some myths about nudity

True nudists are upset. And rightly so. For starters, most of our ideas about nudism are all wrong from the beginning. Especially if our views of nudism were from furtive glances at the inside pictures of an old Sunshine & Health magazine of the '50s.

Most all those lovely ladies and handsome men in the peak of physical perfection were paid and posed models, although some may have also been sun fanciers, too. Part of the whole nudist camp myth.

One of the two greatest men this nation has produced, Benjamin Franklin (Thomas Alva Edison was the other), was an advocate of what he called open-air bathing, which was his wordy and acceptable way of saying walking around in the sun without any clothes on.

Franklin believed in the natural curative effects of the sun and air on the body, as has every accepted and honorable nudist since. They don't go to these camps — the legitimate ones — for a peek show. I discovered this a few years ago when I visited Whispering Oaks nudist camp near Lapeer.

Free Press photographer Ira Rosenberg and I went there and did a story with pictures for the Sunday Free Press Detroit magazine. We both had our eyes opened, and I don't mean that way. The eye of the mind that controls our attitudinal centers, I mean.

Whispering Oaks, which is still in operation, says owner Rita (true nudists only use first names), was one of the more interesting experiences I've ever had. The people there were your honest-to-goodness-dyed-in-the-sun nudists, mostly families of them.

First of all, I had expected that nudists were all exhibitionists, folks who liked to parade around naked in front of other people. Just the opposite. Ira and I were the only naked people there. There's a difference between being nude and naked.

Ira and I joined the others and shed our clothes. I really don't remember much about the first hour because, like all fat people, I was too busy holding in my stomach to remember much of anything.

One thing Ira and I noticed about the true nudist is that they are totally honest people, leaving their purses and wallets just anywhere without fear of someone ripping them off. This total honesty extended to their personal beliefs about everything, which I found, in the main, to be on the conservative side.

I recently got a call from a professional man — an attorney — whom I'd met there. Nudist beaches and sham nudist camps were the subject. "Those types of things, along with these Ms. Nude America contests, have hurt the image of nudists a great deal," he said. "There is nothing sexy about a true nudist camp for sunshine worshippers. But I'm afraid we're going to be lumped into all the current anti-pornography movement."

To a true nudist, it is almost a religion. I met a nurse there who explained that aspect of it to me, plus a lot of other things about the healthful benefits of relieving yourself of your clothes from time to time.

I wish I'd been taking notes at the time because she gave me some excellent quotes. But I was too embarrassed. It was the first time I'd felt embarrassed all day. We'd finished getting our story and were dressed and leaving.

Ira saw one more picture he wanted to take, from a far side of the lake. The nurse and her family happened to be on that side, unclothed of course. While Ira was taking his pictures, I talked with her and suddenly felt very out of place in clothes.

"That's one of the points," I remember her saying. "When everyone else is nude, the ones with clothes are the strange ones." She was more than correct.

After I got over the fat-belly syndrome — I noticed the rest of the pudgy folks just let it all hang out — I was able to observe the most nude human beings I've ever seen in one time in my life.

We are a funny-looking bunch, let me tell you right now. We all have imperfections, scars and other things that equalize us all. Yet none of us are alike.

The attorney-nudist worries that the nudist beaches, which draw your exhibitionist types, will tarnish nudism's already precarious position in society's view. "We never harmed anyone and found a peace in our lives we could find nowhere else," he said, "and now we may be on the verge of losing our privilege to congregate together in our private camps."

He's a lot closer to the scene than I am, since I have not returned to a nudist camp since that one unforgettable experience. But if what he's saying is right, then I would say the true nudist may be in for trouble, which I find most unfortunate.

I could never be a nudist because I like to see how tan I am, and if you're tan all over, there's no contrast. I do believe there is a great rejuvenating process in sunshine on the body. Psychologically, it makes you feel healthier.

I realize that every other magazine or newspaper is telling us the dangers of sun rays as far as aging the skin, causing wrinkles, etc., and, of course, cancer. Everything seems to be a cause of cancer these days.

When Ira and I visited Whispering Oaks, these weren't major issues. I don't think I asked a soul about that. Say, Ira, maybe that's a good reason for us to make another trip to Whispering Oaks. But wait'll I lose another 20 pounds.

— July 13, 1977

Thanks a lot, Bob, I can use the buck

If a perfect stranger walked up to you and gave you a dollar, how would you react?

You'd be very surprised. You'd be surprised, of course, that some fool is handing you a buck. But the way you react will surprise you, too.

As one of the country's legal, card-carrying fools, I spent a few days recently handing out dollar bills to perfect strangers.

I'm sort of a behavioral bozo, mondo category. Or grosso. Or whatever. A registered fool is allowed, for some reason, to get away with these things without getting arrested, slapped or questioned, even.

I don't know why the rest of the fools do it, but I behave the way I do when in the bozo mode for three reasons: one, to check out your reaction; two, to hopefully bring a smile to your life; and, three, to give you something to talk about for the rest of the day.

People need the last two — I need the first. A fair exchange, I'd say. I feed off people, who don't smile enough in general and can always use an anecdote about some fool thing they saw or heard.

When I'm in the fool mode, nothing embarrasses or intimidates me. That, by the way, is how you get to be a registered fool, with a card and all.

I happened to be switching into the fool mode the other day, walking to my parking lot. I had a wad of dollars in my hand as I saw this guy who could pass for Ron ("Barney Miller") Glass' brother coming my way. I was into full fool.

"Have one," I said and handed him a dollar. He took it, kept walking a step, wheeled on a heel and said, "All right," grinned, then wheeled off on his way.

And, after that reaction, I was on my way, too. A fool only needs a wisp of encouragement. So I started passing out dollars for a couple of days. Most interesting.

Walked into a Burger Chef, stood in line and when the girl asked for my order, I handed her a dollar, said thank you and walked out. Would you believe she came running out the door after me, telling me that I hadn't given her my order yet?

At the Detroit Race Course I handed a fellow a dollar. Preoccupied with his Racing Form, he stuffed it in his pocket and said, "Must've dropped it."

Walking out of a restaurant, I handed a waitress — not my waitress — a buck and she gave me one of those surly Big-Deal-Buck looks. I don't think she ever realized she wasn't my waitress.

At a stoplight I got out of my car and handed a jogger a dollar, got back in and drove away without saying anything. In the rearview mirror I could see him standing there, just scratching his head. Think I ruined his jog concentration.

In Oakland Mall I handed a buck to a kid about eight years old and just walked away. In a moment I could feel a tapping on my back and then saw a woman emerge around my right with the kid in tow. "What did you give my son a dollar for?" she asked, looking at me as if I were some dangerous pervert. I just handed her a dollar and walked on.

Walk on is what I had to do in all cases. Best not to linger too long. Just enough to get some sort of reaction. In the same mall I handed a teenage boy a buck, and he asked for another. Another reason for not lingering.

Gave a buck to one of those sweet little old ladies waiting at a bus stop. Would you believe she dropped it! Wouldn't have a thing to do with it.

Another little old lady in a supermarket, a recipient of one of my dollars, seemed to try to keep avoiding me as we carted through the aisles. Maybe she thought I was going to take it back.

I handed a sleepy-eyed security guard a dollar, and he mumbled something, "Where'd you find it?" In full fool mode, I told him they were floating out of a window on the side of his Southfield building. I couldn't help that. Poor soul. An hour later I saw him standing outside his building, still looking up.

I drove through one neighborhood, stopping to pass out bucks to strolling older couples. I would pull up beside 'em, stop my car, jump out — probably scaring them half to death, I think in retrospect — hand each a dollar, jump back in my car and drive away without saying a word. Now, you know they are going to talk about that for a week!

And that's what really turns on registered fools. Most people say, "Please don't talk about me after I'm gone." Fools beg for you to talk about them AFTER.

After this little exercise in fool I've concluded that people in general react in three ways: grateful, greedy or totally perplexed. At least when you pass out free bucks.

The best of all was a downtown bag lady. You know those characters. Walking collections of clothing, bags, makeups, doodads and what-have-yous. Part of the cityscape. A quaint part.

I fell in step beside one, laboring along with bulging bouquets of shopping bags in both hands. I slipped a dollar into her hat band. At the corner, so help me, she catches up with me and hands me two rolls of pennies. Never try to out-fool a bag lady.

I'm going to attach a buck to this column and see what the editors do with it. Probably think I borrowed it from 'em.

Out of my mind on a Monday moanin'

Halloween is that time of the year when the average father, walking the neigborhood with his kids, finally meets the fellow who lives across the street.

There must be some sort of intelligent life in outer space, 'cause you don't see them spending billions of dollars to land on us.

You can count on that new car costing you a minimum of $1,000 more than the lowest advertised price that got you into the showroom in the first place.

Home is really a place where Dad is free to do anything he pleases because no one is paying any attention to him, anyway.

It's more fashionable these days to discuss your bill and insurance policy than it is your operation.

With more and more high school pregnancies I wouldn't be surprised to see maternity clothes in school colors.

I have never known a man who went in a supermarket and bought only the things his wife put on a list.

How liberal a person is seems to be directly related to how far he is from the problem and how conservative a person is directly related to how close he is the problem.

It's strange that some men who haven't kissed their wives in years will shoot a fellow who does.

Men who once wondered if they could afford to get married now have sons who wonder if they can get along without a working wife.

"Black is beautiful" only when it isn't a synonym for "white is ugly."

There isn't a married woman alive who isn't itching to find a mate for every bachelor friend of her husband.

Men always pull in their stomachs and tug at their pant waists to show much weight they've lost and women rub their hands over their hips to show the same thing.

Why do we lie and describe bad manners and rudeness in a successful man as his "color"?

More and more I'm beginning to believe the real Christmas message is "batteries not included."

CHANGES

I'll care if I choose to, but not just to impress you

What motivates you? What turns you on? What causes you to react?

Standing back and taking stock is important, especially these days when everyone is riding along the hairy edge.

I've discovered that I no longer need to play games. I have no compelling urge to try to impress anyone. I'm tired of compensating for this, or justifying that. I don't have this burning desire to belong or be with it at all times I only want to level with myself.

No longer do I feel compelled to read all the latest books to impress my literary friends.

No longer do I find it necessary to listen to all the recorded electronic music garbage just so I can appear hip in the eyes of my young rock-and-roll buddies.

No longer do I desperately try to explain to my black friends that I honestly DO care about them ; either they KNOW or . . .

No longer am I ashamed that I belong to white, middle-class America.

No longer do I feel it necessary to make sure my Jewish acquaintances know that my wife is Jewish.

No longer do I make lame little jokes to explain why we have two color TV sets in our house, and why I watch a lot of TV.

No longer do I think I must defend Barbra Streisand's choice of clothes at the Academy Awards.

No longer do I think I must tell everyone how I feel about the Smothers Brothers being canceled by CBS-TV.

No longer do I have this burning desire to crusade against someone else's definition of pornography and smut and obscenity.

No longer do I fret that certain things aren't my bag when it comes to entertainment, food and clothing.

No longer do I worry that my shirt and tie aren't as up-to-date as my sophisticated pals think they should be.

No longer do I feel I must somehow persuade the students on Unrest Campus to feel that I'm with them in spirit but not in body.

No longer do I feel I must take a stand about birth control or the Pill or the Pope or worry about the changes in the church.

No longer will I answer questions about whether I'd want my daughter to "marry one" or "be one."

No longer do I throw up the Hubbards and Zaks and Crocketts and Lobsingers and Del Rios and Gordons and Wallaces and Goldwaters as examples that your heroes can be as wrong — or as right — as mine.

No longer will I care, get bugged, amused, outraged or delighted by the hair, garb and manners of hippies and militants.

No longer do I attempt to talk with people who reject me because of the color of my skin or the scope of my education or my 33 years.

No longer do I find it necessary to make apologetic little jokes about why I don't drink or smoke.

No longer do I feel I must plan on raising my son sternly and Spartanly so he'll know the value of dollars, discipline or dogmas.

No longer do I worry about whether intellectuals and society types respect my opinions or invite me to their parties.

No longer do I feel compelled to do things just because of what the neighbors may think or do.

No longer do I find it necessary to feign excitement, appreciation or applause over people and things that don't warrant any.

No longer do I get upset when I discover that you don't read me, or that you misinterpret me, or that you get me mixed up with other columnists.

Hang-ups don't have to be a way of life.

I'm going to try to know me and be me.

Maybe I'm growing up.

— *April 18, 1969*

As a longhair, I resent smirks, defy threat of Gestapo abuse

There's something funny about my hair.

The longer it gets, the angrier it makes people.

Friends, family, fans, perfect strangers give me those why-don't-you-get-a-haircut looks.

A policeman in the Carolinas recently eyed my Michigan license plates and my hair, then asked, "What's a matter, boy, ain't got no bobbuhs in Mich-eye-gun? You a hip-pee?" He laughed and I laughed. But it wasn't really funny.

As a matter of damn hard fact, it's a tragic commentary on something tearing up the country these days.

Forget the left vs. right. The black vs. white thing isn't it. Rich vs. poor? No way.

Hair has neatly parted this country — and the world — equally into those who like it and these who don't. And in this sort of polarization, reason suffers.

My hair isn't that long, either. It hangs over my ears and collar, but I could grease it down, slick it back and no one would even notice. But I wash my hair every day, leaving it sort of fluffed out, doing its own thing, if you'll excuse the tired cliche.

I happen to really like the way it looks and does. So does my wife. So do my two children. My employer doesn't care how it looks so long as it doesn't grow on my typing fingers and into my head and brain, rather than out of it.

But the way hair has become a pro-con symbol does disturb me. On one side there are people who equate short hair with God, Mom's apple pie and patriotism. At the other end of hair are these who feel short hair equates with violence, repression and police state.

This simply isn't true. But simple truths don't register on polarized minds and hearts. Unfortunately, simplistic methods and reactions register only too graphically in this environment.

I once laughed at the statement that "hippies are the new niggers." But since I have recently been labeled that, I now know a little how the black man has felt. Because my skin is white I can never fully know what it means to grow up in a white-oriented society.

But because my hair is long I've recently felt that certain alienation, that non-verbalized hate, that unmistakable feeling of not being wanted in areas where there's no reason to reject me.

Hippies — and all young and old people affecting a certain life style in clothing and grooming fall under this label — have become fair game for those seeking ultra-quick and ultra-positive solutions to all manner of problems from dope to recession.

Hippies, per se, are not welcome in Charlevoix, Mich., Atlanta, Ga., Dallas, Tex., Love Valley, N.C., New Orleans, Mexico, France, Japan, etc. The list grows daily.

It makes sense to pick on the hippies, the young students. Police today are wary of clubbing or even touching the blacks because of subsequent court action and public reaction. But a hippie? A student? Bam! Zap! Who cares? Parents don't, so why should they? Zip-zip! Hair today, gone tomorrow.

This is frightening. These Gestapo-like tactics occur in Ann Arbor where hippies were shorn of their hair for no valid reason. I watched it happen in San Miguel Allende, Mexico, where the police shaved both Mexican and American longhairs as a warning that "we want no hippies hanging out here."

Merchants feel hippies scare off tourists, therefore hippies are the cause of the recession and tight money. And hippies (longhairs) are all on dope and swim nude, don't they?

Charlevoix could be the next clip joint, hippies, so beware, and soon the big cities will wise up as to what safe hate-objects you are and then you really will have to hide in caves and trees. You have become "instant solutions" to what ails us. Cutting your hair will let us all sleep better tonight.

What is equally frightening is Vice-President Spiro Agnew's statement that there are people in our society who should be separated and discarded so their ideas and opinions shall have no effect on the rest of society. He was talking about criminals, psychopaths and hard-line dissidents. It is even more frightening that there are people who buy this. They would have also bought the Nazi ovens, and see nothing wrong with Con Son's Tiger cages. Today it's long hair that's wrong. Tomorrow it may be all people with big noses or blue eyes. Or people who laugh too much. Or smile.

Just let your hair grow and You'll see what I mean. And I can promise you that you won't like what you see.

— *July 28, 1970*

Barefaced Bob's back, minus the beard

You noticed!

You didn't notice.

Either way, I'm going to learn some things about you that I didn't know before.

If you ask, "What happened to your beard?" I've got to figure you for one of two things; a super dum-dum or an unimaginative person.

It's as obvious as the nose on my face what I did with my beard. I shaved it off.

If you don't notice it at all that tells me one of two things, too: You either knew me before I grew the beard or you really didn't bother to know me that well after I grew it.

I've discovered that people who have only known the Bearded Bob Talbert recognize its absence immediately. People who've known me for over two years — from those pre-beard, growout days — don't recognize its absence immediately, sometimes for days.

I have also discovered some rather interesting things about pro-and-con reactions to the shaving of the beard.

I can remember that when I grew the beard, there were some violent pros and equally violent cons. Most of the cons equated the beard with hippies and other so-called perversions. The pro-beards equated it with hippies and other so-called free-thinking individualistic things. It all sort of boiled down to your point of view about hippies and hipness.

I really didn't care how you felt. It was my face, my beard, and I chose to grow it, it was my wife Beryl's suggestion that I let it grow to see what I would look like in a beard. It was a change from how I looked for over a dozen years. We both liked the change.

It was a new image, at least that's the way people liked to describe it. The whole bit: mod clothes, long hair, do-your-own-thing, etc. And because most people felt that, I almost grew to despise the new image.

Don't get me wrong. I dig being the center of attention. I thrive on it. And looking different from the rest of the herd can make you the center of attention in a hurry. Ego is my middle name. Vanity, too, I love being recognized. And the beard was an instant badge that said without saying, "Hello, I am — ."

At one point, though, it got to be a pain explaining the beard. I felt like getting a card printed up that answered all the questions:

"Yes, it itches. No, I'm not a hippie. Yes, my wife likes it. No, we don't kiss as much as we used to. Yes, it scares small children. No, you can't pull it. Yes, you can feel it. No, it isn't hot. Yes, food get in it and is a bother. No, I'm not hiding a weak chin or a scar. Yes, it is a conversation point. No, it makes shaving even harder."

I also got tired of being used as an example — along with Abraham, Moses, Plato, Jesus, Santa Claus, Rasputin, Manson, Shakespeare, Castro, Gabby Hayes, etc. — of people with beards, pro or con.

I also got tired of messing with a beard. Beards are a pain if they are groomed beards. Let one grow wild all over and it's no particular problem. Trying to keep one shaped and neat and clean can be a full-time endeavor.

For a couple of months I've had this urge to shave it off. Just a small, growing feeling. I told Beryl about it earlier in the summer. She sort of agreed, too. But not to the point of saying. "Take it all off, hon."

Coming back from vacation the other day, Beryl glanced over at me and said, "I think it would be all right if you shaved it off." That's all she had to say.

Well, I lay awake practically all night in a Lexington, Ky., motel with visions of Super Schicks and Gillette Safetys dancing on my chin. I dreamed of eating pizzas and ice cream and salads without worrying about leaving half on my face. I dreamed of that tingly, bracing feel of splashing on after-shave.

At 6 a.m. with my courage on high and my chin out, I got up and shaved it off. It was wonderful. It was shocking. It was another new me. Some people find their "me" when they're 12, others at 21 or 43 or 50. Some never find their me. I happen to believe each of us are a lot of me's and it's fun to try them all on. Get hooked on one me and you miss a lot.

But I shaved it because I wanted to, not because someone else said I had to, or because some antiquated thinking dictates a clean face or short hair. For example, coaches who insist all their athletes must have short hair and clean faces have a classic generation gap between their ears. It's a shame when hair is hanging up the athletic world. If you ask 'em to play like men, allow them to be men and quit treating them like children.

Anyway, it's fun, now, to hear your comments or lack of comments. I particularly like the ones about looking younger and looking thinner. Who wouldn't?

— Aug. 11, 1971

Rootin', tootin' cowboy movies live in my memory

I didn't care whether his six-shooter never ran out of bullets. I didn't find it strange that every one of his bullets found their mark in an evil heart, while the bad guys shot at him 4,000 times and missed, except one, which nicked him in the left arm if he was a right-handed shooter.

It never puzzled me that his face was always clean-shaven after 10 days on the desert trail. It didn't bother me that he seldom had a past, never paid for drinks and never got the girl. I never puzzled over why he never gambled, never got in a hurry, never started a fight and never had much to say.

I didn't find it strange that it was the same story, same plot, same background, same cliches, same characters, same posses, same chase scenes, same actual footage, same backgrounds, same sidekicks, same villains, same town and same ending week after week. I didn't think about any of this stuff. Man, that was just the way the Saturday morning shoot-'em-ups were. That's what they were all about, were supposed to be and I wouldn't have had it any other way. That man up there on the screen, a tall-in-the-saddle hero wearing a white hat and a fancy pair of guns and holster rig, was my main man. His actions spoke louder than words of others. And justice was a result of his direct actions, not elaborate, entangled legality.

Maybe the West wasn't won that away, pod'nuh. Maybe Wyatt Earp ran a protection racket in the real Dodge City. Maybe Billy the Kid was some runt born in New York City. Maybe all of them were a bunch of drunks and shoot-you-in-the-back-firsters and yellow dogs. I really didn't care.

I paid my dime and knew exactly what I was getting. And if I didn't get all — the long, music-swelling chase climaxed by a leaping off the-horse-tumble-roll-fight-down-a-rocky-bank-into-a-creek — then I would have felt cheated.

My cowboy hero was me. For however many times I sat through the movie (plus a serial, cartoon, newsreel and sometimes a short subject), I was William (Hopalong Cassidy) Boyd, Wild Bill Elliott and Don (Red) Berry and Allan Lane and Tim Holt and Lash La Rue and Sunset Carson. Sometimes I was Smiley Burnette or Pat Buttram or Gabby Hayes or Dub (Cannonball) Taylor or Fuzzy Knight or Fuzzy St. John. Some Saturdays you just felt more like being a sidekick.

But all the time I was Gene Autry and Roy Rogers. Honest. I could walk just like Gene and squint just like Roy. I could outdraw 'em both. Really. I practiced all the time, even when I didn't have my shootin' arms a'strapped to my side. And I also practiced making the sound of Trigger's whinny and Champion's neigh. They were different, and just a few of us could tell.

I didn't even care when Gene and Roy would burst into song. And, honest, I didn't get mad when Dale Evans would run up and give ol' Roy a hug and peck on the cheek. I'd usually head for the restroom or candy counter when these parts came on. I hate to think how many conversations I've carried on with Roy and Gene. I'd also hate to think how many times I'd switch in having one or the other as my favorite. I even remember going through one period when Charles Starett, the Durango Kid, and Warner Baxter, the Cisco Kid ("Hey, Pancho?" "Coming, Cees-Cooo!"), replaced Gene and Roy. But only momentarily.

I can't tell you whether I'm better or worse for having these B-movie stars as my heroes. I do know they were a meaningful and important part of my life. They taught me some good guys-bad guys absolutes that may not sound viable or relevant today. I'm quite sure many minority and liberation groups will find my attitude ridiculous. But I really don't care what they find. I find very little wrong with remembering those Saturday horse operas when men were men, issues were clear-cut and the skies were not smoggy all day.

Those were cowboy movies, not Westerns. Westerns were another breed of film. Westerns cost a lot of money to make and starred John Wayne and Gary Cooper and Alan Ladd. I liked them, too, but in an entirely different way. Sometimes they weren't so predictable, and sometimes they didn't do much chasing and weren't really shoot- 'em-ups.

They've evolved into still another genre of Westerns with more blood than a Red Cross bank. Not only does the cowboy get the girl in the new ones, he gets her right there before everyone in close-up and technicolor detail. And the heroes have mouths as dirty as the villain's faces used to be. Now the hero does the clowning around and rides a bike, of all things. The spaghetti Westerns, the sagebrush spoofs, and the over-realistic "authentic" Western dramas seem to have forgotten about that little boy who needs to have a dream, who needs to have an hour-and-a-half of pure escape without being told every eight minutes about some cereal he should get his mother to buy.

That's why I know that when I wave today at the State Fair to a 59-year-old cowboy hero named Roy Rogers, he'll wave back, smiling that little squinty smile. And I won't even care if he hugs and kisses Dale Evans first.

— *August 31, 1971*

With glasses, I perceive I'm aging

Aging is one of those things universally shared.

We all do it.

We all hate it.

I think.

The reason I say I think is because I can remember in my salad years where I desperately wanted to get older.

The reasons for this were things like being able to buy a beer, or voting, or getting a driver's license.

I wanted to be older in years, but I never really wanted to age.

I certainly am not liking the aging process that's going on with me now.

I was trying to read something in Jimmy Butsicaris' office at the Lindell AC the other evening and was holding it almost at arm's length.

"Here," said Butsicaris, "join us senior citizens."

He handed me his bifocals.

I was astounded. I could read again!

Thanks and no thanks, Jimmy. I'm glad you made me get glasses so I can read again normally, but I'm not thanking you for making me aware of the aging process.

My kids, Dafna, 14, and Jason, 7, have started to help, too. They think I'm getting deaf.

I'm probably unique in this. My kids tell ME to turn down the car radio or the stereo. How do you like that? What did you say? Speak up, I can't hear you.

I have also become painfully aware — damn mirrors that let you see in back of you — that I have a very nice bald spot just to the rear of the crown. Even my permanent won't cover it.

For most of my life I have subconsciously felt I'm around 24 or 25. Young thinker, maybe.

I've found as the years have added up I have done lots of things to hold on to whatever youth is available.

I'm not your normal coat-and-tie dresser, to begin with. I don't dress like my peers, because I'm not comfortable dressed like that. I could walk into the new Brooks Brothers and give them a heart attack.

I dress more like your kids, but not necessarily because I'm trying to stay young.

Don't get me wrong. I'll try anything to stop the aging process. I'd get a hair transplant. I'd have a facelift.

Why not? If you satisfy your own mind and heart that you're looking your best, you are going to feel better and happier. Is that bad?

I'll be 38 at the end of this month.

At one point in time I figured I'd be rich and famous by this age. I figured I'd have written plays and songs and be living someplace like Big Sur.

As you get older you become a bit more realistic about your goals.

You rationalize: Maybe I wasn't cut out to be a novelist or playwright. To be a songwriter you should at least play some instrument, even if you are just a lyricist.

You also get locked into the system.

I've become a slave to the economic system that requires lots of money to maintain a good lifestyle I've grown to love.

And being in a divorced situation, it just doubles the importance of making money because of alimony and child support.

While these are my personal reasons for hanging on to all the security the economic system affords, I'm sure you have yours, have had them, or will have them eventually.

You wake up one day and realize that no matter if you wanted to stop and write a novel, stop and take a camper around the country, stop and open up a candle shop in Boulder, Colo., you can't.

That, I think is the point you begin to reassess whatever it is you are doing and whatever it is you can do considering all factors.

You start thinking: "I'm almost 40 and what?"

What are they — 20, 30, 40, 50, 65? Numbers. Experience. Birthdays. Memories. Reality. Milestones. Turning points.

When I was at that point you got to be an adult at 21, not 18. Got to be an adult. Big deal. I've known 12-year-old adults and far too many 33-year-old children.

And 40 becomes the monster. Life begins there or ends there. You're not sure.

The day after you're 40, will you stop being able to do this and that? Will you not be able to think the same things you thought at 30? Will you fall apart physically? Does everyone look at you and know you're 40?

I can't contemplate 50 or 65. But for some reason I feel 50 must be the easiest age milestone to handle. By 50 you know you can't go back and you've found your 40s weren't so bad. I don't know this for sure, but I sense it.

Getting older isn't so bad, really, but this aging process is a different matter. That's the killer. Literally. It's when you have to start thinking of yourself as a fine wine. Then aging ain't so bad. It's sorta nice.

— May 18, 1974

My super summers with Grandmamma

It is summer and in the soft hanging Spanish moss of my memory is tenderly tangled my grandmamma's attic.

Now, when summers at grandmamma's farm are no more, the recollection is fresh as the warmth of a just-laid egg.

It was one of those things that was just as wonderful then as it is now thinking back to it. Too often the things we recall as wonderful really weren't so wonderful while we went through them.

I sometimes think this is what helps make the various nostalgia fads work so well. For example, the '50s are hot now. When I went through them, I thought they stunk and so did most of my friends. But we love the '50s now because those were the unburdened days. No burdens. No one pulling on your sleeve or punching your clock. Every moment had the potential for being an adventure that may change your entire life.

Now, no adventures — at least not those spur-of-the-moment kind — can do that. These excursions out of normalcy are only to be enjoyed for the passing moment, which eventually dumps you back into reality with a bump and a crunch.

But grandmamma's was special. Particularly in this day and time. I met a grandmother the other day I could not believe. Beautiful. Looks 35, if that. Drives a Corvette. Trim as a slender Salem girl. So "today" she looks like next month's Vogue. The 1974-style Grandmother smells of Shalimar and dresses in jeans, the latest embroidered, sequined kind.

My Grandmamma Beulah Mabe always smelled like buttermilk. Her perfurme was Milking Time No. 3.

She kept her honestly gray hair pulled back, which was practical, not fashionable. She never wore jeans or slacks in her entire life. To this day I don't even know what her legs looked like. They were always covered by high-button shoes and long print dresses.

My grandmamma was of the farm, by the farm and for the farm. The only thing the farm couldn't give her was radio soap opera. "John's Other Life" brought the entire farm to a halt every day while she sat there listening and staring and sharing John's lives, which poured out of the gold-glowing little Stromberg-Carlson radio dial.

That was her contact with the "today" of her time, that radio show and a frosty Dr. Pepper she had every afternoon that I would run a mile to the store to get. Dr. Pepper and "store-bought'n" bread were her two vices.

She wasn't much a hand at reading books and newspapers, but did find time to spend an hour with the Bible every day and some moments with the Sears Roebuck catalog, always a'restin' on the shelf in the "four-holer" behind the chicken pen.

Summer at grandmamma's was the year's trophy, the time when grandmamma taught me about things. Patchwork quilts are the warmest in the world. Pears are to be eaten one a setting, not in stomach-destroying bunches. Watermelons are coldest when left in the stream an hour longer. Cows won't hurt you if you let them know you aren't scared of them. And fried chicken is the "bestest eating" in the world even if you have to wring their necks first.

Nine months of the year I was a little city slicker, but in the summer I was barefoot and free and a prince in a world of trunk-filled attics, earthy-smelling barns and fields rich with tobacco and wheat running to the lip of deep and mysterious woods, with cold streams and moss-covered rocks slashing and wiggling through them.

Grandmamma's lap got smaller as I got bigger, but it was always the warmest and softest place to get sleepy. Grandmamma's barn was a theater and she told me to put my ear "on that cow's stomach" and I can still feel that tight rounding warm fur next to my cheek as I felt the hard thump of an unborn calf kicking and I got that feeling you get in church.

Grandmamma called me "Br'er Fox" and she knew Br'er Fox's favorite place was her attic in the main house. Those mounds of quilts became magic carpets and those boxes of buttons, of all shapes and sizes, were the money I spent in the magical lands those carpets took me to. Maybe the most vivid of all my memories of childhood was watching with total amazement as a mother rat gave birth to a dozen thimble-sized pink babies, a sight the nine-year-old mind can't quite comprehend.

Grandmamma's was the dearest place I have ever known. I can see her now at summer's end as watched from the car's rear window as she stood by the well and waved. I would turn back to my seat and sit there and not say anything for the longest time afterward, and when my parents asked what was the matter and I sighed, "Nothing," they knew and didn't ask anything else.

— June 26, 1974

Do clothes make the man weird?

You'd have thought one of two things: I was either completely naked or else I had developed the perfect disguise.

I've never gotten so much attention while at the same time being totally overlooked by people who've known me almost as long as I've been around here.

It was one of the weirdest experiences I've had since coming to Detroit, a barefoot boy with cheek, from the Carolina hill country nine years ago. And if you have followed this space for long, you know that includes some pretty weird carryings-on.

And if you've been following this space or have ever seen me in public, you know I'm not exactly your straight dresser. My clothes have been variously described as "sort of cowboyish-fag," "a hippie hillbilly" and "a thrown-together mess." I prefer "contemporary tacky."

Rolls off like water off a mallard's back. I love rhinestones and studs and leather pants and pointy-toed cowboy boots. I love real patch jeans and embroidered stuff. I love dashikis and loose-fitting tops that hide my spare tires (you don't know how I hated to have to pluralize that).

Anyway, I dress this close to "strange," OK? Strange by any other standards, I guess, but I'm always perfectly comfortable. As I've written here before, I dress first for comfort and second for shock value.

But the other day, for the first time in I really don't know how long, I went to work dressed in a shirt, tie, suit and vest. Normal standard garb for most of the men you see, right? It's been years since I've had a tie on in the daytime, I know that much.

But you'd have thought I had on the wildest costume imaginable. A couple of folks at the newspaper who ride me the hardest about my bizarre tastes actually brought people from other floors to see Talbert in a suit and tie.

There were such dandy comments as:
- "You must be going on a job interview."
- "He must be dead."

I'll have you know I plan to donate all my usable parts to medical research and then be cremated. And the urn will be rhinestoned. A couple of denim-clad pals whispered "Sell-out." That didn't hurt, either.

Why should it? The damn straight old plain dark blue suit was getting me more attention around here than the one with 1,500 studs in it. You betcha it's heavy. Only exercise I get is wearing my clothes. No wonder I had to pluralize my spares.

It was a riot all day long. Everywhere I'd go people would look at me in astonishment or with a puzzled look on their faces. The astonished were those who have never before in their lives, they claim, seen me in a tie.

The puzzled people were those who thought they knew me, but figured otherwise. The suit was throwing 'em off. Four or five folks I've known almost since I got here walked right by me. I used to live in the same building with one of them.

I cornered him. "I'm Bob Talbert," I said.

"No, you're not," he said. "I used to live in the same building with him." He turned and walked away. But I must remember that even the Free Press tour guides had been so confused they had earlier introduced me as Bob Talbert's brother.

I happened to be at a luncheon with some people who didn't know me from Adam's off ox, regardless of what I'd been wearing. But they must've been amused or confused at people coming up and making a big to-do over me in a suit and tie. Finally, one of the people asked politely, "May I ask how you usually dress?"

I started to go into my spiel, but shortened it to this: "About an inch and a half short of strange." That seemed to satisfy them. They didn't ask any more questions about it.

When people who normally wear a suit and tie every day show up to work dressed differently, do they get the same sort of reaction I got when I wore a suit?

If the open-neck, leisure-suited era has taken you out of a dress-up suit and tie, may I suggest that you give it a whirl again. You'll be surprised at the attention you get. But there are a couple of things I'd better warn you about.

First off, wearing a suit and a tie is not like a bicycle, where once you learn you never forget. For example, on the way out of the restaurant I had to stop by the men's room. Thank the Lord it was one of my dearest friends behind me who whispered, "Talbert, you've tucked your suit coat into your pants." I'll never figure out how I did that.

And I've also had a hard time figuring out how to tie a tie again. This is the best time for me to wear a suit because they now have these little vests and they can hide the fact that you have more little end of the tie hanging down than the wide end.

Many years ago I roomed with a fellow who had a simple solution to this problem of the tie's ends not coming out together. He'd just take a pair of scissors and snip off the too-long short end. Then he'd take off the tie without unknotting it and use that same knot every time. He had quite a collection of skinny ends of ties.

One other thing: I must warn you that wearing a suit and tie may be slightly addictive, especially if you're on the chubby side. Suits slim you, it seems. Don't ask me how or why, but they also make you feel sort of important — and that's nice. Just warning you.

— May 18, 1977

You won't believe
the things I missed

Well, the pictures from the vacation returned, but I think we've already covered — or uncovered — most of them. There's me blistering and Lynn tanning.

I know I promised to show you my vacation slides, but they even bore me. Instead, let me tell you about some things about this place that don't bore me.

It's taken me about a week to get it cranked up again, but in that week I've discovered I truly missed . . .

MY OWN BATHROOM — It may have a "Condemned" sign on the door, it may have a counter crowded with I-don't-know-what all, it may have funny wrong-way handles on the shower, but it's mine. It sits well with me. Perfect.

MICHIGAN DRIVERS — I'll say this for you motorists around here: You get the job done. I think you drive too fast, but at least you know how to drive. Most of you seem to know where you are going. And some of you even let a few folks into traffic at times.

LOCAL RADIO — We have some real pros in this area's radio industry and a variety none of us really appreciates. After listening to "Le Freak" on every station for a week, I can assure you it was a pleasure to be able to punch back into Detroit radio. At least the announcers' voices don't crack.

THE TEMPO — While the purpose of our vacation was to vegetate, my wife's term for laying back and letting the rest of the world go by, it was sort of nice to get back into the metropolitan gear. After a week of not even wearing a watch, it recharges me somehow now that I'm once again its slave. That sounds nuts, probably, but it works for me.

SNOW — I can't even believe I wrote those four letters. But I have to tell you something: Christmas lights on palm trees just don't cut it. I didn't realize how dull Southern Christmases are sans snow until moving here 10 years ago. Soon as we hit the outside air at Metro I got the Christmas spirit.

THE FREE PRESS — You don't really appreciate just what an excellent and readable newspaper this is until you are without it for a week or so. I'm sure I'm prejudiced, but I guess I missed the Free Press more than just about anything. It's a newspaper junkie's perfect fix.

MY BED — I don't care if I were invited to spend a week upon the most glorious bed ever designed, I'd be so antsy to get home to my own bed by the end of seven days I'd be a basket case, with baggy eyes. I only sleep well in my own bed. You, too?

THE TELEPHONE — I can't believe I wrote that, either. Where we go, there is no telephone. That and the sun are the main reasons we go there. Imagine not hearing the telephone ring for a solid week? Heavens. Also, where we go, we don't know anyone to call. Also a blessing. But it has been a treat getting back on the phone and in touch.

LOCAL TELEVISION — I don't care where you go, by the time you've figured out the local TV stations and what they carry, it's time to leave. We may sit here and criticize Detroit television, but compared to smaller markets it's very professional. Compared to small-market local advertising, even Ollie Fretter looks good. Well, maybe that's stretching a point.

THE ENTERTAINMENT — Now I didn't come back and immediately go to a whirlwind of shows, concerts, movies, etc. But the fact that these things are available to us in such a variety — from sports to arts — is something we too often take for granted. And, you can only eat so many oranges and so much barbecue and seafood.

YOU — I missed our daily get-togethers here. I missed reading your letters, thoughts, opinions, ideas, feelings, emotions and spirit. I also missed your complaints, gripes and moans. Did I just write that? Why not? That's part of you, part of us, part of Detroit. Glad to be back.

— Dec. 16, 1978

It takes a special person not to swear

My column of a couple weeks ago about swearing off swearing struck quite a nerve with a great many of you.

In case you missed it, I woke up one day and realized how polluted our language — in public and private — had become. Nothing I can do about the way you talk, but I decided to clean up my act.

Surprisingly, I have been very successful. I say surprisingly because oaths and obscenities had become automatic for me to use in many situations.

Let me share a note from a very highly placed power figure in this community: "The other day, your article about Cursers Anonymous (CA) was a stopper. You really hit home; I'm a confirmed curser who needs help.

"Your column prompted the following — I'm going to try. If a cat like you can try, so can I. It's tough. I tried today. I said a lot of swear words, but each time I remembered, and even mentioned, your article. I'll overcome.

"Consider me a CA with a desire to stop. Keep reminding us CAs, Bob."

It is tough. We live in a foul-mouthed society. It's a sickness that began, I think, during World War II. Several of you pinpoint the war as the time our language began to take a nose dive.

Your letters, matter of fact, have opened up an enormous new field for me to explore. A couple of fields.

Many of you feel that our society's ever-snowballing verbal pollution is the single biggest reason Johnny can't read or write anymore. We don't have to be able to read or write, just memorize the prescribed four-letter words and they say all you have to.

But another area you brought up — verbal abuse — was startling to me in its possible enormity. Verbal abuse is something I wasn't very familiar with. Unfortunately, many of you are.

Young people tell horror stories of verbal abuse they receive from their parents to the point they will not bring their friends around if their parents are home. Sad stuff. Makes your heart break.

"My parents are constantly calling each other names," writes one. "Mean, hurting things. Vulgar words and nasty words. And they turn around and do the same thing to us. Do you know how many times a day I'm called dumb and stupid and lazy? Do you know what that makes you feel like?"

Quite frankly, I don't. I didn't grow up around verbal abuse. And there are only a few instances in my life when I can remember verbally abusing. It's just not part of my makeup or character.

Some of the most touching letters and conversations about verbal abuse came from wives, whose husbands use them as some sort of verbal emotional whipping post.

None of these women mentioned any physical abuse. Many said their husbands wouldn't dare do anything like that, "but he thinks nothing of beating up my mind and my heart with some nasty dig every chance he can get. Sometimes I don't think he even hears what he's saying to me."

I heard from athletes who bemoaned the fact that some coaches resort to verbal abuse as their only means of motivating their players. I heard from line workers, nurses, secretaries, teachers and students.

From the letters I have a feeling "stupid" and "dumb" have become obscenities in their environments. I think I will add them to my list of words not to use.

I mentioned that I had been successful in my campaign to clean up my own mouth. I can count on two hands the number of times I let one slip. And the times I slipped I won't justify in my own mind, even though one of them was when three pounds of frozen turkey legs crushed my naked big toe on the cold concrete.

I actually swore off swearing on March 3. It's been a week or so since I've slipped. Maybe longer. Most of it occurred in the first week. I didn't have my monitoring system fine-tuned.

Now it's in synch — my mind and my mouth. My psyche is also set, as it is set against alcohol. I've taken the stand that profanity pollutes my mind, poisons it, just as alcohol did my entire system.

Rather than spewing out a string of four-letteratti, I've had to start thinking again about the words I use in conversation and communication with others. It's made a better communicator out of me. That surprised me, but also reassured me that I've done the right thing.

I had a fear that if I quit cursing, I'd lose my personality and find out no one liked a clean-mouth Bob Talbert. I joked about it. But I thought about it seriously.

I can't detect that it has changed my relationship with others, although I do find some people act a little uncomfortable around me when they let loose one of those unconscious swears. It's driving my wife a little nuts because she says my lack of swearing makes her realize what a Rachel Rottenmouth she is and she'd just as soon not be reminded of this flaw.

But she's doing better than she suspects. When you don't curse, you hear all the curses others utter. She's just becoming aware of it. That's the important thing. The more you are aware of it, the more you will want to stop.

Why? Because you'll realize that anybody and everybody swears. It takes a special person — a true individual — not to swear automatically. And none of us wants to be just another part of the herd, do we?

— April 2, 1980

Leaving Fat City
on the down elevator

I always get these neat clues that I have gotten enormously fat again.

I'll be walking along a mirrored corridor in a building, glance into a mirror and wonder where that crowd's going. And I'm all alone.

You know how thigh-tight corduroy pants whistle when you walk? Mine play "Stars and Stripes Forever."

When I sit down I turn into a pile of lap and leg.

When my fat friends start looking skinnier.

When I have to step out of the shower, turn around, then step back in to get all sides washed.

When I notice people who just met me walk away and puff up their cheeks and go into a penguin waddle when they think they are out of eye range.

When I find myself standing in the big men's store with the other hippos thinking that if an XXL feels so good, wondering how much better an XXXL would feel and how much more it would hide if I could find it in black.

When I suggest to my wife we need to buy a new scales and she points out that it's a scale, not scales. Funny, I've called it a scales all my life. "Maybe in your case," my wife says, "the plural is correct. You've always needed two scales, one for each leg."

Before someone comes around and paints Goodyear along my side, it is time for me to do something drastic once again — like dieting. All us fatsoes know that when the drastics hit, shedding the suet is soon to follow.

I'm stopping this trip up the fat elevator at this level. I'm getting off and pushing the down button. No express elevator for me this trip. I'm taking a car that goes slow and stops at each floor.

Do you realize there are 90 million Americans on this fat elevator every day of our lives? And at least half of us have to use the freight car?

As so many others with flab affliction, I was born fat and my baby fat never went away — it just hung on, got older and settled around my equator.

All my life, clothes have been a problem. I had to wear chubby-sized diapers and husky playsuits. I graduated from the boys' department when I was in the first grade. My dad was borrowing my sweaters when I was in junior high.

By high school and college I had already started assembling the wardrobe of one who rides the fat elevator. I believe a peek into my closet is a peek into the closets of every tub-O around.

It's time we fatties brought our closets out of the closet.

We all have three wardrobes. First, there's the normal overweight set. Second, the dreaded humongous line, and, third, the one-day-I'll-get-in-'ems.

The last time I pushed the down button and dropped a few floors, I dramatically and foolishly gave away every stitch in my humongous line.

After ripping the crotch out of my last pair of decent pants, I reached into the humongous section of the closet and came up bare.

Talk about your subtle hint!

I need no more hints. Diet it is. I've chosen Thanksgiving as the official starting date because Thanksgiving is the worst day in a fatso's life. Sort of like New Year's Eve to the alcoholic.

Thanksgiving is the only holiday of the year those of us on the fat elevator celebrate, along with our birthdays. On those two days, we lard buckets eagerly agree with anyone that "after all, it is your birthday" or "Thanksgiving only comes once a year" and we become the Mayor of Pig City.

I'm using Thanksgiving as an excuse to begin a diet this year, not a reason to get off one. The holiday season will be a true test of my willpower and resolve.

If I don't know by now what makes me fat, no one could. I don't need any new fad diet, pill, regimen, hypnosis, behavior modification or book to tell me what to do. The professional fatties never do.

Oh, yes, we're talking about your professional plump-Os. We've spent most of our careers being fat. There's nothing you can tell us, show us or teach us about fat. We know what puts it on us, and we know what will take it off.

Just a matter of making our minds do for our bodies what our hearts want done. You have to get your mind, heart and gut in sync. It's really as simple as that.

The only goal I'm setting is that next Thanksgiving I won't have to write a column like this. After I step on the scale this morning, I'm stepping into the down car and not getting off until next Thanksgiving.

I also promise you that I will not bore you with the agonies or my dieting. That's so boring. Maybe a progress (or lack of progress) report from time to time to keep me honest, but that's all.

I'd like to thank one and all for the subtle hints you've dropped. Especially you cheek-puffing waddlers. Didn't think I saw you, did you?

— Nov. 27, 1980

No more tears for halcyon days of youth

I buried my youth at a four-hour lunch with my oldest friend while I was on vacation.

Every year in the spring Lynn and I go south and spend a week at my momma Pearl's in Spartanburg, S.C.

And every visit, I'll spend some time meandering about this small Southern town looking for my youth.

I wander around town with this where-have-the-'50s-woebegone? look on my face.

I don't walk up to everyone and say, "Say, friend, I'm Bobby Talbert, Bob Talbert's son. The Carolina Theater's Bob Talbert. Where'd my youth go?"

There's no Carolina Theater anymore. And the man who ran this ornate movie palace is not even a memory to most of the people in my hometown now.

I'll take solo sojourns down long forgotten streets and sigh when a memory is flushed by an aging, but I-remember-that! landmark.

I'll search the faces of people I suspect are my age and wonder if I should know them. Sometimes I see a young person who is a dead-ringer for someone I grew up with.

But I never stop them and ask. It would also be easy to pick up the phone and call some ol' buddies. A lot of them are still around. But I don't ask and don't call because I'm afraid they won't care as much about replaying the past as I do.

Momma and my sister Mary Jane Sanders and nephew Craig usually have our dance cards pretty well filled when we get there and there isn't a lot of free time, particularly in the evenings when old buddies like to have you over for for dinner.

This year was different for some reasons. The old tried-and-trues like my favorite barbecue place didn't come up to memory's snuff or spice. The fish camp of my youth was laboriously slow and the fried catfish not so sweet as yesterday.

The fields and forests I roamed are now long-established subdivisions close to malls. Downtown, which I didn't even recognize, was trying to go through a rebirth and the downtown I remembered is nowhere to be found.

I had to talk about it with someone who would appreciate it all, my oldest friend, attorney Joe Hines Jr. Unannounced, I waited at the back of the court for Joe to come out.

When he did, we both did double takes. I would have sworn I was looking at Joe's father and he was sure he was looking at the Carolina Theater's Mr. T.

What happened to young Jodie and young Bobby?

We laughed at the remarkable resemblances.

Later at lunch, we laughed and cried and groaned and moaned over the antics and anxieties of our youth. Those side-by-side goal line stands we made for dear ol' Spartan High. Those steamy double dates at the drive-in movies.

The beer drinking contests. Our old cars. Hanging out at Wade's. Smitty's, Fernwood, the NuWay, the Beacon, Frog's and cruising the main drag and dragging out Pine Street.

I've always suspected my drinking escapades would be remembered, but I didn't know they've become part of the town's legend when people gather and recall crazy people.

We passed by one of our favorite haunts and Joe asked, "Remember, 'Smile this off,' fat boy!'? Happened right there.

" 'You wanna smile one off.' It's still a saying around town when someone's sassing you or looking at you with a crooked smile."

Joe and a couple of our other buddies were trying to sober me up one night in the DeLuxe Diner on hamburgers and black coffee, but I was more interested in asking this total stranger about the "Mom" tattoo on his scrawny arm.

The stranger, half my size, got enough of my smart mouth and invited me outside, to which I was cheerfully responding when skinny Mr. Tattoo uttered the famous "Smile this off, fat boy" and split my grin and lip in two.

The sight of this little fellow dumping me on my can with one punch seemed like the funniest thing in the world to me and I sat there on the sidewalk laughing through a split lip. We all started laughing, including Mr. Tattoo, until the police came to arrest us but couldn't find a laughter violation on the books.

Joe brought the tears out with talk of suicides of some of my favorites, divorces, our friends with problem kids, our friends in jail, those who are drunks and unfaithful and unhappy. He brought smiles with tales of the improbable success and the late bloomers.

More importantly, he brought an end to my search for my youth. When I think about it now all I have to do is reach up and touch the faint scar on my upper lip. And I'll smile one off once again.

— *May 21, 1982*

Out of my mind
on a Monday moanin'

The only thing wrong with clock radios is the song that awakens you sticks in your mind all day.

The honeymoon is over when the fellow who once whispered sweet nothings whispers nothing sweet.

No one ever pays attention to the first time you notice a coat's button is loose and your car's tires are getting slick.

A million years ago Mother Nature had no idea we'd be wearing glasses, but she sure placed our ears in the right place.

How come when you visit those exotic islands you never see all those sexy girls the airline ads used to entice you to come?

Best way to cool a teenage daughter's romance is for Dad to praise her boyfriend.

If all the shoppers in all the supermarkets were placed end to end, I'd be the one at the back of the line with my carton of milk and loaf of bread.

The best-seller lists show that today's hot books are about sex, politics, medicine,, astrology, religion, dieting and crime so the ultimate would be: "The Politics of Dr. Sex and His Crime Dog and How They Found God Through Dieting and the Stars."

When parents say, "My child is really smart, but just doesn't try," I never believe them.

Truest way to judge a man's character is to watch how he plays games with children or adults clearly his inferior.

Letter-to-the-editor writers who are the most pious in tone are also the most narrow, intolerant and vindictive in their opinions.

I could listen to Gordon Lightfoot's "If You Could Read My Mind" a thousand times a day and not get tired of it; same goes for Tammy Wynette's "Stand By Your Man."

Men who don't cry aren't worth crying over — I never trust those emotionless fellows.

It shouldn't be against the law to let the air out of the tires of a motorist who parks in the middle of a two-car space.

You know you're successful when people tell you you're a lot smarter and wiser than you know you are.

MIDDLE AGE

Middle age: The unloved phase and how to recognize it

The most maligned, misunderstood, misquoted and messed-with group in the country is the middle-aged. Compared to middle-agers, teenagers, senior citizens and young adults have it made.

Middle-agers grew up with this constant threat from their parents: "You better — or else!" Today their kids tell them: "You better — or else!"

Some hairy-headed, surly-lipped, smart-mouthed little snit is always saying, "Never trust anyone over 30." I must admit there are times when I feel like agreeing. Like, for instance, when I realize that middle-agers have allowed one man to run a union from a jail cell, another to run for Congress from Bimini, and another to run an entire state from a background of "B" movies.

But for the most part, middle-agers are bum-rapped. They get blamed for anything and everything that goes wrong. A little probing shows that middle-agers control very little and make even fewer decisions. Everything these days is being run by either the old Establishment or the young rebels. Middle-agers are caught squarely in the — where else? — middle.

Middle-agers are like the inmates at the zoo. They aren't taking the tours nor are they conducting them. They're the ones being toured.

They can blame it all on themselves. They have no spokesmen. No one will admit to being a middle-ager. In fact, most middle-agers prefer to not even bring up the subject. I know I'm that way, although I'm not about to admit I'm a middle-ager.

Once upon a time I used to believe that middle age had something to do with how many birthdays a person racked up. But the more I rack, the less I figure it that way.

I recall that 30 once seemed to be the point at which decline started. I know now that was a lot of nonsense. Middle age can't possibly begin until at least 46 or 48, maybe even 50. I've recently attended two retirement dinners for fellows who called themselves middle-agers.

Women, by some strange quirk of nature, never go through middle age. Somehow they go from sweet young things to little old ladies. I think the magic lies somewhere between two-way stretch and cosmetology.

Studies report that middle age is a state of mind, which is a researcher's way of saying he doesn't have the vaguest idea of an answer. Two rather observant people have told me that middle age begins with "a wife, a couple of children and your first mortgage," or "whenever you get your third credit card."

For what it's worth, and to help you prepare for it, here is a primer to let you know when middle age arrives.

It's when you've learned how to take care of yourself and intend to start any day now.

It's when you hate to see dust on the furniture so you take off your glasses.

It's when the only thing that can lead you down the garden path is a seed catalog.

It's when you think that in a week or two you'll feel as good as ever.

It's when you no longer get what you pay for in a beauty parlor.

It's when your wife tells you to pull in your stomach and you already have.

It's being able to remember when Elizabeth Taylor's big love was a horse.

It's lying down on the couch at 11 p.m. to watch the news and having a daughter awaken you at 1 a.m.

It's attending the wedding of a young woman whose father was two years behind you in school.

It's figuring up your bank statement and trying to convince yourself that you really don't want to be rich after all.

It's taking your wife out to dine and dance and not recognizing any of the songs they play, nor being able to eat the rich foods.

It's feeling bad in the morning without having had the fun the night before.

It's thinking your barber charges too much for the little haircut he gives you.

It's checking the age of people in obituaries.

It's not minding when you're called Mister and are told, "Yes, sir."

It's having a feeling that you've been through it all before.

— *June 19, 1969*

Arise! Fellow middle-agers, stop being put-down minority

Every time you turn around, turn a page, or turn the dial, there is something or someone telling us how important the youth vote-voice is. Or how much money the old and the young control in this country. All the surveys indicate everyone who counts is under 26 or over 60. Anytime the young or old feel rained on, they point the finger at us middle-agers for hiding the umbrellas or something.

I keep hearing that middle-agers are in command, the movers and shakers of this country. From all I can gather we're the commanded, the moved and the shook. Looks like to me the young Turks and old Establishment run it all. And the reason we don't have the handles and the buttons is that no one owns up to being a middle-ager. We treat it like a disease.

Another problem is that no one I know has ever known just when middle age starts. At one time I can remember thinking 30 was ancient. And 40! Wow, a 40-year-old was ready for Medicare and Social Security. It is usually about 10 years older than you are.

All that was before policemen and doctors started looking younger than me. That was my first wave of Future Shock. When the cop who stopped me to give me a ticket was younger than I and when a young whippersnapper "kid" wanted to perform some minor operation on my daughter, Dafna.

Another face has now gotten younger, the airline pilot. That shakes me up, too, 'cause I like those graying-templed fathers at the controls. And all of a sudden I feel surrounded by juvenile politicians. Mere kids, hardly old enough to cast votes, much less seek them.

Another thing that jolted me was the nostalgia fad. All the kids are grooving on the 1950s and punch me in the ribs and say, "Man, that's your era! Don'tcha just love it?" Nope. I didn't like it the first time around and am certainly not going to fall all over myself pretending to dig it warmed-over and caricatured. I've never understood how the hangers-on-to-yesterday and dreamers-of-tomorrow can possibly get through the todays.

Since it seems the biggest problem of middle age is not knowing or admitting when you join it, I feel it is my duty to offer this little primer to clue you into when you become a middle-ager:

It's when you can remember understanding the entire lyrics of a popular song.

It's when you pay more attention to the menu than the waitress.

It's when it takes you longer to get the mower started than to cut the grass.

It's when you realize you've collected so many recipes that you couldn't possibly live long enough to use them all.

It's looking at Perry Como or Danny Thomas and thinking how young they look.

It's thinking when people say, "the war," they mean World War II.

It's thinking of Friday as the end of the week, not the beginning of the weekend.

It's friends you haven't seen for years fishing for a compliment by telling you how well you look.

It's clothing sizes getting smaller, summers hotter and winters colder.

It's when most of your friends look as tired as you feel.

It's wondering almost daily "What do THEY really want?" and "Just who do THEY think they are?"

It's thinking the news headlines seem like repeats every day.

It's sitting around thinking up definitions of middle age.

— Aug. 28, 1972

The revelations of middle age

Middle age is . . . discovering everyone is hiring children to do jobs that you can remember young adults like yourself once doing.

Middle age is . . . finding you listen more to your inside voices than the outside voices of others.

Middle age is . . . clothing cut tighter, summers cut shorter and winters cut longer.

Middle age is . . . waiting for the 11 o'clock news to get tomorrow's weather rather than tonight's scores.

Middle age is . . . realizing that politicians and football coaches seem to get changed about as frequently as a car's oil.

Middle age is . . . when prejudices surface by reflex, and it doesn't bother you anymore.

Middle age is . . . when the faults of the other sex are more evident to you but you are more tolerant of them.

Middle age is . . . when days trudge along like caterpillars but the years flit by like butterflies.

Middle age is . . . loving the music by the Beatles and the Rolling Stones but recalling how you first rejected them as too loud and you couldn't understand the lyrics.

Middle age is . . . having climate rise on your list of priorities.

Middle age is . . . waiting for the prime of senility.

Middle age is . . . wondering if Johnny Carson goes to sleep some nights, as I do, while watching "The Tonight Show," even though I fully intend to watch each show through.

Middle age is . . . discovering tennis balls bounce twice as high as they used to.

Middle age is . . . taking three times as long to find your car in a mall parking lot because all cars look alike to you these days.

Middle age is . . . your body treating you so much nicer, the nicer you treat it.

Middle age is . . . realizing patience is perhaps the finest of all traits to have or cultivate, if you're lacking it.

Middle age is . . . swapping a kid's eyes — bigger 'n-his-stomach — for man's eyes — bigger 'n-his-pocketbook.

Middle age is . . . hating to throw away anything that is only half worn out, so your storage area looks like Salvage City.

Middle age is . . . seeing all those children of your movie heroes become the TV heroes of your own children.

Middle age is . . . wondering if you'll ever again get something worth what you pay for it.

After all is said and done, middle age is just about the best of your lives — this time around, anyway.

— March 4, 1978

Here in the middle of my age . . .

All my life I've wondered how I would know and how I would react to it. To answer the first part, I think it's a matter of adding up the little things that happen and you recognize.

Realizing that hardly a weekend goes by that we aren't going to the wedding of a son or daughter of a friend of mine. Kids I remember as being knee-high-to-a-grasshopper. Grown. Getting married. Starting families of their own. Ker-chunk. It registers.

Sitting in the stands at a high school football game and realizing one of the stars on the other team is the son of one of your co-workers — another contemporary, whose son has become a star athlete. I thought the kid was still in Pee Wee ball. Ker-chunk. Ker-chunk.

Walking into a friend's office and realizing his new receptionist reminds you of your own daughter, a high school senior. He tells you the same thing: She reminds him of HIS daughter. Ker-chunk, for both of us.

Reading about someone dying every day — someone for whom you have a great attachment — and thinking more people are dying today than ever before. Damn death. Why does it take so many of our old pals and heroes and people we enjoyed? Why does it start to hurt so much? Ker-chunk.

Standing in my favorite record store and exclaiming out loud over finding some old Bird and Pres jazz tapes and having a lady nearby do the same thing about finding some old Mario Lanza tapes for her husband. Ker-chunk for me and a ker-chunk for him.

Bowling for the first time since last fall and having my 10-year-old son beat me fair and square with no handicap in the third game — 128 to 119 — and something else fell in place. Ker-chunk!

Having the folks from Channel 56 remind me that this year will be the 10th anniversary of the dynamic auction which supports our educational TV net. Ten years ago in the Tel-Twelve Mall. Such fun. Was it that long ago? Ten years? You mean I've been around this place for one decade? Ker-chunk.

Watching a show on television about Hollywood and World War II and it's still not history to me but part of my childhood that seems to flood much of my memory these days. I remember mashing those metal cans flat, saving paper, scrap-metal drives and being convinced John Wayne won World War II. Ker-chunk!

These are just a few of the ways I know I have settled comfortably and without too much trauma into middle age. I'll tell you this much, I sure dreaded it.

More than I even realized. Last summer I was the oldest 40-year-old I have ever met. Right this moment, I don't know of a younger 41-year-old.

When I wrote last summer on hitting 40 that "I didn't realize 40 hit back," I sure wasn't kidding. I seemed to fall apart. And I was depressed. For us over-achievers, 40 is a terrible year if we haven't set the whole world on fire or haven't made enough bread to retire as we once dreamed of doing.

Somewhere over the winter I began to realize all of these things were in my mind. After all, by the census bureau accounting, 40 is a few years past a man's midpoint anyway. My own old man was 40 or 41 when I was going through high school, but I didn't even think of him as being any age at the time. Bet you were the same.

You can't really relate to your own parents' ages until you reach those ages yourself. Age is a mind trip all your life if you think about it. We've been programmed that old is a no-no and youth is the only thing worth coveting.

Age is a mind trip, all right. At a Pine Knob concert this summer — one you could say I was exuberantly into — someone behind us leaned over to my wife and asked, "What's your husband going to be when he grows up?"

I'm just glad I can let go, loosen up and boogie like a 22-year-old. I'm also glad I can escape into an all-afternoon game of Monopoly with a son who gets into that game as exuberantly as I do.

I'm also glad I can sit with a younger friend asking for advice and be as wise to him as a friend of mine who is 66 seems to me when I go to him for advice.

Only now do I think I can answer the second half of the initial question I've been wondering about: How would I react to middle age? From what I've observed from others, I've reacted normally and predictable. (That, in itself, may be the toughest thing for the ol' ego to swallow.)

The initial trauma, then the settling in, adjusting and finding you are comfortable, really, acting any age required of you. You can go either way, up or down, and not be intimidated by growing old or not acting your age.

Perhaps the most surprising thing of all about learning to love middle age is how so many cliches come true. Take it from a one-time screaming liberal, you do become more conservative the older you get.

I find myself preceding many of my statements to younger people with, "Hope this doesn't sound reactionary, but . . . " Ker-CHUNK!

It has taken me two decades as an adult to finally get it all sorted out and discover that things have a perspective that only those 20 years can create. I became an adult when I was 21 because they told us that's when we could be adults. You are how you are programmed.

I can take a look at today's 21-year-olds and know they are far more adult than I was at 21. I just hope, for their sakes, when they get to be 41 they can say the same thing and also be a whole lot smarter than we 41-year-olders are now.

— Sept. 24, 1977

Out of my mind on a Monday moanin'

Have you noticed that all women on any list of "most admired" or "best dressed" are all prime candidates for the "married well" list, 'cause dear ol' hubby pays the freight.

Why is "aeroplane" archaic and "aerospace" isn't?

There are two kinds of people at every party: Those who want to leave early and those who want to stay late, and they're always married to each other.

The color and length of one's hair seem to bother the most the people who have no hair or hair with no color.

People who say religion has nothing to do with politics know nothing about politics and completely misunderstand religion.

People who say "There are two sides to every story" have already rejected yours.

Bachelors looking for wives who cook like their mothers wind up with girls who dress like their fathers.

People who ask "Do you know what I mean?" never know what they mean themselves.

Question You'll Hate to Ask and Answer Yourself: "Would your spouse remarry you?"

Most men believe a woman's place is in the home and expect to find her there 30 minutes after she gets off work.

Anyone who says he's too old to learn new things always was.

With all those jets flying around half-empty, how come we still can't find a parking place at the airport?

When really big money talks, no one notices whether the grammar is bad or not.

One of the basic differences between sexes is that females can go into sheer rapture over an empty pair of panty hose.

LIFE

Send your kid to summer camp in a lovely tenement block

It is high time we did something about summer camps for the kiddies.

These skeeter-infested water holes tucked in distant mountains or carved out of some sandy shore advertise themselves as places to give the city kids a taste of sunshine, swimming, horseback riding, supervised recreation and general communication with the great outdoors.

But these days you have so many kids living in the suburbs that they get all the outdoors they can use in their own backyards. So what we ought to start is a summer camp for suburban kids to give them a taste of the delights of city dwelling. Face facts. Eventually these kids will grow up and have to come to the city for one reason or the other. It's inevitable. They better get used to it early.

So what I propose to do is take one square city block and designate it as our camping area. On one side you would have a section of street undergoing repairs and a row of schlock stores. This would be the sports and recreation area.

On another side there would be some second-rate apartments, almost ready for condemnation: living quarters for the campers.

A parking lot, an abandoned warehouse and a building under construction would be a third side: auxiliary rec area. The fourth side would include a factory, some ethnic taverns and bars, an Afro book store, a Chinese laundry: the cultural and educational area.

The camp would give the suburban kids all that a city can offer: bad air, congestion, traffic, crowding, anonymity, pollution, noise, corruption.

Daily classes could be conducted in dodging traffic, jaywalking (they've got to learn somewhere), name-calling, meter-feeding, drunk-rolling, fender-banging, police-cursing, adult-baiting and petty stealing. Some of these courses would be optional, depending on the camper's age, speed and persuasion.

There would be a well-rounded staff of counselors, including a mom-and-pop who run a corner drugstore and sell pot, pills and pornography under the counter.

One of the classes would be led by a beer drinker in an undershirt with no sleeves and egg stains on the front who would periodically come off the stoop and whack hell out of any kid who strays too close.

One of the counselors would be an old hag of a woman who hangs out of a fourth-story window, and screams that the kids should quit bounding their blank-blank-ball off her bleep-bleep wall or she'll call the beep-beep police.

There would be nature walks through the alleys where the kids would get to see some of the city's wildlife — rats, bums, winos, hookers. There would be field trips to a nearby urban campus to watch the students revolt.

All of the campers would be required to spend one hour a day smelling the dirty exhaust fumes of buses, cars, diesels and the dirty belches from factory smokestacks.

In the evening after a good vesper service of a honky-tonk jukebox blaring away for hours and campfire service of burning down a building, the campers would get a good night's sleep in an airless, 90-degree tenement bedroom.

The camp kitchen would serve a steady diet of grits, greasy potatoes, stale bread, hot dogs, candy bars, soft drinks, warm beer and beans.

Take advantage of these camps now, while they exist far away in the Inner City. Chances are if you wait very much longer, some branch camps just like them will begin to open up in the suburbs, whether the suburbs want them or not.

All in all, it's just the thing — a truly valuable learning program — for the suburban child. Applications are now being accepted.

— April 29, 1969

Our new specialist society gives a special pain in the neck

I was extremely vulnerable.

Tilted back in the chair at a helpless angle, my mouth was open and filled with a shiny array of periodontal hardware.

My eyes were filled with the top of the dentist's head as he rummaged around in my mouth.

"Huuuummmm," he hummed. "Looks like that wisdom tooth has to come out."

"Pmrpliuvhtopit," I said.

"What?" he asked, removing his hand and standing back.

"I said, Then pull it!"

You would have thought he'd grabbed a live 220 wire the way he started jerking.

"Do what? You can't mean that!" he exclaimed in semi-shock as if I had asked him to commit murder.

He drew himself up in all his tailed white silk efficiency and said, "I don't pull teeth. Your dentist will have to do that."

I wanted to ask him what the hell he was if he wasn't my dentist.

But I had struck a nerve. He hadn't spent all that time and money (his mother's or wife's probably) learning how to be a periodontist to pull a mere abscessed wisdom tooth. He was a gum man, a surgical specialist.

And it dawned on me right then and there that the American public is also extremely vulnerable at this point.

We are being specialized to death.

I took my television set in for some minor adjustments and was informed that it would be two weeks because the minor adjustment man was on vacation. The man talking to me was a picture tube man himself.

I needed to get my lawn mower blade sharpened and discovered that it would cost me $7.75 and 10 days to have some chubby high school lad take the blade off and sharpen it. "Bring us the blade by itself and we can do it in 10 minutes for a buck seventy-five," they admitted.

Just try to buy a complete chicken at a supermarket. You can get packages of legs, thighs and breast, but you won't find them connected any more.

While getting a yearly checkup at the internal medicine man's office, I wondered out loud if I could have a small cyst removed. You'd have thought I'd asked to see their Medicare rolls.

To give my car a similar checkup, I was informed that the ring man and the carb man weren't talking to the chassis man so I'd have to wait until next week.

We once had a refrigerator stand idle for weeks because the world's largest department store had only one man on consignment to install refrigerators.

I checked into the consignment matter and discovered that every store has a ratio of 50 salespeople to one man who makes actual delivery and one man who does the installing.

These consignment people are in cahoots with the specialists and the rest of us are doomed to suffer with things that we can't get repaired because the man won't work on the premises or the man who turns all Phillips-head screws is on an extended vacation.

I fully expect the parking lot attendant to refuse to get my station wagon because he drives only two-door sports cars.

A shoeshine boy has already refused to do a pair of my buckled boots.

I met a model the other day who gets $50 a hour for her hands to hold up lipsticks. Even her parts are specialized.

In the ice cream parlor the other evening, the counter boy said I'd have to wait until the banana-split maker came back off his break.

Go into a fancy restaurant and ask for a glass of water. Unless you grab the lowliest culinary slave first thing, you'll die of thirst.

To get a sofa reupholstered one has to hire an interior decorator, a fabric specialist, a carpenter, someone to measure the sofa, someone to haul it to the upholsterer, and someone to haul it back.

Even baby-sitters refuse to sit unless you have color TV, a frig stocked with Diet Pepsi, and no more than two children, both of whom must be potty-trained.

And we're the nation that landed men on the moon and brought them back to earth. On consignment and by specialists, no doubt.

— *Aug. 20, 1969*

Here's a brave man: He dares to put the knock on golf

A lot of wives and children will want to run me for President when I'm through writing this. Their husbands and fathers will went to quarter me over some sand trap and 6-iron me to death. To the womenfolk I am the last resort between them and a divorce court. To the men, I'm going to be the subject of a libel and slander suit.

Golf to some guys is a four-letter word like live and life. Like life? Brother, it IS life and death to these fairway fanatics. Like love, no one can really explain how or why it takes hold. Golf is a grabber, a gotcha, but good. The mid-iron maniacs wake up with a running case of the putts and there is no known antidote or cure.

The golfer is the world's most amazing nut. There have been cases of a fellow staggering up to the 15th tee, holding his side, saying apologetically to a group preparing to tee off, "Mind if I play through, fellows, my appendix just burst?"

Golfers are not to be believed. They never give up. They will golf you to death with replays and poison you with rehash. They four-putt every conversation. That's all they seem to know or care about.

It's amazing how they treat you when you tell them you don't play golf. They look at you as if you had a contagious social disease, bad breath or dandruff.

"That's un-American," a golfer once told me when I told him I didn't play nor did I think very much of the game. "It's obscene. You're part of a dirty, rotten, subversive Commie-rat-fink-plot."

Golfers have accused me of lacking married parents, masculinity, virility, veracity and lots of other things they seem to miraculously acquire from scrambling around 18 holes.

If I could honestly say that I don't know one end of a golf ball from the other, it would be easy for you to excuse me as a mad, but harmless fellow. But I have been a golfer. In fact, I was as hooked and sliced as no one you've ever known before or since. I was mainlining with 3-wood.

Just looking at a new buckles-all-over golf bag and all those shiny irons and rich woods sent me into mental orgies. I've fantasized my way into making a 22-foot putt on 18 at Augusta for all the Masters' marbles or clobbering Palmer, Nicklaus, Player, Casper and all the rest in the Open.

At the same time I was a slave to the 6-iron, I was also sitting at the bridge table with a No Trump on my back. I spent my days on the golf course and my nights at the contact bridge table. I played them both for blood — my opponents' or partner's, it didn't really seem to matter which.

I think I knew I'd had it the morning I woke up and reach for a golf club and a four of clubs before I grabbed a cigaret and coffee.

"Look," I said to me, "these are just games. You shouldn't play like they are war. No game on earth should become this important to you. A game is a game is a game. If you can't treat them that way, you'd better give 'em up or forget about ever accomplishing anything but a Master-Point ranking or an invite to the Masters."

I quit bridge and golf the same day. The withdrawal pains were akin to having my fingernails and toenails pulled off. If memory serves, I stayed drunk for six weeks, trying to get over my need for birdies and little slams. Later when I quit drinking and smoking, it was a breeze compared to giving up golf and bridge.

I have been a better man since I gave up those impossible games.

A better man, a better husband, a better father, a better person toward my fellow man. Like so many evangelists I have devoted part of my life since then trying to convince my friends to quit before it's too late.

My campaign has been completely unsuccessful. Indeed, my friends and enemies are embracing the game as never before. They have even got women playing it now. Children, too. Families may soon resemble a set of matched woods.

They seem to spend more time on golf than the government does on war, an equally senseless pastime. They spend every waking moment trying to figure out how to trick those little white balls into those cups. They dream of the Even-Par Promised Land with no sand traps and bunkers. Golf makes arrogant boasters out of pleasant sorts. It turns charming couples into bloody, vengeful bores.

And don't let them kid you. Golf is not a game or a sport. It is, in fact, a disease, a plague upon the land. Man will never conquer space, cure cancer, eliminate poverty, or find lasting peace as long as there is golf to shift him off course. Mankind will die with a 12-handicap.

— April 8, 1970

Honest, gals, I'm on your side, but I don't dig humorless lib

One of the city's underground papers, the Fifth Estate, takes me to task for what it implies is my anti-women's lib stand and "inane" attempts at humor in this area. The paper also says that the women of Detroit have singled me out to crusade against, and the undergroundling adds that I must have a problem.

I do. I happen to think that men and women are different.

At least, I've thought this up until recently. I'm beginning to wonder NOW.

My life has been a chorus from "South Pacific," singing that there is absolutely nothing like a dame. While I think it's a catchy tune, I never bought Prof. Henry Higgins' "Why Can't a Woman Be Like a Man?" from "My Fair Lady."

Most of the men I know are puzzled and a little bit hurt about this women's liberation business. Most of us worship the ground you gals walk — and now protest-march — on.

I, for one, have always preferred the company of women to the company of men. I can even assure you I'd rather be with an ugly woman than a pretty man any time.

I can't figure what's happened to women. Men are quite willing to accept the difference between men and women, but women aren't. Women are better looking, are sweeter acting, smell better and are more delightfully put together than men.

The first bit of reasoning my son Jason, who is three, did was understand that rhyme about girls being made of sugar and spice and everything nice, while boys are made of snips and snails and puppy dog's tails. On his own he figured out that you don't hit girls. You tattle on 'em, but don't hit 'em.

This women's lib thing has pointed out to me the one big area women are truly inferior to me. The lack of humor in the mass of women — lib or not lib — is amazing. This humorless characteristic corresponds to the mass male's lack of sensitivity. Both traits make it hard to love them.

I get letters from uptight frustrated ladies (I hope you don't mind me calling you "ladies") who see nothing at all humorous in jokes about women's lib. "We are tired of being treated as objects," they cry. "We want to be treated as equals." It may sound like a joke, but for most of the women I've known, equality would be a demotion.

The women's lib people, when confronted face-to-unmade face, get around to the biggest thing in their craw, not being paid on an equal basis with men doing the same jobs. Most of the time those men doing the same job have more wives and kids at home than females do and the fellows need more money. I don't want to get into this area, but I do think that just as much discrimination occurs in smart-dumb, young-old, experience-inexperience, black-white, pull-non-pull situations as male-female.

Equal rights for all.

Equal rights for all people would be a fine thing if all people were equal. They aren't. Some people are always more equal than others.

If you'd listen, I'd tell women's lib people not to try to be equal to a man because he's eventually going to tell you to prove it.

Whatever women's lib is after, it'll get because men are inclined to give in to women, even pampering them (heaven forbid!). But I'll never understand these women's dissatisfaction with themselves, with their own virtues, that make them go around imitating the worst characteristics of males and demeaning their own attributes.

From listening to women's lib, I get the feeling that men are the only things that stand between them and success in every area of their lives. I know of absolutely no collusion, stated or unstated, among men to exclude women from anything.

The truth is that men, being far lazier than females, would gladly pass the work of the world onto the ladies and lie on the couch dozing. But the woman keeps waking us up and asking, 'What's wrong with me anyhow?" And when we say, "Nothing, dear," you don't believe we mean it. And you won't let us doze on the couch, either.,

I'll never understand why a woman wants to give up her strength and glory, the ability to love and her capacity of patience, to adopt man's sense of values — position, money and power.

Money doesn't seem to hurt women, but power and authority are seldom becoming. Women in power are mean to each other — far meaner than men. Almost always women use more authority than is necessary to accomplish the job.

Women are the best when they are feminine, not feminists. Women are best when men can't figure them out. When women become equal with men, we'll have you figured in a millisecond and where will you be then? You'll be just like a man, and I doubt if that's what you want.

I don't care if the hand that rocks the cradle now cradles a rock aimed at my head. Go ahead and throw, but please smile. I don't care what they say, you ain't very pretty when you're mad.

— *Aug. 26, 1970*

Let's wage battle to preserve fairy tales and fantasies

It's high time we got some things straightened out about all these myths and fairy tales we live with. We've got to stop living these lies and passing them on to our children.

Let's tell the truth. Let the chips fall, the cookies crumble, and Gibraltar tumble.

Porky is a male chauvinist pig.

Orphan Annie is an Aunt Tom.

Senator Claghorn is an elitist.

Sir Galahad was a woman-chaser.

Paul Bunyan had a glandular disorder.

Sleeping Beauty had mono.
Snow White lived in a commune.
Alice in Wonderland was an acid head.
Winnie the Pooh had diabetes.
Little Miss Muffett was schizo.
The Emperor with New Clothes and Lady Godiva were exhibition-ists.
Jack and Jill weren't married.

Those are for starters. Wait'll the research is in on this stuff.

It looks grim for the Brothers Grimm. Seen the new bumper stickers: "Stop Aesop!"

I'm not being a wise guy. It's happening and you don't even know it. All the various rights groups, for example, are going to clean up the classics and the comics. They are de-mything us.

Civil Righters think little Black Sambo should be burned. Women's lib would ban Cinderella, Snow White and all the Mary Poppins and Dr. Doolittle things. These books are full of racist and sexist thoughts. A pox on their publishing houses.

Not long ago in one of those South American countries — they all look and sound alike to me — a left-wing group proved that Donald Duck has a sadomasochistic relationship with Huey, Dewey and Louie, his nephews. Scrooge McDuck, of course, is a capitalist imperialist.

A California minister recently attacked Charlie Brown and all the Peanuts gang for not getting involved in what's happening in the streets and neglecting the problems of the urban areas.

Schroeder, I guess, should play more like Elton John than Beethoven. Charlie Brown's little redhead girlfriend should stop flaunting her sex appeal in the kindergarten play yard and Lucy should write women's lib pamphlets. Linus is a blanket-junkie and should be dried out. Snoopy's parents were never married.

Are you ready for all this? I wasn't and I'm still not.

To insist that comics and fairy tales become politicized is my idea of the decade's prizewinning bad suggestion. Of all periods in history, today is a hysterical exclamation point that needs comic relief.

With so much relevancy and reality shoved at children, it's nice to have an Old Woman Who Lived in a Shoe to think about. But wait a minute, the Planned Parenthood crowd would be after that Old Woman's neck. How about welfare reformers? Think of the check she must've received every month! Wow!

Jack Spratt's wife would immediately be enrolled in Weight Watchers and Vic Tanny would grab ol' Jack and build him up.

Remember the Ugly Duckling? Elizabeth Arden would work wonders with the feathered friend. The No-Doz crowd would love to get hold of Sleeping Beauty.

The health food industry loves Miss Muffet, since they're the only ones who know what curds and whey are, anyway. Maybe they know what the Three Bears put in the porridge. And if the truth be known, Goldilocks was probably the Avon Lady in disguise.

Little Red Riding Hood was a hooker and you just think that was Grandma's house.

If we really investigate this stuff it'll come out that the Phantom was a CIA agent. Robin Hood and his Merry Men were the Hell's Angels of Sherwood Forest, and were Mafia-controlled. King Arthur and his Knights of the Round Table were the first Gay Liberation Front.

Johnny Appleseed was anti-union. The Three Blind Mice are products of the ghetto and spread disease with Mickey Mouse. Old King Cole was a despot. Mary Mary Quite Contrary was anti-ecology.

And Parker Brothers is going to have to clean up Monopoly. Those houses and hotels must be turned into condominiums. When you Pass Go, you have to Pay $200 in property and school tax. Free Parking is now $7.50 a day. Boardwalk's rent is $600 unfurnished.

All right, friends, you see the task before us. Let's get busy. Free the fairy tales! Make Charles Schulz have Charlie Brown "token up" and shout "Power to the people!"

— July 17, 1972

Today we spin the flip side, shower you with happy talk

I must admit I've found myself in an angry bag lately. "Somebody sure licked the red off your candy," a caller said the other say after an El Gripe-o column. "I told my wife somebody must've tromped on the boy's toes," another caller said. Being angry is too easy these days. Let's turn the frown upside down. Let's put on a happy face even if it's a yellow paste-on with black/grins and dot-eyes. Let's get happy. But what is happiness? (And if that isn't a great column lead-in, I've never seen it.)

Happiness is an extra pack of McDonald's french fries you eat on the way home just like in the commercial.

Happiness is listening to Stan Getz play "Con Alma" on the sweetest tenor sax in the world.

Happiness is getting your water glass refilled in a restaurant without asking.

Happiness is picking a surface road instead of a freeway at rush time and getting there faster.

Happiness is having both Greg Landry and Bill Munson as Lion quarterbacks.

Happiness is Wrigley's opening its supermarkets 24 hours a day.

Happiness is sitting down in a pair of shorts and your sweaty legs not sticking to the chair fabric.

Happiness is listening to a fun nut like WDEE's Deano Day and his telephoners in the morning and switching over to the sanity of WJR's J.P. McCarthy to find out what's happening in Detroit.

Happiness is going into a store and the Tiger game is on the radio.

Happiness is having the Fratello Larcos serve you up the finest Italian food in Detroit at their famous McNichols restaurant.

Happiness if finding a shirt you've been looking for in your size on sale and it's the last one.

Happiness is watching the rent-a-cops and real ones look the other way when kids take up a joint at a Rolling Stones concert and nobody gets hurt by it.

Happiness is a dinner conversation without someone mentioning busing — a subject that just can't be mentioned calmly anymore.

Happiness is being away at camp and getting a letter at every mail call.

Happiness is a new boss remembering your name the second day at work.

Happiness is the first time you learn to write your name or tie your shoelaces and feeling all-grown-up.

Happiness is your first checking account and the very first check you write and you don't want to cash it.

Happiness is pulling into a parking place with 20 minutes still on the meter and all you need is 15.

Happiness is finding a $5 bill wadding up in the pocket of a summer suit you left there last summer.

Happiness is flipping a cigaret or a piece of paper litter at a target and hitting it dead center — a trash can, of course.

Happiness is watching a pretty, glad-to-be-alive girl in long legs and short shorts walk proudly down the street with hair and hips swinging happily.

Happiness is a dentist saying, "No cavities — see you in six months."

Happiness is a patrolman saying, "Well, I'll let you go this time, but watch it from here on out."

Happiness is watching a base-runner turn a double into a triple.

Happiness is the fun and laughter at Fran Rodgers' Pinkey's on the Boulevard every single night — happiest bar on Jefferson.

Happiness is not having to listen to a successful dieter or someone who has successfully quit cigarets for the first time.

Happiness is a small son watching you shave and pretending he is, too.

Happiness is mom at last being able to play some for-real "dress up" in her daughters' mod clothes.

Happiness is a newspaper or newscast without a story on Bobby Fischer's or Henry Kissinger's latest moves.

Happiness is liking the nickname your friends gave you.

Happiness is walking into the coolness of a bank's lobby from the hotness of a city street.

Happiness is a banjo-blanket party and cold fried chicken.

Happiness is having a flatter-chested friend.

Happiness is her always having to say she's sorry.

Happiness is a newscaster flubbing a line and not getting flustered.

Happiness is thinking money won't buy happiness.

Happiness is a hand to hold at the scary parts and a heart to be near at the love stuff.

Happiness is having someone to agree with your opinion of movies like "A Clockwork Orange" and "Portnoy's Complaint."

Happiness is not playing golf or tennis and not caring that you don't, either.

Happiness is knowing for sure how you are going to vote.

Happiness is just happening to turn on the TV and there's a rerun of a show you wanted to see and missed the first time.

Happiness is a taco from Jack-in-the-Box.

Happiness is not having to wear socks with loafers.

Happiness is not having to wear loafers.

Happiness is being able to write a column like this once in a while.
— *July 21, 1972*

Skip that talk about unity, mankind is a great divide

OK, we know the world is divided into two kinds of people: "them" and "us."

Agreed? Of course you do.

But we can break it down better than that.

Lots better.

People are one way or the other today.

No middle ground. No middle road. No middle brow. No middle-class, 'cause who would admit it?

No one wants to be average.

Two kinds of people. Barbra Streisand should sing about that.

Our world loves labels. Pigeonholes. Niches. Slots. Categories.

Without 'em we wouldn't know who the hell we are, and we'd go crazy trying to figure out who they are.

You remember "They," don't you? As in "They say . . . They will . . . They predict . . . "

I know for a fact that each and every one of us can find ourselves in this two-kinds-of-people world, this either-or society.

First, there are winners and losers. Even if they lose, winners win. Same for losers. No matter how much he wins, the loser eventually loses.

There are givers and takers. Unfortunately, they never seem to get together. Two takers or two givers never make it with each other. But a true giver with a true taker is a happening.

We read all the time about the Ins and the Outs. There is no way an Out person can ever get to be an In, but Ins can become Outs with no trouble at all.

There are Day people and Night people. Never have you heard of Dusk and Dawn people.

There are Tub and Shower people and neither would be caught dead in the other.

The world is divided into Doers-of-Things and Watchers-of-Things. It works well, 'cause the watchers love watching the Doers and the Doers love being watched.

Every day we become more aware of the Haves and Have-nots. Without going into the socio-economics of the matter, just let us realize we will always have these two groupings.

There are Yes people and No people, who instinctively adopt a Yes or No (Pro and Con) attitude toward everything. And their Yesses never mean No, nor do their Nos ever mean Yes.

There are people who Care and those who Care Less. Once in a great while a Care Less does Care, but those who Care are always caring, thank goodness.

We have those who Remember and those who Forget, everything and always. I think we are born one or the other.

There are the Full people vs. the Empty people.

There are the Whole people and the Broken people.

There are those who love Onions and those who hate Onions. Except when they date each other and sometimes compromise.

We have Daredevils on one side and Scaredy-cats on the other.

People come in two sizes — Fat and Thin and two lengths — Tall and Short. No average person, 'cause no one is ever satisfied with their present shape.

We're also divided into those who love to live in the city and those who love the country.

Some people are Readers and do so constantly, while others are Non-Readers and never, but never read anything other than directions and menus (with possible TV listings thrown in).

There are the Fancy people and the Plain people, and no matter how much money you spend, a Plain can never really become a Fancy, and Fancies always stand out even when they try to be Plain.

We have people who have their thing Together as opposed to those who are Apart in their thing, which I assume the Hip and the Un-Hip will figure out.

The world is populated by the Neats and the Slobs, those with Taste and those who are Tasteless.

There are the Energetics and the Tireds who are this way no matter the time nor the activity.

There are the Healthies and the Sicks, the Smarts and the Dumbs, the Pretties and the Uglies. The Glibs vs. the Silents.

There are some people who are always Bright and those who are always Dull. Some like 'em With Almonds or some Without.

People are either Hard or Soft, even if they constantly try to disguise this.

Life has its Pros and its Amateurs in everything.

We're divided all right. Polarized. Either-Or. It works.

But you can't predict that a Shower person will be a neat Carer and a Soft with Onions. We swap and switch and cross over, and even change in some instances.

The only division I worry about, really, is between the Positive people and the Negative people, 'cause Negatives make too many Positives Negatives and seldom can Positives turn Negatives into Positives.

— July 27, 1972

Her first day in school, a lifetime memory

It was the biggest day in her life.

You can't imagine how big, unless you're 42 pounds and six years old and it's the first day of school.

That big.

Psychologists say the major crisis in a girl's life is her wedding day. Try to get a six-year-old to believe that on her first day of school.

Nothing compares to that first day of school.

It's the all-time champion day of feeling happy-scared.

Forever and ever Angie will remember every single second of her first day. And 50 years from now it will seem like yesterday.

Let me pause a moment. Angie doesn't live here.

Her first day of school was several yesterdays ago. But on a day like today Angie and I are remembering her first day.

It started the night before.

Well, to be honest, the first day of school starts in the middle of the summer. You think about it every day until the night before and then you begin living it.

Your head won't stop wondering about the what and who of it. The where and why and how are of little concern.

Angie's cute little head couldn't stop thinking about that mysterious room No. 117 — with its doorway into a whole new world.

Angie's heart felt like it would thump right out of her chest.

Sleep just wouldn't come . . . but all of a sudden there was Angie's mother learning over the bed and saying softly, "Time to get up, dear. You know what today is."

Did Angie know what the day is?

Did God make little green apples and six-year-old girls?

Pretty little girls in pink dresses with puffy little sleeves and new see-your-face-in-them patent-leather shoes and a carry-in-the-hand purse?

A carry-in-the-hand purse always helps in times like this.

A girl should never, ever go anywhere unknown without a carry-in-the-hand purse to hold. It's good for snapping open and shut when you don't know what else to do. And squeezing tight.

Angie's parents were up earlier than usual so Angie could have a big breakfast and have some time to get her hair just right.

Women, even at six, will do nothing important unless their hair is just right. It is the law of the land and men will be well advised never to forget this.

Angie began to wonder about the other children as she sat still while her mother put the matching pink ribbons in place.

Would the other girls' mothers be fussing with their hair, too?

And there would be boys there. Really, terrible boys who probably don't even know how to act in school. Boys who tease you a lot.

And the teacher who smiles and smiles and smiles.

They had met the teacher earlier when they had gone to school to get enrolled and get Angie's books and a box of big, fat crayons and a tablet with blue lines on white paper.

That was the day they had walked to the school and Angie remembered every single step of the two blocks.

Every step she would be taking all alone today.

Angie remembered the teacher showing her the way to the bathroom and what if she forgets today?

"Oh, Angie," her mother smiled, "that's too silly to worry about. You'll remember. If you don't, someone will help show you again."

Angie's mother began telling her about all the fun things and recess and lunch and the friends she would make and learning how to write her name and read the words in her new books.

All the happy talk was helping.

Angie's heart was still thump-thump-thumping but she was used to it now.

Angie's daddy stood around and smiled and told her how pretty she looked.

That's what daddies do best on a six-year-old girl's first day of school. Daddies are also best when they hug and squeeze you and let you know everything's going to be all right.

Everyone looked at the clock.

The time had come.

Time to walk those two blocks to school and the brand new world it promised to a six-year-old girl on a beautiful September morn.

Angie's mother checked her over for the final time. Her father gave her a big kiss and a squeezing hug.

Angie looked back over her shoulder at the two people she loved and who loved her. The two people she wanted to be proud of her.

She couldn't see the happy and proud tears in their eyes as she turned up the sidewalk.

She could only see the school yard and then a blurry shadow at her side and someone spat in her face and shouted:

"Go way, nigger! We don't want no niggers in our school! Go 'way!"

Forever and ever Angie will remember the day she helped integrate the schools in a small Southern town.

— Sept. 6, 1973

TV may be entertaining, but it's unreal

Just once I'd like to see someone on TV pick up a ringing phone and it's someone calling a wrong number.

Just once I'd like to see someone on TV circle the block and not find a parking place.

Just once I'd like to see someone on TV receive a bouquet of flowers and not be able to find a vase of the right size and shape at her elbow.

Just once I'd like to see someone on TV have to fumble around and find a credit card to buy something.

These things never happen. And they never will.

Time's too precious to waste getting a busy signal unless the busy signal furthers the plot. Time's too precious for the hero to stop to fill out a check.

And it's far too precious for anyone to pause to go to the restroom. Anyway, everyone knows TV actors and actresses don't have bladders. It's written right into their contracts. And TV children are born without 'em.

TV refrigerators are always full of ice, sandwich stuff already sliced, and never ever a milk carton sneaked back in empty by the last person to use it.

TV cars always start, always have plenty of gas and pickup when needed. TV light bulbs always light. TV beds always magically make themselves. TV streets are always well marked.

They always will be.

Just as you can always be sure that TV male stars will fall into one of two categories: dudes or boobs. And TV's female stars are either great looking or funny looking.

The only place on TV you'll find ordinary people is watching it. Speaking of that, have you ever noticed that almost no one on TV is ever watching TV? That's how most of us spend every evening, but that's sure not how most people on TV spend theirs. In fact, you rarely even see a TV set on a television series set.

TV males either look like Mike Connors or Carroll O'Connor. TV females look like Mary Tyler Moore or Lucille Ball in drag.

Somewhere in the rules it says "No ordinary people on TV shows." This has been amended lately with this clause: "Put the ordinary people into TV commercials."

But the agencies go too far with the Ordinary People in Commercials. They make 'em too damn ordinary.

My head has never felt like it had a block of concrete around it, and I've had some real doozies of colds, believe me.

I've never had a dinner party saved by a bottle of detergent and I hope to God I never attend one that is.

If some fellow stopped me outside a supermarket and wanted to rummage around in my shopping bag, he'd get bagged all right.

So help me, if a chick ever sings about my ring-around-the-collar I'll wring her neck.

And you can rest assured my sex life isn't determined by sucking on those candy breath hickies.

Nor will I ever buy one single thing shown to me by someone who dresses up funny, like a man wearing a woman's clothes.

Anyone who talks to me in a heavy accent, be it Swedish or Jewish or Hillbillyish, is going to talk me right out of their product.

People who drive cars in television commercials are either gloriously glamorous or grotesquely comic.

Just show me some Saturday afternoon slob in a parking lot struggling with a seat belt or a parking place or a dieseling engine. I'd buy that car in a minute.

Women in the car commercials have hair that looks like Vidal Sassoon just did them, or they are in curlers. Never someone in-between, which is what most women are.

And kids on TV — commercials and shows — are too cute or too rotten. No in-betweens there, either.

So what do we get? We get an abnormal view of life and people. We get Bigger-Than-Lifers or Big Laughers. Extremes. A Mannix or a Bunker.

Maybe television has us figured out better than we could ever figure out ourselves. Who wants to look at some ordinary household at night when you live in one everyday?

And most of us are ordinary looking, with images fashioned by some facial cookie-cutters. Instantly forgettable, which is a TV no-no. None of us dress as well or as funny as the way wardrobe garbs its TV people.

This is the new TV season, one that I'm told has made a concerted effort to go for the average types. The "uglies" as the ordinary people are called in the TV trade.

But no matter how bald, how fat, how bad-eyed or bad-tempered they make them, they won't be us. They can make them mumble and fumble, sweat and forget, but we won't identify with them. 'Cause, baby, we watch TV. We sure don't want it watching us.

— *Sept. 14, 1973*

Here's my certified druthers list

I would rather read my mail than answer it. I would rather take a shower than a bath. I would rather buy groceries than put them away when I get home.

I'd rather watch sports than participate in them. I'd rather wash dishes than dry them, and rather put them in the dishwasher than take them out.

There are lots of things I'd rather do. I'd rather make up a list of things to do than do the things on the list. I'd rather sleep in than get up early. I'd rather browse through a hardware store than a gift shop.

I'd rather write with red or green ink than blue or black. I'd rather take out the garbage than put stuff in the garbage bag. I'd rather walk along a beach than just lie on it.

I'd rather listen to good stereo than hear bad live music. I'd rather have a glass of cold milk than any other liquid. I'd rather be 38 than

48 or 28. I'd rather have my feet treated by a podiatrist than my hands treated by a manicurist.

I'd rather pay cash when I buy than have to sit down and pay bills when they come in. I'd rather have a late lunch than an early lunch. I'd rather half-finish a crossword puzzle myself than finish it with someone else's help.

I'd rather shave my full face than mess around manicuring a beard. I'd rather wear jeans than tailored pants. I'd rather have the TV turned on as background noise than be in a totally silent room.

I'd rather place the blame than accept it but I'll accept the blame in a moment if it will prevent arguments.

I'd rather be in light snow than a hard rain. I'd rather drive the freeways than the surface streets.

I'd rather shop Tuesday morning than Saturday afternoon. I'd rather read the newspaper in the morning than the afternoon.

I'd rather talk to someone I don't know than talk with someone I know too well. I'd rather hum than whistle.

I'd rather give fits than receive them. I'd rather watch any talk show than watch an old movie. I'd rather watch anything in color than anything in black and white.

I'd rather eat French fries than baked potatoes. I'd rather eat ethnic food than steak and salad. I'd rather yawn than sneeze. I'd rather wait in line in my car than stand in line.

I'd rather write columns about one subject than write an odds-and-ends column. I'd rather read an odds-and-ends column than a one-subject column. I'd rather listen to other new opinions than hear my own old ones.

I'd rather work downtown, but I'd rather shop in the suburbs — parking, you know. I'd rather sleep under heavy quilts than an electric blanket. I'd rather have drapes than curtains.

I'd rather read a contemporary novel than a historical one. I'd rather have one bite of a dessert than pass it up completely. I'd rather eat the house dressing than any of the standards they have for salads.

I'd rather drive a big car than a small car. I'd rather be driven than drive. I'd rather sit and listen to music than get up and dance to it. I'd rather use a handkerchief than a tissue.

I'd rather wear colorful sports shirts than turtlenecks. I'd rather never wear a tie than wear one anywhere. I'd rather clean a bathroom than a kitchen.

I'd rather read about a politician's wife than about the politician.

I'd rather listen to an ex-quarterback do color than to an ex-lineman. I'd rather just enjoy Detroit than try to convince bad-mouthers that you can enjoy Detroit.
you can enjoy Detroit.

I'd rather float on my back than swim a lap. I'd rather wear sunglasses than reading glasses. I'd rather eat barbecued ribs than prime ribs.

I'd rather stretch than scratch. I'd rather read about a Fanne Foxe than a Martha Mitchell. I'd rather rap with a liberal than a conservative. I'd rather see a cop than be one.

I'd rather sleep in a vacation motel than camp out. I'd rather eat something you make with a blender than with a grill. I'd rather not have a cold than have one, but I'd rather live with a cold than try to get rid of it.

I'd rather have an artificial Christmas tree than a real one. I'd rather listen to FM than AM. I'd rather have a woman sell me something on TV than a man.

I'd rather like to do this kind of column from time to time, than not to do it and forget about a lot of things I'd rather do.

— Dec. 28, 1974

High on my list is just plain ol' ridin' 'round

If you were to push me to the line and ask me to name three or four things that I love doing, one that would be high on the list would be plain ol' ridin' 'round.

Just ridin' 'round.

I love it.

It's my time alone. My time to lay back and sort it all out.

The things I do take me on freeway and surface jaunts of up to an hour in length. They are wonderful little segments of the day I appreciate.

A 30-minute time for me before I get out and join you or others in finding the handle on what's happening, what's going on.

These little journeys are addictive.

And also necessary.

I honestly don't know how I could cope with my schedule, the worlds in which I run and walk, if I didn't have my ridin' 'round moments.

I'm of a very big opinion that we all need to slow down.

I don't know about you, but I suspect you are like yours truly here — always feeling like you are flat-out and rushing here and rushing there.

A couple of years ago I knew I couldn't keep up this pace.

I had to have pockets of time for myself.

For only me. I would try to grab 30 minutes here or 30 minutes there and it seemed I rushed through these periods like I rushed through everything else.

Then it dawned on me. Utilize the time you spend in your car.

Most of the time most of us drive is combat time. Literally.

The rush traffic hours before 9 a.m. and every afternoon from 4 o'clock on are virtually combat. We are forced to drive defensively and the tension mounts.

Tensions and frustrations. How can you enjoy ridin' 'round?

So I started scheduling my life before and after traffic.

A little morning and afternoon ridin' 'round.

The more and more I get to do my ridin' 'round thing, the more convinced I become that it's the best therapy possible. Don't come down on my back about the energy shortage and that I'm wasting a lot of fuel.

Nothing's a waste if it helps your mental attitude, if it unjangles your nerves. But my ridin' 'round is also how I do my thing, going to and fro to find out what's happening to you and to your neighbors.

And you can't get that information just by sitting behind a desk and picking up a phone.

I have a theory that this entire country and the world, for that matter, should just do some ridin' 'round. First of all, we all need to slow down.

We should all shove it up into cruise gear and take the time to look around and really see what we've been looking at for years.

I have discovered you can accomplish this by driving five miles an hour under the posted speed limits. You'll practically be alone, be it on freeways, surface streets, or back country roads. Drive 50 and you'll find the road is practically yours. No traffic around you because most people are still locked into that hurry-up-and-wait style of driving.

I have found my slowing down on the road has enabled me to slow the rest of my life down, many r.p.m.'s worth. Outside of extreme emergencies, there is nothing in life worth rushing to get to or away from.

I love to put it in cruise, tune into some radio station — music is a vital part of ridin' 'round — that gets some good sets rolling, and just sort of lay back and observe the passing world.

Care to join me?

Ah, yes, Marvin Gaye is singing his oldie about how he heard it through the grapevine. Today's grapevine, connecting up people, is our vast interconnecting system of streets and roads. The backyard fences are intersections and cloverleafs and parking lots.

There are some kids over at that service station standing around their new old van. A rock group, peacock-proud of their names written on the side of their van. Maybe one day they'll be making music for ridin' 'round.

See those two bikers over there, standing by the bike with the For Sale sign on it? Two hours ago I saw the short one wipe it out in some gravel. He came close to having his leg run over by a car. Complete little story right there.

There's a funeral. Ten cars maybe. Who died? How? Your mind races and that's all right. There goes a young couple with a rental truck and a station wagon, loaded down to the limit of their shocks. Are they happy they're moving? Where are they going? Where did they come from?

An elderly man and his wife are changing the marquee in front of their store. The ladder's awfully tall and he's awfully old. He makes it. Is he as happy about it as I am for him?

You just keep ridin' 'round and wondering about the people and things you see. And you forget about your own problems.

— June 25, 1975

When football season comes, I always think of Coach

Standing on the sidelines of a high school game last Saturday, I thought of him. I always do in the fall. I've talked about him before and I'll talk about him again.

To me, he was football, even though he spent his lifetime in the game's bush leagues. You may even know him.

He never heard 100,000 fans raise their voices in that tidal wave of praise that follows a successful touchdown drive.

What he heard was a couple thousand folks in a plank-seat

stadium talk about business, crops, weather, socials and, incidentally, a halfback's fine zigzag run following an end's clean block.

Down through the years he never had much in the way of assistants. Only occasionally would a math or chemistry teacher fill in as a line or backfield coach.

He had to teach his assistant how to "crab block" and to understand what an over-shifted formation was before he went out to teach it to his boys.

His boys. Oh, how he loved his boys. He always told people that even if he lost all 10 games he'd have "11 fine gentlemen out there. Hard-nosed gentlemen, I might add."

Hard-nose was his favorite word, in those pre-face mask days. "Show me a kid with a scabbed-up nose and I'll show you a kid who can play for me," he'd say. And you better believe we all wore those badges all season long.

He drove his players hard, insisting over and over again that football was a game of blocking and tackling and hard work and guts and sacrifice. "If you don't give them girls and cigarets up," he'd say, "you'll give out on me in the fourth quarter every time, so I don't want you."

That was first day of practice. And he stood there until the smokers and the jitterbugs left. He'd walk down the exercise lines and look each player in the eye and repeat his statement.

If you could look back into those cold gray eyes you could stay, but if your eyes wavered he'd tell you to turn it in.

He knew that most of his players would spend most of their lives taking orders from other people. That's why he'd say: "When you get through playin' under me, son, any boss in the world will seem like an angel and you'll have no trouble adjusting."

His budget for the entire year was what it costs to put on one of the halftime shows at a pro game today. He taped a thousand ankles and patched a thousand cuts a season because there wasn't a trainer, just ol' Doc So-and-So who'd sit on the end of the bench at home games.

He even washed the dirty uniforms and patched a few to get by from season to season and he'd get up the morning of home games to line off the field himself.

He was coach, trainer, groundskeeper and equipment manager all rolled in one. And he wanted it that way.

He took a fierce pride in being one of those underpaid, overworked, harassed high school coaches of an era which slipped silently into history a couple of decades ago.

Oh, he had a name, but it didn't matter. He was Coach to everybody in town, from the preachers to the panhandlers on the square and around the train station.

And Coach looked like a coach. Pickle-barrel chest, a set of Arm & Hammer baking soda arms, a grip like a vise, and a pair of spindly legs that bore the countless scars football had hacked across his shins and calves.

He scrimmaged with his teams until he was 45. At 55 he could lay a punt out there consistently at 50 to 60 yards and could cut a corner so sharp and slick the ground seemed to crease under his cleats.

He took his first job at school that didn't even have a field. His squad consisted of 13 hard-nosed gentlemen. He won 10 straight.

He watched football change from straight-up runners and bent-down blockers to straight-up blockers and bent runners.

He lost many games, some for titles, because his star sat it out for violating one of Coach's ironclad rules or curfews. He once benched his own son, a starting line and half a backfield and suffered a 78-0 defeat as the scrubs got a lot of practice lining up to receive kickoffs.

He would say "winning's not everything" as if the words were a wonderful discovery he had just made and wanted to share with the rest of the world. But he hated to lose and that's why his boys did not often make him experience that feeling.

He tasted all the thrills he wanted from football and suffered through the disappointments the sport contains. He never let on when a good play really pleased him, but he never failed to let you know when one didn't.

He insisted his athletes go to college for an education if they were lucky enough to get a scholarship — and "don't look at it as a free ride 'cause life ain't arranged that way."

He had some who became starters in college and a few even became stars. But he had thousands who became starters in life — that was his greatest contribution.

When he died, his boys turned out from all over the country. Big men, crying big tears. Going into the church, one of them tossed away a pack of cigarets and said, "Sure as shooting, Coach would rise up in his casket and say, 'Son, let me see what you got in that pocket.' "

That was Coach. Bet you knew one, too.

— Sept. 17, 1977

Why do we believe in generalizations?

What do you believe? Why do you believe what you believe? Ever think about this?

I've been putting my mind to it of late. Thinking about our beliefs and notions. Philosophies and myths. Truths and lies. Facts and fancies. Certainties and assumptions.

How do we get to know all these things? Is it osmosis? Absorption? Are they inherited? Do they come from environmental exposure and parental repetition? Personal experimentation?

I've been talking to a lot of people in a lot of different settings, asking them why they believe some simple statement they just made. Here are some of them:

"The Japanese make a far better, more economical and much safer car than Americans."

"A woman is complete, whole, fulfilled once she has found a man to share life with, but a man needs more needs goals, work, a career."

"I never met a crew cut who wasn't a narrow-minded conservative."

"All white cops are racists."

"To really be successful in business, a woman has to use sex and sexual ploys, because it's only way men can relate with women."

"Right-handers hit better against left-handers and left-handers hit better against right-handers."

"You have to have a violent and brutal streak to want to be a cop."

"New wave rock is nothing more than simplified, bare-bones rock-and-roll."

"To break a record in this market you have to pay through the nose — something for the disc jockey's nose, that is."

"Everybody on welfare today cheats because everyone else is doing it."

"All politicians are owned by someone, in someone's back pocket."

"Marijuana and beer are openly consumed in the Tiger Stadium bleachers and that's why all those young people act so crazy."

"The easiest thing in the world to do today is fix a horse race."

"Newspapers don't care about giving both the sides of the story any more. They report just the side that sells more papers."

"You Southerners all like country music."

"The biggest joke and the saddest thing about this current presidential race is that our choice is between Carter and Reagan. America has no great leaders anymore."

"There is absolutely nothing worth watching on television these days. And all the news is so bad, even the news isn't worth watching."

"Detroit will never have winning sports professionals sports teams with the current ownerships."

"The Coney Islands at the American and Lafayette Coney Islands in downtown Detroit are still the best."

" I don't care where you go or what you are, it takes forever to get waited on these days."

"Nothing ever starts on time any more."

"The 'bad cops' in the various forces are really very few in number, but these are the only ones that get media exposure."

"America is the softest it has ever been in every area and you watch and see if the Russians don't exploit this very knowledge throughout the '80s and '90s."

"I honestly believe we're in the midst of a male-vs.-female war and don't even know it."

"Only Cubans Castro is letting into this country are criminals."

"The public would be surprised and disappointed to discover just how few 'welfare cheats' are on welfare rolls."

"Grosse Pointe is filled only with preppies and Princeton types."

"The new rich in West Bloomfield and Bloomfield Hills have no style, other than one-upmanship."

"Detroit has more good restaurants per capita than any time in its history."

"The media seek only the sensational and if they can't find it, they create it."

"Big oil and world conglomerates control everything and everyone, when it comes right down to it."

"All newspaper columnists are on the take in some way."

"Teachers care more about extra benefits today than they do teaching."

As I said before letting you eavesdrop on all these statements, I stopped these people in mid-conversation and asked them to tell me exactly, precisely and in detail why they made these statements.

Some of the statements are trivial, while others are heavy. They all were explained in some manner. In some instances the belief growing even stronger as they explained it.

Others? The stammering ones compromised. The majority admitted that — possibly — they were generalizing. Overgeneralizing, maybe, I suggested.

Perhaps this overgeneralization and our accepting it as the gospel is one of the core problems our society faces. And I'm not overgeneralizing.

— June 4, 1980

Maybe our generation had life too easy

All my life I have been listening to older folks, from older generations, tell me how much harder they had it coming along than my generation has had it.

I mean, all my life. I can remember when I was a kid listening to my parents and their friends tell me how rough it was when they were young, and I thought how lucky I was to have shoes and three meals a day.

I've heard this all my life. I sort of accepted it as the way things are. The way things have always been and will always be. And the way the older generations said it should be.

Each succeeding generation is supposed to have it easier than the one preceding it and a whole lot easier than the even-older generations. Isn't that one of the foundations of the American Dream?

While our fathers did go on endlessly about how we kids had it made, reminding us how far they had to walk to school and how they "worked for pennies and were glad to get 'em," we always had to agree with them.

My generation, born before World War II of parents born around the turn of the century, did have it made. Whether we have it made at this moment may be an arguable point.

But I think most of us who grew up in the Depression '30s and war '40s will agree we had it a lot easier than our parents had it. And most of us have directed our energies to the proposition that our children should have it easier than we did, right? The American Dream?

Of course I'm right. But my generation is the last of the had-it-better generations. My generation is the culmination of the American Dream. For my generation — up until now — it had been good times. Maybe, the *best* times.

My generation will be the first generation ever to confess to younger generations that yes, indeed, "we sure had it easier than you folks have it."

When I was 21 and even 31 the world was an oyster irritating a pearl just for me. Had my name on it. To today's 21-year-old, to the 31-year-old, those irritants in the oyster-world don't turn into pearls. They just remain irritants.

My generation had all the advantages. We grew up talking about standard of living rather than cost of living. As each of us from my generation set about to become whatever, we didn't start with handicaps such as out-of-hand inflation and a world on the brink of oil wars.

When my generation was establishing itself as the establishment the good life was still affordable and reachable. It was almost to simple. All we had to do was work hard and the rewards would come.

Today's young person must have a numbing feeling that even if you work hard, apply yourself, the only reward on the horizon is survival.

And what of the world the young person is competing in? The Wall Street Journal just had a story on the fact that nothing seems to work anymore. And repair and service industries are backlogged with business.

Once upon a time when I was growing up we had quality products, quality goods, quality services. Granted, our products weren't as complicated or sophisticated as those manufactured and produced today, but they worked.

There weren't as many things to go wrong with a washing machine that basically washed clothes and didn't know anything about rinse cycles and pre-soaks.

Our cars weren't a mass/mess of wiring, wrought by push-button this and digital that. Repairing cars was a simple process, usually done at home or at some shade-tree mechanic's shop.

Multi-rinse cycles and push-button windows are the American Dream-come-true for my generation. But is it anything like what we thought it would be?

And is this American Dream — one we've hardly realized we've achieved and are enjoying — now coming to an end? Is there a new American Dream out there? Wonder what its prime rate is?

Heavy questions. If one American dream is coming to an end, surely another will come along to take its place, won't it? We don't really have a clue because we've only had one dream to reckon with up until now.

My generation is slowly but surely asking itself another heavy question: Where did we blow the American dream? And the biggie that follows that: Should we be held to blame for blowing it?

What have we done with the world we've inherited? Have we made it a better place? An easier place for the next generation to deal with?

If we are honest with our answers we're going to feel guilty about how we've prepared the way for the future generations. I think we'll find that a big thing we've taken away from them is our American Dream, with nothing coming along to replace it.

Maybe younger generations are now trying to redefine that dream to one in tune with their needs, their future. One more in sync with the world running out of raw materials, leadership, purpose.

My generation was handed its dream on a silver platter. Maybe that was our problem. Maybe we didn't have to work for it. Maybe it all came too easy.

— Jan. 18, 1981

Did I have things to say to the pollster!

All my life I've wanted to be surveyed and polled.

I always read the results of these public question-askings with a great deal of envy. This is especially true when it's a question about a subject I'm en expert in.

Once our household was a A.C. Nielsen rated family for a month, except the head of the household was listed as my wife Lynn, so she was the official one being polled about what we watched on television.

In this mega-marketing era of consumer-society, research is the creed, drones the huckster's screed. Heavy-duty stuff and I'd never been a part of any of it.

"Our research shows . . . " these ad types say and proceed to tell us exactly how many of us like to do what with which and why and to whom and who knows where or when.

I've always wanted to be a what with which or a where or when. That's part of being an American, isn't it? Getting your two cents in, having your opinions recorded, even if you wind up in the undecided column.

But up until the other evening, I'd never been stopped on the street, quizzed in an aisle or buzzed on the phone by a pollster.

So what a thrill it was for me when the researcher for the coffee advertising industry called from New York, asking if I had a few minutes to answer some questions about coffee.

Coffee! Now that's something I can go to town on. Been drinking it every day for 30 years. Love it. Need it. Crave it. Did I ever have some things to say to her.

The questions she started asking were general. How much coffee do you drink a day, where do you drink it, how is it made, etc. What do I think of non-caffeine coffee.

I hate it. I drink coffee for the caffeine. I wish they'd put more caffeine in each cup. Enough to open my eyes for a week. "Tell 'em to double the dose."

Her next question made me wonder if she were even listening: Would I buy non-caffeinated because of the price, advertising or promotions like coupons?

"If I hate it, I certainly wouldn't buy it, would I? They could give it away, advertise it non-stop and enclose a coupon to heaven and I still don't want it."

She wanted to know if that would be a none-of-the-above?

Uh-oh!

So this is the wonderful world of advertising research. This is what I've felt left out of all these years? A pollster who can't deviate from her script, even though she's getting all these great quotes.

Oh, well.

Then she started to ask me a series of questions about the brands of coffee I used.

"We buy two eight-ounce jars of Maxim 100 percent Freeze-Dried Coffee at a time because a good heaping spoonful knocks our socks off in the morning. We've done this for years because Maxim doesn't fool around. It gets the job done. It's a great laxative, too."

That obviously glitched-off her computer terminal. She was upset.

She decided to skip the advertising part and proceeded to ask whether I remembered any of the commercials for every brand made, I think. What did I remember about Folger's?

"She's a naggy old busybody and I've wondered why someone hasn't punched her out."

Sanka?

"Did you know they canned Marcus Welby? No wonder. He's become as big a pain in the butt as Mrs. Folger. No one likes that constant nagging. I'd like to tell 'em to pour it in their ear."

Could I describe coffee commercials for Maxwell House?

"Is it still good 'til the last drop or something like that?"

Hills Brothers?

"One's tall, another's sort of short. And then there's a chubby one and the other fellow. Are there five of them?"

We kept this up for a quite few minutes.

But I could no longer give her a straight answer. I wanted to get a rise out of her, some reaction. Some sign that I wasn't talking to Roberta the Robot.

But it didn't seem to matter. She never laughed. Never deviated from her questionnaire. When we concluded she thanked me and said I sure was different from the rest of the people she'd called.

Ah, I thought, I did make an impression! How was I different?

"Oh, you're the first one who didn't hang up on me."

So much for becoming part of the wonderful world of advertising research.

— September 3, 1982

Out of my mind on a Monday moanin'

Husbands who brag about their wives' attributes cheat with females who have none of the same attributes.

The average motorist is a person who will drive carefully for two miles after seeing a bad wreck on the freeway.

The hardest thing to give is in.

Why is everyone in such a hurry to get right up when they fall or slip down?

I firmly believe that you are what you hate.

People who write, "Will write at length later," never do.

Dinners at 8 that start at 10 are a sin.

All electric cords should have at least one foot added to them for starters.

Censors are people who think they know more than you ought to.

There's nothing neater than a well-stacked lumberyard.

WORDS

Meaningless phrases take the worry out of talking

"You know."

I doubt if you do. But at least 43 times a day someone will inform you that "you know."

Another 23 people will tell you sincerely "I mean."

Still 17 will follow some statement with "Right? Right!"

In between all this you will hear groovy, uptight people turning on and off, freaking out, doing their thing, or finding out that where it's at is out of sight. You better believe they will be into their bag, which may be a confrontation, a dialog, or a hangup. They will talk about — are you ready for this — the "you-fill-in-the-blank" problem and the lifestyle of it.

Would you believe? Sorry about that, you know.

People have stopped talking.

They've substituted all manner of conversation crutches — current and not-so-current cliches which make the talker think he's an instant wit.

These little phrases take the worry out of being conversationally close for people not equipped to string more than eight words together of even second-grade intelligence.

I cringe every time someone approaches me with "Would you believe . . . " because I know that some unfunny nonsense is sure to follow.

And I could strangle the waitresses who foul something up royally, then expect me to forgive and forget just because they say with a silly smirk, "Sorry about that!"

Well, I am sorry about it. I am fed up about it. Would you believe that? You know.

Of all the verbal hangu . . . er . . . illnesses, the "youknowitis" is the worst disease of them all. I just wish people would go back to saying "duh" and "uh" when they need to punctuate their conversations to get their thoughts in order, or whatever it is they're doing when they "you know" you to death.

I have never had the experience of someone saying, "you know," then pausing long enough to give me a chance to say,"No, I don't happen to know." Most of the time I do know, but I don't care to be told so 16 times in one silly anecdote about a wife buying her husband a shirt and tie.

I wish they would hesitate, because I would say, "I don't know. Explain it to me." They would die. Right there on the spot, they would collapse like a ruptured balloon, or run down like a record turned to a slower speed.

It would be wonderful to catch these clowns with their "you know's" down.

People steal these little cliches and crutches from those they consider clever and hip — TV comedians, militant spokesmen, young rebels, and newspaper columnists. That ought to tell you all you need to know about the sources.

There's a psychiatrist in California who has gone into this subject a lot deeper than I care to, but on the "you know" business he makes a telling observation.

"People characteristically repeat interjectory phrases such as 'you know.' It is a repetitive, compulsive expression of enfeebled groping for a relationship through verbal contact. It establishes mutual sharing of knowledge. It is a child's plea for understanding and acceptance on the one hand and adult secret code on the other, filled with subtle nuances of what one knows and chooses not to speak."

You understand that? I think what he means is that the "you knower" is trying to get on your good side by giving you credit for knowing something, while all along it keeps him from having to explain something he either doesn't or can't express.

You'll find more "you know's" in conversations between people of differences — different colors, different ages, different backgrounds, different bank accounts. The "you know" fills both communication and other gaps.

I have never understood exactly why people use these same old phrases over and over again — the same unoriginal things everyone else is mouthing at the moment. I hate to say it, but I believe it's because people don't have the least bit of faith in their own wit and humor. They can use these safe gags without fear, carving out a fine local reputation as a funny fellow with the brillant repartee. They're the kind people are talking about when they say, "You just have to meet so-and-so. He's so funny."

Those are just the people I don't want to meet. Their conversations are one-line standoffs. I've yet to meet a very funny fellow who came billed with a reputation as a very funny fellow. People who make their living being funny — are at least trying to be funny — have absolutely nothing in common with the "funniest guy in our crowd."

In a way, I wish I weren't right about why these conversational crutches are employed. It's a little sad to think of people so desperately wanting to be clever and witty, the life-of-the-party and failing so unoriginally.

You know what I mean. Right? Right! Beautiful!

— July 10, 1969

Let each be his own man; save labels for catsup bottles

We could do this country a favor if we'd all lay off the word "the."

That simple three-letter word is at the bottom of today's biggest problem: Stereotyping.

It has other names: categorizing, labeling, slotting, and either-or-ing.

Americans even have a stereotypes hall of fame for classics such as the Irish Cop, the Southern Redneck, the Token Negro, the Jewish Mother, the Italian Gangster, the Rude Yankee, the Dirty Hippie, the Dumb Polack, the Lazy Mexican, the Cunning Oriental, the French Lover, the Stingy Scot, and the Rich Texan.

There are dozens and dozens of other equally erroneous images that we accept.

Not all newspapermen drink. Not all male hairdressers are "thweet." Not all teachers are brains. Not all athletes are dumb. Not all divorcees are man-hungry. Not all cops are pigs. Not all Negroes are militant. Not all teenagers smoke pot. Not all long-hairs are dirty.

But we can't seem to get "the" stereotypes off our minds or out of our hearts. The Poor. The Rich. The College Student. The Parent. The Negro. The Whites. The Jew. The WASP. The Catholic. The Hawk. The Dove. The Liberal. The Conservative. The Swingers. The Squares. All conjure up to instant images.

Advertising pumps them at us all day and night: The Beautiful People. The Chargers. The Switchables. The Safe Tire. The People Movers. The Lively Ones. The In Crowd. The Flavor Grabbers. The Dependables. Richard Nixon was elected President with the slogan:

"Nixon — He's the One."

It eventually gets to the point where things and people become THE something: THE quarterback. THE team. THE disc jockey. THE decision-maker. THE final word. THE candidate. THE store. THE dress. THE singer. THE band. THE body. THE answer. THE party. THE club. THE song.

This stereotyping and "labelese" has reached epidemic proportions. Labels become more and more handy as the world grows more complex. They reduce things to very simple terms, eliminating explanations and the need for communication.

Putting people into "either-or" slots is also a substitute for thinking. To uncomplicate our life, we stick labels and stereotypes on everything. Stereotyping ranges from the most basic to the most introspective, from the ridiculous to the sublime.

"Either-or" may be the only stereotyping with any validity. For example, most of us are either day people or night people. Or shower people or tub people, tea or coffee drinkers, cake or pie eaters, and letter writers or telephoners.

Most of us either save things or throw them away, prefer steak or lobster, bourbon or scotch, horror movies or Westerns, hamburgers with or without onions, cats or dogs, small cars or large cars, and paint or wallpaper.

We either salt-first-and-taste or taste-first-and-salt. We either read maps or follow our noses. We like living in houses or apartments, having a family or remaining single, locking doors or leaving them open, carry matches or lighters, reading Time or Newsweek, doing things now or postponing them until tomorrow, paying cash, or charging, and we either tear things or clip them.

Just try linking these various characteristics and tastes together, and the art of stereotyping gets even more complex. A night person becomes, also, a coffee drinker, telephoner, tub-bather, horror movie fan and a postponer who leaves doors open.

But in all this I think we forget we're just people. Human progress depends on the "just people" of the world. The "just people" who don't belong to this or that, them or us, the good or the bad, one side or the other.

The "just people" aren't against labels, categories, organization, or social order. They just refuse to be forced into these things that deny them options or individual differences.

Maybe they are the most alienated of us all. Maybe they have a deep belief that the world's problems can be solved without dividing

up sides. I know this, they are the only group I'd like to join.
— *July 18, 1969*

With 625,000 to choose from, we use the same old words

You would think that given the choice of more than 625,000 words in the English language I would have no trouble finding the right word or combinations of words for people and things.

That's just it. Too often we have to put words into lengthy combinations to describe something that should be covered by a single word of not too many syllables.

The average American can recognize only 20,000 words, and has only 1,000 in his hard-core vocabulary, with 250 of these being slang or profanity.

But this same average American says something like 40,000 words a day which means some words are getting as overworked as some jaws.

The most common word in our language is, of course, the word "the." The rest of the top 10 most-used words are (in order): of, and, to, a, in, that, is, was, and he.

The top 10 nouns are: time, man, year, people, world, life, day, house, home, and school. The top 10 descriptive adjectives: little, good, great, old, small, high, united, young, national and important.

Hardly imaginative list. I sometimes feel the same way about the language. Not only does it tend toward unimaginative usage, it is sometimes most confusing.

Look up "best" and "worst" and you'll find that both can mean "to defeat." Try "cleave," which can mean "to adhere closely" or "to separate into parts."

And it seems to me we natives don't handle our own language as well as non-natives. I once told a waiter in a French restaurant that there was a fly in my soup. He said, "No, monsieur, there is a fly on your soup. If the fly is in the soup it is the fault of the chef, but if it is on your soup it is an act of God!"

The people who put together dictionaries very rarely come up with the new words that are most needed. Sure, slang expressions and political terms are quickly recorded. Words used in nuclear, lunar and space activities find their way into the books with no trouble. But these technical terms and language slices don't always get the job done. Most of the time advertising copywriters and headline writers shove these words into our language whether we care for them or not.

And I sometimes feel there are people who do nothing but sit around and dream up words and terms for various culture and lifestyle groups. They obviously compete to see who can have this week's in word.

Maybe we should solicit their assistance in dreaming up words for things that, up until now, have no single term.

There should be a word, for example, for athletes-who-retire-but-not-really-a-la-Joe-Namath.

There should be a word for today's contemporary music that's a mixture of rock, roll, rhythm, blues, gospel, soul, country, western, classical, jazz, folk, etc.

There should be a word for a happily married man, and likewise, a word for unhappily married men. Same for women.

There should be a word for men who are married but pretend they aren't when they get around pretty girls.

There should be a word for people whose names and pictures are always in the papers.

There should be a word for the sound the ocean makes.

There should be a word for someone who has been married many times.

There should be word to describe why a wife say she's buying china while the husband says dishes.

There should be a word to use when you ask someone to move over a little bit so someone else can sit down.

There should be a word for that helpless feeling when you forget the name of someone you are about to introduce at a party.

There should be a word to use between calling an acquaintance "Mr. So-and-So" and his too familiar first name.

There should be a word to describe the lateness of mail, the way a woman looks prior to a beauty parlor appointment and after, the feeling you have when you quit smoking and the disgust with yourself when you fall off a diet.

Children, probably better than anyone else, come up with great new words. When she tipped something over, dumping out its contents, my daughter Dafna described it as "tumping." She also combined squeeze and crunch into "scruntch," which is what we need to do to a lot more of our words.

— *August 12, 1969*

Getting-along glossary aims at heart of what's the matter

Just getting along is becoming increasingly difficult these days because it's so hard to figure out what the other fellow is talking about.

Here is my Getting Along Glossary aimed at helping you to close or cope with the communication gap:

POWER STRUCTURE — Them; Us, if we're eventually lucky enough.

THE ESTABLISHMENT — People who have more money than you have.

HARDCORE — Stubborn.

CITY PLANNER — A college graduate who can't decide on a career.

LIVING COLOR — A subliminal trigger to make kids of black-and-white-set owners beg for a color model.

SEX APPEAL — Anything that makes dog food, toothpaste and coffee sell better.

ONE-OWNER CAR — His name was either Avis or Hertz.

BLITZ — All-purpose word for use by TV football commentators who missed the play and are covering up.

ROLLING WOODS — Name for a flat, treeless subdivision.

CLOSE-IN — Anything approximately 35 miles or 35 minutes away from everything.

CONFRONTATION — Surrender, or else.

SEX EDUCATION — What those who oppose it never had.

LEADERSHIP QUALITIES — Having a loud voice and being related to the owner.

DIALOG — Argument.

PUBLIC DEMAND — Something a campaign contributor asked for.

NATIONAL INTEREST — A favor for a lobbyist.

ACTIVE SOCIALLY — Drinks a lot.

CONTEMPORARY — What you call an art or music form when

you don't know enough about it to describe it properly.

RELEVANT — What you say when you forget viable.

VIABLE — What you say when you forget relevant.

TEAM SPIRIT — Nobody's a star.

NEW IMPROVED — A newly designed package, container or box with a change of colors.

OPINION LEADER — Someone who gets advance copies of Time and Newsweek.

ORIENTATION — Moving around until they can find something to do with you.

COORDINATOR — An executive with a desk between two expediters.

MERGER — Putting one or more executives out of jobs.

LOW MILEAGE — Driven little, but towed a lot.

ANTIQUE — Anything more than 100 years old; anything more than 50 years old; anything more than 10 years old; anything.

TEENAGER — A means of distribution and consumption in the food, clothing, cosmetics and music industries.

SEX SYMBOL — Anything.

RIOT — A means of exchange.

KITCHENETTE — A room with no room for kitchen furniture.

FAMILY ENTERTAINMENT — A myth.

FAMILY — Another myth.

POLARIZE — What you say when you forget the word meaningful.

MEANINGFUL — What you say when you forget the word polarize.

NEW MATH — Theory developed by textbook publishers.

OVERREACT — What They do when They misunderstand Us.

MILITANT — People who disagree with us.

ACTIVIST — Militant spelled differently.

GENUINE — Any silver plate, plastic or vinyl.

CONSUMER — Someone with some money left over and you wonder how.

CLASS — People who brush after every meal.

CHARISMA — People who don't brush after every meal but fake it.

EXPERT — A good-taste measurement kit, containing one Informed Source, two Qualified Observers, a Leading Authority, several Men-on-the-Street, an undetermined number of Insiders, and Nine-of- 10 Doctors.

QUALITY — The cheapest we can make a copy of our competitor's best selling product.

GENIUS — You can't figure out how he does it.

EQUALITY — What others have.

ISSUES — Things that attract clouds.

LAW AND ORDER — Answer to police brutality.

POLICE BRUTALITY — Answer to law and order.

MIDDLE-CLASS — Either what we wish we were, what we're afraid we are, or what we're scared we'll be thought of as.

— Sept. 11, 1969

Out of my mind on a Monday moanin'

Has anyone ever really cared whether a ballpoint pen writes under water?

Most people walk around an art museum as if they were in church.

Nurses invariably ask you a question the second after they pop a thermometer in your mouth.

Men who wear both beards and short hair look funny, like half-finished pictures.

People who say, "I hate to say I told you so," love to say, "I told you so."

You get old in a hurry when you discover your children are studying in history class what you studied in current events.

Honesty's hardest moment: Describing yourself to a blind date.

At the end of a long motor trip the man will invariably talk about how many miles to a gallon the car got and the lady about how much distance was covered.

Isn't it funny how the laziest people always know the correct time.

No one will ever convince me Muhammed Ali could have beaten Joe Louis.

Some husbands never discover their wives consider them financial geniuses until they get into divorce court.

Parents used to tell children stories to go to sleep, now children tell parents stories that keep them awake.

I'm thinking of forming a Society Opposed to More Ice Than Soft

Drink in a Paper Cup.

Why does "nurse" have to be a feminine noun and "mechanic" male?

If you stare at a braless female long enough she will eventually fold her arms across her chest.

There's nothing quite as disturbing as a room full of young kids suddenly quiet.

Nobody, but nobody, works as hard for his money as a man who marries it.

Baked Alaska is my idea of a just dessert for class people.

I've never seen anyone refuse a Life-Saver.

If justice and the courts were swifter we would see a lot more public support of the death penalty, but the long time lag between apprehension, trial, sentence and execution has turned the public off.

Anyone who builds a better mousetrap today has to worry about patent infringement, suits, material shortages, design difficulties, collective bargaining, work stoppages, collusive bidding, discount discrimination, taxes distribution, lockouts, not to mention the SPCA.

No one can quit smoking without telling someone, lose 10 pounds without asking if you notice, or buy a new car without telling how much they paid for it.

I'm always convinced the judges of TV beauty pageants must know something that I don't about the contestants because they never pick the ones I do.

Any woman who says, "Oh, my husband is just a salesman," doesn't deserve him.

No place on earth can match a metropolitan airport for people wearing odd, strange, colorful, bizarre, weird, wild, beautiful, chic, slick and head-turning fashion.

I don't care what they say, no one can get a really close shave with an electric razor.

Nothing makes you madder than seeing an item on sale you bought last week at the regular price.

The most frustrating service problem of all is trying to get waited on five minutes before the help changes shifts — impossible.

Many marriages are held together by the children — he won't take them and she won't, either.

What the world really needs is a TV set that would interfere with power tools.

ON BEING A PARENT

Courage of explorers pales beside stamina of parents

The world's great explorers have nothing on the millions of Americans who are going through that annual back-to-school exploration which engulfs us every fall.

This is not one of those knowledge-found-in-books, learning process discovery pitches.

If you don't know by now that "knowledge power" is where it's at then you need more help than I can offer. Just watch a dropout try to write a letter or fill out a job application.

But if you are a first-timer to this annual phenomenon, here are some of the great discoveries in store for you, whether you are a student, a teacher or a parent.

You will discover that it is possible in one morning before school to read and write a report on "War and Peace," find all the material and things to make a dress, construct a science project which proves water can run uphill, and sell (or buy) 20 tickets to a PTA spaghetti supper.

You will discover that they don't manufacture matching socks anymore.

You will discover the agony of trying to explain the functions of three branches of government and its system of checks and balances as the rest of the family watches "Laugh-In."

You will discover 722 different ways to prepare peanut butter-and-jelly sandwiches.

You will discover that peanut butter and French fries are the American staff of life.

You will discover your name scrawled in chalk on the sidewalk and discover you have an admirer who loves you, but can't spell.

You will discover the greatest answer in the world is "Go ask your father."

You will discover the second greatest answer in the world is "How should I know? Go ask your mother."

You will discover how easy it is to get lost while trying to find Room 224 and winding up standing in front of the entrance to the girls' locker room.

You will discover pencil points break only when you know the answer.

You will discover after a week that you and algebra just can't make it.

You will discover after the second week that you and algebra had better get along — or else.

You will discover that one of mankind's most perplexing questions is: "How come just ONE of the shoes is always missing?"

You will discover that oranges aren't good to put in lunches because they're hard to trade for cookies.

You will discover that Fritos and potato chips trade almost as good as homemade cake.

You will discover that writing a theme about what you did all summer makes you realize what a dull time that great summer really was.

You will discover that no one really knows what the new math is all about.

You will discover you spend more time collecting money for various fees, funds and projects than you do teaching.

You will discover a million excuses for ripping the knee out of your new pants.

You will discover losing forms parents are supposed to fill out is the easiest thing in life to do.

You will discover getting on the wrong school bus is the second easiest.

You will discover it's not so hard to write a book review on a book you never read.

You will discover there is always one teacher who will insist on addressing you by your full formal name in front of the snickering class.

You will discover your kids tell the school nurse they subsist on "Goofy Grape" drink and doughnuts.

You will discover that "Where's my underwear?" is the same as saying "Good morning!"

You will discover the joys of being volunteered for PTA duty by your child.

You will discover that, at last, everything is finally back to normal.

— *Sept. 2, 1969*

Kids may be hip and heavy, but their profanity isn't

Today's youth may be hip, glib and heavy when it comes to creating a working slanguage, but in the area of sweating or describing a state of intoxication, young people take second place to the Establishment.

I listen to kids talking about the drug scene and am amazed at the lack of imagination they use in their descriptions. Whether it's pot, speed or smack, the kids refer to being high or stoned. Some talk about the buzz or getting strung out or spaced out and flipped out. Zonked and tripped are rather descriptive but these terms can't compare with the old-fashioned synonyms used for intoxication.

I hesitate to even bring up the subject because there's nothing worse than a reformed drunk talking about his old drinking days, but one of the few things I miss about not drinking is not being able to discover new words to tell people how drunk I was.

I cannot describe to you the pleasure I used to derive from springing a new word on my crowd: "Boy, did we ever get fried last night." Or, "I was really on a toot!"

How sweet it was to describe the condition of a boozer as being "knee-walking, naval-gazing" drunk. There was also a great challenge in thinking up clever new terms for a drink, such as "Can I get you a little taste?" How super-smug that one was. Or, "How about a little smile?" So clubby and ta-ta, unnnh!

Some enterprising soul, not too long ago did what must have been some epic hangover-producing homework to come up with 1,400 synonyms for intoxication in the English language, which is far and away the leading language for describing drunks or the glow, buzz, high, etc., brought on by drinking intoxicants.

If you think that's a lot of words, just pick any letter and see the number of slang words that come to mind. "S," for instance, includes sloshed, soused, sozzled, stinking, smashed, snoggered, squiffed, stinko, soaked, etc.

One of the favorites of my crowd at one time was polluted, which doesn't seem to be used in that connotation today. I think of all those tales told about being bombed, wiped out, creamed, destroyed, potted (how about that one, hippie friends?), swacked, gassed, tanked and so forth and I come to one conclusion:

Virtually every one of the descriptions we used implied that the drunk is a helpless victim or was happily overindulged. Very few of the terms applied to a common drunk or drinking ever had an air of real disapproval about them. They still don't.

I used to be amused by the terms drinkers would use in describing various levels of intoxication. Women invariably go for the cutesy terms like "tipsy." Most men like the vivid crunchers like "boiled."

Some recent research in Mexico enabled me to discover you can be booked for eight different degrees of "ebrio" or drunk. If you are "ebrio impertinente" you have a fairly mild case. "Ebrio indignado" means you talked back to the police. "Ebrio escandolso" can be loosely interpreted that you were rip-roaring and created a helluva scene. There are other degrees for drunk-and-fighting, drunk-and-fighting-and-you-won, passed out, and the worst of all — "ebrio insultos al gobierno" — drunk and insulting the government. Our own language falls short in this area.

When it comes to swearing, cursing and profanity, today's young people seem to be hung up on certain four-letter words and derivatives. Quite frankly, I'm getting sort of tired of hearing it come out of young mouths and watching braless girls wear the word on their T-shirts.

I have long admired good swearers, but have yet to meet a young person who has even a rudimentary knowledge of profanity.

Spiro Agnew, regardless of anything else, seems to have rejuvenated the grand old sport of blasphemy without resorting to profane or vulgar terms. He certainly seems to get under the skin of a great many people without casting doubts on the marital status of their ancestors. He can goad the fool out of folks without using any references to personal habits or anatomy, which is no small accomplishment these days.

Today's writers — young and old — are too lazy or dumb to bring a vivid style to their invectives. Nothing Norman Mailer has written can compare to O. Henry's "May his liver turn to water, and the bones of him crack in the cold of his heart. May dog fennel grow upon his ancestors' graves, and the grandsons of his children be born without eyes. May whiskey turn to clabber in his mouth, and every time he sneezes, may he blister the soles of his feet."

The great curse and put-down can also be succinct as Dorothy Parker once really did in a friend with: "She knows 18 languages and can't say 'no' in any of them."

Maybe the young people are just naive and feel the "graphic fours" communicate contempt better. I guess maybe we are all naive. For years I thought people who called me SOB meant "Sweet Old Bob."

— Aug. 19, 1970

A behavior guide for parents, as discerning children tell it

What if there were no rules, no laws?

Children hate rules more than anybody. More than criminals. More than professional revolutionaries. More than interior linemen. More than shyster lawyers. More than corrupt cops.

But children also know we need rules and laws more than anybody. What if there were none?

"Lots of terrible stuff would happen," the child answers. "It would be a crazy place."

What makes a rule, a law, right?

The child knows precisely: "If we are both being bad, we should both get yelled at."

Simplistic? Maybe so. But how many times have you said, "No fair" or "That's not fair" in your lifetime? Almost every day. You said it out loud as a child, thought it as a teenager, and now sound off about it somewhere as an adult.

The child wants the rule explained, the why of the law spelled out.

And the child also wants to know an alternative. "Well, if we can't talk, then what can we do?"

Ask the child who makes the best rule — rules that are most right, most fair, rules they will follow? You'll hear mother first, father second, and teachers and policemen, an interchangeable third.

When you ask for specific people, you'll find the child will follow the rules and behave better for someone the child trusts, rather than fears.

It's so basic, so simple.

But somewhere it's been missed.

Somewhere rules, laws and values have been taking a beating.

The value of property, public and private. The value of another's opinion. The value of individuality. The value of privacy.

And it all starts with the way the parents treat the child.

None of the parents realize they're raising a revolutionary, a rioter, a looter, a hijacker, a kidnapper, a pusher, a pimp, a prostitute or an addict.

How do these parents do it? Easy.

The parents set no limit on gifts, either to be received or to be given at Christmas or birthdays.

The parents make sure their child has new notebooks for school every year, with all the fancy covers for the books, and all the latest styles in clothes.

The parents stand by and watch the child blow his "hard-earned" money on an absolutely dead-end project or item and say, "After all, it is his money."

The parents pay for good grades, and accept grades below ability and continue privileges.

The parents let the child be a front-runner in every fad from a drawer full of troll dolls to a garage full of minibikes.

The parents pay the child for routine family chores.

The parents never level with the child and simply tell him the family can't afford something.

The parents try to be buddies with the child, instead of parents.

The parents use discipline as punishment, not as correction, but even then they relent on the punishment before the time is up.

The parents insist the child go to the right school, dress in the right clothes, date the right people, join the right clubs, without letting the child seek and find his own level.

The parents never try to see the child as others see the child — teachers, playmates and other parents.

The parents defend their child first before hearing the other side, and continue the defense even when their child is wrong.

The parents are consistent in only one thing, their inconsistency in the handling of the child.

The parents let the child quit a job or project he wanted and accepted before the child's commitment is complete.

The parents insist on having confidences with the child, rather than inviting the confidences and letting the child make up his own mind.

The parents stereotype all other young people, usually in a derogatory fashion, while holding their own child out as an exception.

The parents cry "scare tactics" in areas they don't understand like drugs and sex and youth identification and rock music, then panic, misunderstand and despair when the child samples the forbidden fruits.

And the very same parents will watch the TV news and look at newspaper pictures of "wanted" kids, murdered kids, and dead kids, and say, "Wonder what their parents feel like? They ought to do something about the parents. At least I know one thing, it'll never happen in our family."

— *Oct. 16, 1970*

The parent's lot is not a happy one

I don't know where this originated. I ran across it almost two decades ago. It was an editorial in the South Carolina State Penitentiary's inmate publication, "About Face." It was titled "How to Raise a Juvenile Delinquent" and listed these 12 points:

1. Begin from infancy to give the child everything he wants. In this way, he will grow up to believe that the world owes him a living.

2. When he picks up bad words, laugh at him. It will encourage him to pick up cuter phrases that will blow the top off your head later.

3. Never give him any spiritual training. Wait until he is 21 and let him decide for himself.

4. Avoid the use of the word "wrong." It may develop a guilt complex. This will condition him to believe later, when he is arrested for stealing a car, that society is against him and he is being persecuted.

5. Pick up everything he leaves lying around — books, shoes and clothes. Do everything for him so he will be experienced in throwing the responsibility onto others.

6. Let him read any printed matter he can get his hands on. Be careful that his silverware and drinking glasses are sterilized, but let his mind feed on garbage.

7. Quarrel frequently in the presence of children. Then they won't be shocked when the home is broken up.

8. Give the child all the spending money he wants. Never let him earn his own. Why should he have things as tough as you had them?

9. Satisfy his every craving for food, drink and comfort. See that every desire is gratified. Denial may lead to harmful frustration.

10. Take his side against the neighbors, teachers and policemen. They are all prejudiced against your child.

11. When he gets into real trouble, apologize for yourself for saying, "I never could do anything with him."

12. Prepare for a life of grief. You'll have it.

I take this out and read it to myself from time to time. I think, if you can read between the lines, you, too, will find this to be as helpful advice on parenting as you'll find anywhere.

Be honest with yourself and read the list over again. Let's suppose you have yet to be confronted with Nos. 11 and 12. Concentrate on the first 10.

Being as objective as possible, I find that I am weak in four of the first 10 areas — categories of parenting that I really have to bear down on.

Parenting is not the easiest thing to do these days. Would that raising kids was as easy and as delightful as creating them. It does not surprise me to read that the latest poll of parents shows that a majority of them indicated that they would not be parents again.

Most of the parents I know shouldn't be parents. I mean that. They are either good-time buddies with their kids, or they are ultra-strict almost to the point of being tyrannical owners of the child.

Why do we have children, anyway? Not for the reasons we once had them — to serve as free hired hands. I don't think my Grandmother Mabe would have had 10 children — nine girls and one boy — had they not needed them to help bring in the crops.

How do I know this? She once told me that the nicest thing she had found about growing old was that she didn't have to worry about some kid being fed and she didn't have to suffer through another Southern summer pregnant.

I told her that, if they thought they had to raise 10 children, most women would have a nervous breakdown. "I often thought about having one," she said, eyes still sparkly sharp, "but I was too busy between having children and getting four cash crops in every year to take time off to have a nervous breakdown."

I asked a few people to give me some reasons for having children. Here are some of their responses:

" . . . to live a life you never had through your child. The old stage mother bit or jock father pushing a son into sports . . . "

" . . . to aid and comfort you when you get old. Sometimes I'm sure that's why my mother had me . . . "

"...curiosity — to see what someone with your genes would look

like. It would be the only compelling reason for me to be a parent . . .
"

" . . . someone to leave your business to or your possessions and treasures. Why amass a fortune or establish a business and have no one to carry it on . . . "

" . . . to prove virility in males and womanhood in females. In some cultures to this day, this manhood and childbearing attachment is still a prime reason for having children . . . "

" . . . to have someone really and truly need you and your love, someone to be dependent on you and your love . . . "

" . . . some people just love children — love having 'em, raising 'em and being with 'em . . . "

" . . . reasons? Hey, most people find out they're having babies before they ever think of the reasons for having them . . . "

Do you find yourself in any of these reasons? Did you find yourself in any of those first 10 points we began with?

Maybe you're not in any of these lists. Maybe you're Super Parent. Even if you are, it doesn't hurt you to review these things from time to time because so much new happens, and attitudes change between times these days. Today's parents have problems their parents never dreamed of. That's something else my Grandmother Mabe told me.

— Sept. 21, 1977

Out of my mind on a Monday moanin'

Was women's lib really started by a small group who got tired of dancing backward?

Above every door this sign should go: "Everyone brings joy — some by entering, some by leaving — and the choice is yours."

I've never met a seer or astrologist who didn't swear he or she predicted John Kennedy would be assassinated.

But a woman of 40 will never look 30 dressing like 20.

If you think for one minute you can understand teenagers, you have it timed about right.

I doubt if there's a soul anywhere who hasn't walked off with someone else's ballpoint pen by mistake.

Farmers and firemen are supposedly the biggest moonlighters, but I have never met a cab driver who didn't have at least one other "regular" job.

I never believe crowd estimates at sports events and parades, gold record sales figures or program heights and weights.

Remember when Tupperware ladies were the only ones who had pot parties?

A real music fan is someone who goes to hockey games to listen to the organ music.

If the world's people don't learn to get along without war one of these days war will teach the world how to get along without people.

Kids who mope around today are sent to a $50-an-hour psychiatrist for what a 25-cent laxative used to cure.

I'll bet: The same guy who designs bridges with two-foot steel beams right where the view would be the most spectacular is the same guy who designs auto headlights so you can't tell when they're on high or low.

I've got to believe the word "license" is in the running as the most misspelled word by amateur sign letterers.

People who pose for portraits with props or pipes or hands on their chin will also overact in everything they do.

You wouldn't worry about what people think of you if you knew how seldom they do.

Is this fair? A girl's best friend is a diamond; man's best friend is a dog?

The Man of the Year, any year, is the fellow who appreciates his own time too highly to waste the time of someone else.

For fixing things around the house and yard nothing beats a man who is handy with his checkbook.

Happiness is: Hearing Hugh Hefner is a square . . . Getting a 24-hour virus on rainy days . . . Having a fatter friend . . . Seeing leading men actors getting bald . . . Seeing the TV show the night before everyone's talking about the next day.

That menu item you almost ordered always looks better on someone else's plate than what you finally decided on.

As a kid I was told I'd learn if I listened to old people; as an adult I'm told I'll learn if I listen to young people.

The best time to make friends is long before you need them.

Ladies, do you wonder how your mother survived without clothes dryers, frozen food and "Sesame Street."

A "Business Is Lousy" Sale would be honest and a success.

FAMILY & FRIENDS

Watching the children sleep, a father's Valentine dream

It is four in the morning and the snow piles softly outside. I'm standing at the end of the upstairs hall and can look into the rooms where my children sleep.

In the fuzzy pre-dawn darkness, daughter Dafna seems so still in the soft pastels of her bed. At nine years old, she's a tangle-haired princess with happy, pretty dreams. She will probably be picked on today by some snaggled-toothed Prince Charming with the knee ripped out of his jeans.

Son Jason, just turned two, seems so small and content in his fresh "jommies" and full, fat tummy, with his chubby hands tucked tightly under a dimpled chin, clutching his tattered yellow blanket. He knows an untroubled peace.

At nine and two there are only good things to think about, good things to dream. Daughter Dafna's dreams are filled with the memory of her first trip down the ski slope this night and how proud her Mommie and Daddy were. Son Jason's dreams — if two-year-olds have dreams — are about whatever new thing was intriguing his imagination before he went to bed.

How different their worlds are — nine years and two years — but how close they are, too. Their irritations are minor — wet noses, broken crayons and skinned knees — but their basic protests are major in volume and intensity. They protest bedtime and get-up time and whatever's for dinner and what's not for between meals.

Standing here watching them, I'm glad they know nothing of bills and war and taxes and prejudice and bigotry and poverty and crime and society's other sores and scars and pock marks.

I wonder, as I watch them shift ever-so-slightly in their sweet sleep, whether it would be possible for them never to have the larger irritations and heartaches which life hands out. To never experience fear and hunger and hurt. To never have to hate. To never undergo anguish, anxiety and anger. To never have to stand in the middle of their own hall someday and wonder about their own children's future.

My children, ages nine and two, did not ask to come into a world filled with all these frightening obstacles. They had no choice. But now they are here and so are the obstacles. And how do you explain to them about these things?

Daughter Dafna and her mother Beryl were talking about the Vietnam war. "Why," asked daughter Dafna, "can't God just make them stop?"

Son Jason has just discovered that word "Why?" He's tested it, worked it around on his tongue a couple of times and found it is an attention-getting magic word. Pretty soon that couple of times will be up to a hundred times a day. If we are lucky, very lucky, we will be able to answer one-fourth of his "Whys?" to his satisfaction.

As I stand here and watch them in their slumber my mind hurries forward to what they have in store. I've been told that by the time we reach the age of nine, we have all the impulses and equipment necessary to become whatever it is we will become. I'm not sure how this conclusion is drawn, but it makes sense. It has to be true that we don't keep growing up all our lives, although some people never even start.

But somewhere in the exciting process of climbing life's mountain we do seem to stop learning, stop growing, stop wondering, and stop living at all. The dates vary from individual to individual, but the first sign of it in anyone is the moment we stop talking about how much better we plan to be, how much more we plan to do, and begin talking about how much better things used to be. That is when we begin to die.

I look at these fragile, peaceful children and get scared. At nine years, Dafna seems so unprepared to become anything but a trusting, honest, open, loyal little darling. She is just now reading everything she sees written anywhere, but she still can't get her shoelaces and boot buckles tight enough. Apple sauce is the only surefire thing she'll eat at any meal. Apple sauce and peanut butter. And they say she's supposed to be ready to become whatever it is she will become.

At two, son Jason seems unprepared to become even three. He is so dependent on the knowledge and skills of his mother. He's beginning his solo flights and maiden voyages — dozens daily — and there are bruises and scars for medals. He, too, is such a simple, unspoiled, uncomplex being. He probably owns the happiest, most honest smile in all creation.

I stand here and watch them and wish for a second that time would stand still and let it be such sweet dreams forever for them. and wonder what to give them for Valentine's Day. Two things, I think, will do. All the love they can hold and a wish that the world ahead of them will become one in which they will never stop growing up or learning or wondering.

The sort of place children deserve, but adults never seem to give them.

— Feb. 14, 1969

The midway's for memories of the fairest days of all

Jason let me know in no uncertain terms he could sit on his hobbyhorse without all that help from me.

All he wanted was my reassuring hand on his back as he clutched the brass pole while his highly glossed steed went up and down to the waltz-me-around strains of "The Loveliest Night of the Year."

The Michigan State Fair whirled and twirled around us as we rode the magic merry-go-round, and for the first time I didn't feel silly just standing there.

There's a way you can do your eyes so that everything on the sides gets blurry while you focus on a pinpoint straight ahead.

There's a way you can do your ears so that all the sounds seem to be way off in a tunnel and you select those you want to hear. I did this.

As we turned faster the midway became a psychedelic, stop-action, slow-motion, kaleidoscopic fantasy of spiraling, whirling lights and scary screams and pulsating rock music and happy, shrieky laughter and looking.

It all seemed unreal, as if I could reach out and touch the memories of other fairs in other years.

Back to the time when I was 2½ and my dad stuck me on a pink-and-gold horse and his reassuring hand was at my back as I hung on for dear life.

Back to the first bite of cotton candy and how strange it melted and left a sticky reminder of its nothingness.

Back to the first time I got enough courage to go into a girlie show and how matter-of-fact I tried to act when the half-naked girl bounced on the stage.

Back to the time my stomach met my throat when I took my first roller coaster plunge and how happy I was to get off.

Back to the bump car I got my first time and it wouldn't work and I've never cared for that ride since.

Back to burning my tongue on a hot French fry, but not caring because nowhere on earth do French fries taste better.

Back to that "for-the-first-time" day when I really enjoyed looking at the free agricultural and prize animal exhibits.

Back to that tragic afternoon I lost my entire $6 in the first 30 minutes and had to spend the rest of the day watching the other kids ride and have fun.

Back to being cajoled by a giggly, button-nose blond into trying to win a stuffed panda and spending 10 times its cost to do so.

Back to feeling sorry for the freaks in the sideshow because they seemed to be the only ones at the fair not having fun, then wondering all the way home how that leather-skin lady stuck those pins through her arms.

Back to appreciating for the first time how much that blue ribbon meant to the young lad who had devoted his last year and a half to his prize calf.

Back to that one fleeting moment when I almost asked that weathered young roustabout how I could go about joining the fair.

Back to that numbing excitement as Dad struggled into a parking place and we could hardly wait to get inside the grounds.

Back to that first sailor hat with "Bobby" sewn on it better than I could write with a pencil.

Back to going to sleep on Dad's shoulder and waking up in my own bed and forgetting I'd ever been to the fair.

Back to the first time I looked at the family of a ride operator sitting lonely and sad-faced in a battered truck and being glad, honestly, that it wasn't me sitting there and I had a home to go to.

Back to all the fun and frustrations, the thrills and disappointments. State Fairs freeze time and images in your . . .

Suddenly my eyes were refocusing and my ears opening up as Jason urged his spangled mount to go "More faster!"

Will he remember as I am remembering?

Will he care about it and will he take his son?

When he's 33 in his man-on-the-moon world will there even be State Fairs?

I think so. As long as there are daddies and painted horses and sons who need reassuring hands on their backs there will be State Fairs.

As long as that.

— Aug. 29, 1969

On the death of an old, wise friend

Part of my childhood died last week.

You didn't know Henry Childress. But I'll bet you know someone like him. He was my father's best friend. He taught me how to start a cranky ol' Evinrude and how to put the hook in just the right place above the minnow's spine so it would give you lots of action in the water.

Uncle Henry. Not really blood kin, but every bit a fine uncle to have. The finest.

He died at the age of 79. Worked right up to the day he died. He was the projectionist at the Carolina Theater my father managed in Spartanburg, S.C. Had been since 1926 when the theater opened. In a tribute to Henry in the hometown paper, my mother wrote, "He never missed a reel changeover."

If you know what a projectionist does, you know there could be no finer tribute, especially for one who started changing the reels when they had no sound tracks. Projection equipment is so improved today that one man can run four movies from the same projection booth complex because much of it is automated.

But Henry grew up in the industry when it was done by hand, including the minute adjusting of arc lights to keep the film bright. Reel changeovers were once done by hand and eye, as the projectionist would have to watch for a little code mark in a corner of the film and do this every 20 minutes or so.

I used to love to run up to the projection booth and sit and watch Henry do his thing. It took great skill and he would have answers to my millions of questions.

Henry's boy Buddy was some fine high school football player and I'd tag along with Henry and Daddy to watch Buddy play. We'd always stand in the end zone. Henry was shy. Shyest and least ego-centered man I ever met. If we'd sat in the stands everybody would have been bragging on Buddy to Henry and this would have embarrassed him too much.

Henry was Daddy's fishing partner, another place I was allowed to tag along. What joy! I can remember every trip individually and there must have been hundreds. We'd always stop first at the bait ranches and the men would stand around and talk fishing and where they were biting. I got to help scoop the minnows and count the night crawlers.

Mostly we fished at Buzzard's Roost, S.C., one of those backed-up lake dams for electric power created all over the South. We were crappie and bream fishermen mainly. Still fishing. Watching a bobbing cork for hours on end.

I guess those two men talked about everything under the sun and moon, never holding back because I was sitting in the boat with them. I don't know where all one's education comes from, but I do know a bunch of mine must have come as I sat there cork-watching and listening with hungry ears.

Henry was the best fisherman I've known and a fine teacher. His patience ranked a close second to Job's. A nine or 10-year-old boy is perhaps the most impatient creature known to date. For years I waited for "one of these days" to happen. Henry would always say, "Mister Tee, one of these days Bobby's gonna be a fisherman."

When he finally said I was a fisherman, I was the proudest 15-year-old in the universe. He acknowledged the moment by opening me a beer and passing it to me. Daddy didn't say anything. Kids weren't drinking buddies with their parents in those days. That symbolic beer broke a lot of ice and communication gaps.

The projectionists' union is also the one that includes stagehands and I used to work side by side with Henry on any of the major road shows, ice shows, etc., that came to Spartanburg. Each of these shows would have road managers of such varying temperaments you wouldn't believe. Henry taught me how to judge these people. He taught me how to lift things without hurting myself, how to run a light and sound board. Even how to follow a skating star on center ice with a tiny spot.

Henry also taught me a lot about what a real friend is. He and my father shared a friendship a book could be written about. Even though they had a boss-employe relationship — Henry always called Daddy "Mister Tee" — they shared a mutual bond and understanding they both cherished.

Henry, in addition to being shy, wasn't an emotional man outwardly. He held it all in reserve. While well-read in many areas, he wasn't what he would have called an educated man, he said. That was one of the few things I ever knew him to be wrong about. He was educated all right, and an educator to boot.

The only time I ever saw him reveal an emotional side was at Daddy's funeral. There he was, standing in the back, in the end zone still. I walked over to him and the tears rolled down his cheeks as we hugged for a full minute.

He looked at me with a shared warmth and whispered, "Mister Tee will miss us, too, Bobby."

The wisdom of those words! When death takes us, as it invariably does, what can be nicer than to know your close relations will know that you miss them as you depart this vale of tears, as the poet said. It says so much about the relationships that are shared.

A part of my childhood died and I think it will miss me, too.

— *Oct. 5, 1976*

'Sorry, can't handle it' works wonders

A few questions for a few of my friends and yours:

Has someone close to you expressed concern about your drinking lately?

When you eat lunch or dinner out, do you automatically stop at the bar before entering the dining area?

How early in your work day do you start thinking about that first drink you're going to have?

Even if you don't plan to drink very much, do you find yourself going only to restaurants that serve booze?

Have you ever come in contact with the law because of your drinking?

Do you find yourself — because of booze — having to tell a lie to cover another lie you told which covered another lie, etc.?

Have you ever required medical attention because of an accident you had while drinking?

Has drinking affected your relationship with your spouse sexually, emotionally, physically and romantically?

Do your kids avoid having their friends over when you are drinking?

Have you ever experienced a blackout — the total loss of memory while still awake — while you were drinking?

How many times in the past month have you failed to keep promises to yourself about cutting down or controlling the amount of drinking you do?

How many times in the past month have you let anger or depression or boredom or frustration give you an excuse to get drunk?

Each of these questions is addressed to a certain individual, 12 friends of mine I know are drunks. They don't know I know it.

When I'm around them, not one will look me directly in the eye and discuss these matters. They know how I stand. They also know that I will not stick my nose in their personal lives unless asked.

Asked directly by them — not by their friends, loved ones, wives, husbands and children. Taking that first drink was their choice and taking that last drink must be their own choice, too.

I've discussed their drinking problems with those around them. Oh, yes, your drinking problems are discussed, whispered about and cried over. Behind your back, because you won't admit you have a problem.

These people dearly love you and will help, but can't until you admit you need help. Therein lies the rub and the nub of most alcoholics' initial rejection of reality.

Egos prevent them from looking at their lives realistically. They don't want to admit that something as "helpful" as booze is whipping 'em every time they climb in the bottle with it.

I was there. I know the torment. The anguish. I know the false comfort booze brought at that time in my life. How terrifying it was not to be able to say no when I knew in my heart I should be saying, "No thanks, I'm an alcoholic."

It was hard to say that. At least I thought it was. I thought I was going to be considered a loser. A bum. Unworthy. Helpless. I thought I was going to lose my friends, my job, my life.

Outside of taking that first drink, that's probably the dumbest time in an alcoholic's life. But I've got news for all of you. None of what you're thinking is true.

I've yet to have anyone pat me on the hand and say, "Oh, you poor loser." But I've had countless people grab that hand and give it one of those proud-of-you shakes. And when I looked deeply into some of their eyes, I read two things you may be interested in.

First is true admiration. The sort where you know the other person considers your accomplishment something the other person could never do. That'll boost the ol' ego.

Search that window to their soul long enough and you'll see the second thing that can send your ego soaring — envy. That's right, envy. That's one of the reasons those 12 people won't talk with me about their problem.

I remember that look of envy in each of their eyes when I first met them and my alcoholism came up, as it always does when people ask, "Can I get you a drink?" Or insist on it.

I've dealt with this directly for 17 years. Put it out front with people. For years it was, "No thanks, I'm an alcoholic." Then I shortened it to ex-alkie or the simple, "Sorry, can't handle it."

That last one says everything, I think, without making a big deal out of it. For one thing, few people in this world will admit to not being able to handle anything. They know you're damn honest when you say it and must have a good reason for saying it. And that's usually where they'll drop it, with an admiring nod or some little half-joking, half-serious reference that they can't handle it, either, but what the hell, they'll have a scotch anyway.

I addressed those above questions to 12 different people. But in many instances they can all be addressed to one person. You may know that instance. If so, make sure this gets in the proper hands for reading.

"Sorry, can't handle it" works wonders. Believe me. Especially with those around you — those you want to love and who desperately love you.

— July 21, 1979

Have you had your dozen hugs today?

I could tell my friend had lost it totally. He had been relating a suicidal moment he had just experienced. I watched him fall apart.

Those uncontrollable sobs take over. Body-wrackers. Tears in torrents. Trembling all over.

I reached out and gave him one of those "pour it all out" hugs. I give great hug. A specialty. Only magic I can do.

Hugs are magic. They can work wonders unbelieved and untold. I personally believe they may be mankind's single best form of communication. The compassionate embrace, the reassuring hug, speak all languages.

I could feel it calming him. It was several moments before sobs became sniffles-shudder-sniffles and a final shudder-sigh. We parted and were silent for awhile.

"Thanks," he said. "That's the first time that's happened to me."

"The first time you ever broke down and cried?" I asked.

"No," he said, "that's the first time I've ever been hugged by a man in a situation like that."

My friend has brothers. A father. What about them? No one ever hugged in their family. "Just wasn't done," he said, astonishing me, "and I've never seen my mother and father hug each other."

We immediately related this to his problems that had built up to that moment of contemplating suicide. My friend's no dummy. He took the hug to heart.

I saw him recently and I can tell you that suicide was the last thing on this happy fellow's mind. We discussed how he had gotten his life back together, his personal new image, his future busy plans, etc.

"I'll tell you," he said, "that hug you gave me started something. It's turned me into a hugger. I hug everyone I see now. I'm driving everyone crazy . . . "

My friend then launched into a joking, anecdotal shtick, his honest and true way of showing me his appreciation. Hugged one brother, who told a sister he thought he was turning gay. We laughed till tears started to come.

"And tears!" he screamed, and that broke us up even more. Here's a man who once wouldn't have allowed even one happy, humor-invoked tear to trickle down his tight cheek. Now here he was, a laughing, wet face.

My friend with his cork out, not off. A relaxed man. Laughing at himself, his family, his behind-him troubles, his future problems, etc. A man discovering that it's all right for a man to cry, both happy tears and sad. That there is nothing wrong with sharing an embrace.

I just could not imagine not living in a world without hugs. Thank goodness there are a lot of us this way. Hopefully we can pull hugging out of the closet.

I know Father Larry Valentine, of St. Rene Church in Sterling Heights, will join the movement. Fact of the matter is, it was my friend's experience and something Father Larry wrote in his church's bulletin that spurred me to get this hugging movement off the ground.

He wrote: "Hugging makes people happier and healthier. That's the conclusion of author and social worker Virginia Satir, who shared this secret with 4,000 people gathered for the meeting of the American Orthopsychiatric Association in Toronto recently.

"The therapist says four hugs a day will chase the blues, but four is just a minimum daily requirement for survival. Eight hugs a day are necessary for maintaining a vigorously healthy body and mind. Twelve hugs, she says, are needed for sustained growth of the mind, spirit and body. All of this indicates we have our work cut out for us!"

Indeed, we do, Father Larry. How many of you get your dozen hugs a day? Thought so. To get 'em, you got to give 'em, you see.

I'm a hugger. Of course, I don't go around hugging every person I see. That's some kind of a nut who does that. Make it every other person.

'Specially men. I'm into turning them on to hugging. Not enough of them are into it, I've discovered. I'm a hugger every time I see old friends, folks I haven't seen for awhile. Makes some uneasy. At first.

Or sharing special moments with strangers. That throws 'em every time. "Expression of joy" will cover it and most probably think you're still some sort of nut. Pick your spots with this one, fellow huggers-to-be. Grand-slam moments.

Friendly hugs, reassuring hugs, confidence hugs, go-get-'em hugs and thank-you hugs. Do you believe in magic? You will. Hug Power! 'Tis amazing what a hug can do.

My friend was winding down his hug stories, with one about hugging his company's president, who happens to be a woman, and her taking it the wrong way.

Our tears had stopped as we both had to be on our ways. "Hey," he said, "I really want to thank you a lot for being there. That meant a lot. Really did. Wish there was some way I could show you how much I appreciate what you helped me do."

I told him to just be there to hug somebody who never knew they needed hugs before. You can do it, too. This thing can spread.

— *Nov. 27, 1980*

There are friends and there are . . .

Friends, to me, are people you can confide in, depend on, who understand where you are coming from, and need the same thing from you.

My more pragmatic wife puts it simply, "Friends are people who don't have to call you on the telephone to remind you they are your friends."

I like her definition better. It gets the nub of it. The kernel of true friendship, I feel. It goes without saying, writing or etching it in blood or bronze.

The unstated statement between two people bound by affection and esteem is what true friendship is all about. I'm sure you can add to this definition your own little nuances of what friendship means to you.

Some people have more of a capacity for friends than others. Along with this ability to handle so many friends, these people have an inordinate need to have lots of friends.

But this trait, tendency or characteristic doesn't last a lifetime, I know. For a long period of my life I suffered with an almost terminal case of the "friends," a disease I thought to be terminal.

I use the term "terminal," as "friends" can damn near kill you if you let 'em. I'm not talking about killing you with kindness, either. I'm talking absorption. "Friends" will absorb you if you don't watch out.

Let's lay in those quote marks around "friends" of that ilk. These are the people who are constantly abusing the rights of friendship. They stop the sharing and begin the demanding. I sometimes wonder if these people keep a calendar for themselves and one for you, too? They so busybody your life.

For many unfulfilled reasons I once needed these busybodies cluttering up and meddling with my life. I needed their needs. Had to have 'em. Daily dosages of mega proportions.

I was trying to find myself in all these friends — oops! — "friends." I had no idea who or what I was so I tasted from many, many cups. And since I wasn't clearly defined, I was able to be a friend to all these "friends." All right, go back and slip those quote marks around my "to be a friend."

Maybe I couldn't have been a real friend to all that many people but I thought I was. That was the important thing at that time of my life. It was a real thrill to be involved in all those other people's lives. That way I didn't have to get involved in my own life very much.

But when I did get involved with my own life, and became whatever definable being I am, I found the thrill was gone. Thrills had become a bloody drag, an energy-sapper, an emotional-drainer.

So you become more selective.

Energy and emotion are two things, I've discovered, that friendships demand. If anybody defined friendship as being undemanding, you don't even understand the subject. Study up some more and come back better prepared the next time. Nothing can be more demanding than a true friendship.

That separates the wheat-like kernels of true friends from the useless, shafting chaff. Friendships aren't measured in "did he come through for me," but in rather, "did I come through for him." And that takes your energy and emotion every time.

Those are two commodities on my market that are rationed out now. Use to didn't matter. So the well ran dry by the end of the day. It would be replenished the next day, wouldn't it? True, but you come to another point in your life.

That's when the day's over and you want a little energy and emotion for yourself. You look around and there's nary a drop of the stuff left. All your "friends" took 'em. Sucked you dry of the good stuff and left you with their hangups and hangnails.

Cut! Snip! Clip! Sever those drag-you-down ties. Who needs it? You come to that point where you know it's either you or them. Well, I wasn't about to let them kill me. But too many of us continue to succumb to "them." And they deserve the suspect of quotes.

When whatever's left of your day for you finds you drained of all energy and emotion, don't necessarily blame your job or work, although they are so easy to blame these days. Is anyone happy at what they do? I mean totally happy.

If you find you have none of the Big E's left for yourself, then I would suggest you cast your critical eye in the direction of your friends. There is a point where "loves" become "leeches." You seldom ever know until all the blood is gone.

So you wind up with a handful of friends, tops. You can clutch one or two tightly, grasp several or juggle up to a half dozen maybe. In the winnowing-out process, you don't necessarily discard the rest.

Hopefully they can become the more comfortable "acquaintance," which no one uses any more, preferring the more personal, chummy "friend." I bet people are always throwing a name at you and telling you that you must know them because they said they were a friend of yours. Right?

And then you sound like some halfwit when you stammer around about the name or person until added info is given and it clicks. And it always turns out that you hardly even know the person they're talking about. Maybe just met once or twice, even.

I think in the coming new era picking of one's friends will become of prime importance once again. And friends will be friends again — meaningful relationships that cut both ways. It is truer now than ever what the great sage George Santayana once wrote: "One's friends are part of the human race with which one can be human." That ranks up there with my wife's definition.

— Nov. 15, 1977

Both my friends, but they hate each other

"Tell me something. How do you stand that arrogant creep?"

I'd been waiting for that. I'd known since the middle of lunch that she was going to ask me something like that before we parted.

We'd been in a midmorning committee meeting and decided to grab a quick lunch at a trendy new spot she'd heard about nearby.

But we failed to beat the noon lunch bunch. As we pondered whether to wait six deep in line for a table, another friend of mine, who had beaten the rush, spotted me and insisted we join him at his table.

I didn't think anything about it until mid-lunch when I realized these two friends of mine would never, ever be friends with each other.

Friends? They wouldn't last five minutes alone together. Let's talk your major personality conflict. The supreme clash. They were getting under each other's skin, and not the way Frank Sinatra sings about it.

I spent the last half of lunch nervously steering the conversation along lines that prevented their teeth-gritting hostility and animosity from becoming full-scale war. It was apparent the only thing they shared in common was my friendship.

I happen to like both these people very much. Known 'em both for a long time. I really enjoy their company, appreciate their skills and talents, and always benefit from listening to their opinions.

Before the after-lunch coffee arrived I knew I was going to be grilled later by both of them. I could tell by the little private takes they flashed me. Eye rolls and jaw clinches.

Feeling guilty for this unholy luncheon alliance, I grabbed the check as we all split to go our separate ways. In the parking lot my female friend asked the question I'd been waiting for.

Although I knew the question was coming, I also knew I had no answer that would satisfy her. No way on this earth could she fathom how anyone in his or her right mind could stand this fellow.

I started to give her some mumble about how you have to get to know him and don't go by first impressions. Lines that always begin "Deep down, he's . . . " But she wasn't listening, wasn't waiting for my explanation. She was sitting on ready-to-rip-him.

"Look," I said, "you're my friend, right? He's my friend, right? Friends shouldn't have to explain other friends to friends, right?"

"I guess you're right," she said, "but I also guess there is no accounting for taste or lack of it. But I can say that because we're friends, right?"

We smiled and parted. By the time I got home he'd already called and left a smart-mouth message on my answering machine about that "uptight bitch."

I was relating this little episode to still another friend, who happens to love this sort of thing. "What you should do," she said, "is have a dinner party and sit them side by side. Better yet, I'll have the party and you can sit across from them."

This lady is notorious for putting enemies together in social settings to see what develops. Some of her best stories involve the celeb fistfights and socialite eye-scratchings resulting from her devious mismatch-ups.

She said, "How boring my life would be if all my friends were like me or were like each other. Can you imagine anything more dull? How utterly dreadful. How dull. I pity people whose circle of friends are nothing more than carbon copies of each other."

She mentioned a certain crowd we both know. I'm friends with the people in it, like each of them individually, but find I really can't take 'em for long stretches as a group.

"Know why?" she said. "Because they are clowns and clownettes. But they like this. It's safe. Everyone's predictable. They love being alike. No one's threatened. Status in their group is quo."

The conversation returned to my luncheon friends, the uptight bitch and the arrogant creep. "The more I think about having a party and having them there, the more I love it," she said.

"In fact, no one in this town has more friends-who-would-be-enemies than you. You know that's true. You happen to have more friends from more walks of life than anyone I know. As you have just discovered, they don't all see eye-to-eye with each other.

"Why don't we put them all together and see what would happen. How about a weekend house party on some lake? Perfect. Wouldn't that be marvelous? Can you imagine the fights and backstabbing that would go on? Divorce at 11."

This is not the first time she's brought up this idea. Each time I beg off because the consequences would be horrendous. The lunch I had just experienced was bad enough. Picture that multiplied by a factor of 10, 20 or 100. I'd be a nervous wreck trying to keep everyone apart.

I have a feeling the same thing would occur if you, too, invited all your friends to the same cookout or beer bust. You'd spend all your time refereeing.

But you have to admit, it sure wouldn't be a dull party. I'm tempted.

— March 10, 1981

Going to Momma's —
full speed ahead

On the road to Momma's . . .

. . . Every time I head south and hit a certain section of I-75 below Monroe — where Michigan has a welcome center a few miles north of the Michigan-Ohio border — it happens. It's my vacation-rush spot. We all have them.

It's when I finally allow myself to say, "I'm on vacation." That particular welcome center is the official landmark putting Detroit behind me and telling me I'm on the road to Momma's.

And it's always at this point in the journey I realize I have two homes. Detroit is home, but Spartanburg, S.C., is my hometown. There are a great many of us on the road this holiday season, with this knotty bit of allegiance tugging our hearts.

. . . This annual cross-country pilgrimage to momma's house is an American way of vacation-life for a lot of us. For many Detroiters, it means this trip down I-75 back into the South, the land where we were born.

We ease off the mainstream of the interstate and into the blue-green Kentucky fields, the rolling Tennessee valleys, the lush North Carolina mountains and the red-clay South Carolina hills. All going home to momma's.

. . . Every time I go through Ohio I'm more impressed. If they ever need to take a picture of Middle America's rural farmland, I suggest they do it along I-75 between the Blue Lick and Stop Eight exits. Love those names.

. . . If you've been wondering where the vans and campers of America are, I can tell you they are convening by the droves at rest areas along the interstates. I think they must breed there overnight. The machines, that is.

. . . I'm sure Cincinnati would like to be known for more than this, but Lynn and I both say "WKRP" when Cincy's skyline appears around us. Why do I expect to hear Howard Hesseman on the radio?

. . . Ten minutes into Kentucky some spring splashes of pink begin to appear on the unfurling southern face as budding dogwoods apply blush-on to the greening hills. A hint of the overwhelming color to come as we begin to meet spring coming north.

The tree and flower fairy did a number on the South and timed it all to explode Easter week. Spring is one big reason for planning this Carolina vacation. The Carolinas do spring and Easter better than anyone.

If they need to take a picture of this, Momma's backyard is the spot. It's a smother of pinks and whites and reds and greens — azaleas and dogwoods so thick among the tree canopy the ground looks covered in technicolor snow from the falling petals. Lynn and I couldn't wait.

. . . Lynn also couldn't wait for her all-days in the sun. And me, I couldn't wait to meander into my past. This trip, I planned to search for me in the places of my childhood, the venues of my youth, the haunts of my teen years. Would they be the same? I'm certainly not.

. . . Spring's trumpets play a glorious tune at the Gatlinburg exit where the Tennessee-North Carolina mountains begin to shoulder up to the snaking expressway and range as far as the eyes can see. You can hear the rolling echoes and rushing streams, nature's own synthesizer of sight and sound.

Question of the moment to ponder: Which do you like best, going up a mountain or coming down? If you prefer the vista from the top, you're right beside me.

. . . A thought about freeway fudging on the 55-m.p.h. limit: We all do it. I'm a notorious never-over-55er normally. Saves fuel and saves lives. But the open road is another thing entirely, isn't it?

On the interstates, we drive in clusters. Pull in behind some

trucker with a CB or camper with a Fuzzbuster. They know where
the patrolmen are. Slow down through every interchange and at
every weigh station and rest area, but hang out around 65 the rest of
the time you're in the parade.

Still makes me feel a bit guilty as I speed through the mountains
and valleys. But we are making good time and we *do* want to get to
Momma's for dinner.

. . . Momma's cooking is another reason for this vacation. It's the
real stuff. Down-home cooking. A mess of turnip greens simmering
in pot likker, a nearby pone of golden-crusted cornbread still steamy
from the iron skillet, and another pot filled with string beans, 'taters
and fatback. Seedy sliced 'maters, crunch-fresh onions and tongue-
tart coleslaw. My mouth can't wait.

. . . With the Great Smoky Mountains just behind us and the
rolling Piedmont terrain just ahead of us, Detroit's flatness and
concrete seem so far away. Can I unplug from the city I now call
home and re-enter that world I once called home?

We just went through the place, Asheville, N.C., author Tom
Wolfe once wrote about, about how "You Can't Go Home Again."
It's only an hour away from Momma's house.

Maybe Wolfe was wrong. Maybe he wasn't. That's something we
all have to investigate sometimes.

— April 22, 1981

Another jewel of a mom, my Mother of Pearl

One day this past winter my momma had a heart attack, but it
took seven days before she noticed it.

Then, while recovering in intensive care, she stayed busy making
and selling Pearl's Clowns to the nurses and other patients.

Only way that heart attack slowed her down was that the doctor
told her no digging in the yard and garden, but I just know she's getting in a little secret spade work and limb trimming.

She's an amazing woman. I've been shaking my head in wonder at
her ever since I met her 45 years ago the end of this month.

She defies all rules, all categories, all descriptions, my mother of
Pearl. Always has. Always will.

Approaching Mother's Day — one of our more civilized made-up holidays — thoughts of Mom are uppermost in our minds, particularly those of us who live some distance from her.

Once upon a time mothers didn't live great distances away because they lived with their sons and daughters. We built our homes with this in mind. A spare bedroom for Mother, when it was eventually time for her to come live with you.

My daddy's mother alternated — living with us six months a year and his brother six months. On Momma's side, Grandma Mabe lived with two of her eight daughters, my spinster aunts, Mae and Mary Jane Mabe, when she could no longer tend her chickens and slop the hogs.

It would be nice having my mother live with me but do you think she would move out of her Carolina home of the past four decades? Leave her yard? Are you crazy?

She won't even hear talk of it. And don't dare mention her moving into a smaller, easier-to-keep apartment or duplex with my sister Mary Jane. Don't even think of suggesting a nursing home some day.

That's not Pearl's way. Ah, yes, Pearl's way. The right way, the wrong way and Pearl's way.

I suspect there's some of my mother of Pearl in all mothers about her age of 70-mumble. I promised no exact age. She thinks I have a hang-up about her age. She's right. I've always resented the fact she's younger than I.

These are women who got married and began their families in the Depression; raised their children through World War II and its aftermath. Mothers who've done the biggest chunk of their living in the proud but modest old homes they live in today.

Women who never had time to be liberated. Women who never had time to have nervous breakdowns. Women who had no identity problem with staying home, raising kids, keeping house.

Women who've seen their kids move out and away, starting their own families. Women who turned that empty nest into a perfect place for their husbands and visiting grandchildren.

Women who then outlived their husbands and had to adjust to a life alone and becoming independent as their families scattered throughout mobile America.

Women whose lives have been one adjustment after the other. But through it all, they've kept their base of operations — their home — the same. That home has been their foundation, their strength, their security, their very lives.

They are legion about this great land, living alone in matured neighborhoods. Their pre-WWII homes are solidly built, but small and unfashionable, except for the personal touches and landscaping they added themselves.

Mother Nature and Momma Pearl created a marvelous flora and fauna setting for her little home, one tree she raised from a broken hoe handle. Every time I tell this tale about my momma, people think I'm making it up.

The green power in her thumb is so intense she actually stuck the broken end of a hoe into the ground and the thing took root and grew limbs and is now the only hoe-handle tree in the world I know of. A true story.

But momma, sometimes, is not satisfied with nature. On a recent trip home I couldn't get over one of Pearl's patented touches. She can take a scrap of this and a bit of that and make most anything, like those wonderful clown dolls.

She'd taken a piece of red leather, fashioned this into a bird, a cardinal by Pearl, and nailed it to a tree. The statue of St. Francis of Assisi feeding the birds and squirrels in the flower bed below is bad enough, but isn't a leather bird a bit much, Momma?

About that time, so help me, a cardinal flew up and started talking to that red-leather bird. "See," was all Momma had to say. I swear those birds started laughing at me!

People always laugh when I tell 'em my momma cured every known childhood disease I ever had with things like baking soda, Vaseline and vinegar. Somehow they worked for Pearl, astounding doctors then, much as her recovery from a heart attack astounds them today.

Momma's a treasure trove of home remedies and things done "the country way."

A very special Mother's Day thank you to these women who broke the mold, a remarkable breed who were this nation's secret strength for five decades.

— May 8, 1981

Father and daughter:
A marriage that will last

Have I ever told you how lucky I am that my daughter Dafna adopted me as her father?

It was legally written right there in the adoption papers that she adopted me. And for years after when we'd pass the lawyer's offices where the papers were drawn up, Dafna would point it out as "the place we adopted Daddy."

When Dafna's mother, Beryl, and I were married in 1964, four-year-old Dafna stood right there between us and the judge asked her if she'd take me to be her father and she said yes, and I slipped a little ring on her finger, too.

As the three of us walked down another wedding aisle on June 27 I thought of our other wedding ceremony 17 years ago. Oh, the tears wanted to come. But her mother and I had promised. No tears.

I'd already had my little cry earlier that morning. I was standing alone under the tent in my backyard, which in a few hours would be transformed into a joyous celebration of my daughter's marriage to Keith Abrams.

The tears poured out and trickled down into the corners of my grin. I was crying and laughing at the same time. A magical emotional release.

For 2½ months Dafna and I had lived and breathed this wedding. Every waking moment, it seemed sometimes, and even a dream or two of a monsoon hitting the area. I know we don't have monsoons in this hemisphere, but outdoor weddings can make you crazy, even your dreams.

For 2½ months I'd been the mother and father of the bride, as my ex-wife, Beryl, had moved back South last summer and wasn't on hand for the day-to-day planning and hand-to-hand combat over these plans.

Let me tell you, Dafna and I did have our moments during this period. I didn't know, for example, that when a young lady receives an engagement ring from her fellow, it's her inalienable right and prerogative to dwell on nothing but weddings and bride's stuff until that magic day arrives.

We got to the top of our voices and tears only twice, which, in checking with other mothers of brides, I discovered was remarkably low. In fact, several of these mothers, so taken with how smoothly our production went, suggested we write a how-to-do-it-yourself outdoor wedding handbook.

A short book: Hire professionals and pray for good weather.

Well, maybe I'm exaggerating a little. There's more to it than that. There's having an understanding, helpful wife like Lynn. There are all those wonderful relatives who pour in and pitch in and take over splendidly when the final countdown approaches. It's Keith's family and Dafna's family getting along just fine.

So there I was the morning of the wedding on what had to be the most gorgeous summer's day we've ever had. The relatives and pros would be taking over soon, whipping the backyard into beautiful shape, organizing this and timing that.

It was now out of my hands. The 2½ months Dafna and I had lived this wedding was over. So I had myself a good cry. The happiest sort of tears.

That's why I'm so lucky Dafna adopted me. Those are the only kind of tears my daughter has ever caused me to shed, happy ones filled with love and pride as I've watched her grow up into a beautiful, responsible young lady.

Of course, I'm prejudiced. That's the prerogative, may I point out, of all fathers of the bride.

As we walked down the grassy aisle — Beryl on one side and me on the other giving Dafna away — there was a simultaneous hug between us as we handed her over to Keith while the family's paparazzo seemed to be taking a million pictures.

And, as a matter of fact, I'll be glad when the pictures get back so I can see what went on. It has all become one big marvelous blur to me. I was the blur, never sitting still for a moment, moving about like some tuxedoed mother hen making sure her biddies were happy and having fun.

I'm told that's what I was doing because once the wedding began everything became a montage of toasts, congratulations, smiling faces and warm hugs. I spent the evening grinning. But that, too, is the prerogative of the father of the bride.

The next day someone asked if I'd cried at the wedding and I said I held back because I'd promised Dafna. My son Jason, 14, wondered why in the world anyone would every cry at such a happy occasion.

We talked about how sometimes you cry these happy tears without knowing why. They just come on you unexpectedly. You have no control over them. They are triggered by special moments, special feelings.

I explained that I'm such a sappy person I've even cried at a TV commercial or watching a baby waddle-walk for the first time. Tears that cleanse the ducts, wash the soul and nourish the heart.

One day Jason will understand it better, maybe when he's standing at the altar awaiting his own bride. Or even better, one day when he, too, will be adopted by a daughter. Maybe he'll be as lucky as I am.

— July 8, 1981

A boring Christmas would be a real gift

The Talberts are downright bores.

You heard me right — bores, as in b-o-r-i-n-g!

Compared to our friends, we are Dullsville, Ho-Hum Time. So dreadfully normal that it's downright disgusting to others and embarrassing to us even to talk about it.

When friends and acquaintances ask me how's the family, I can hear, see or feel them turning off and tuning out as I begin my honest, grinny-faced, everything's-just-fine, couldn't-be-better speech. Maybe it's the grin.

My kids are doing well. Daughter Dafna and her husband Keith Abrams are happy, no problems. Son Jason is happy, no problems. Lynn and I are happy, no problems. Everyone's doing just fine.

People don't want to hear this kind of talk. They'd much rather hear that the newlyweds have split, my son was arrested in some teenage dope hangout and my wife and I are having affairs with a commune of midgets in Ypsilanti.

After all, that's the sort of stuff they tell me about when I ask them how's their family. And most of the time I don't even have to ask.

But I'll always ask 'em, because I know I'm going to hear one that'll make my toes curl and my ears ring. Sometimes they even make my toes ring and my earls curl.

That's why I love to listen to them. When you and yours lead such a dull life, you need others to add some spice with their daily soap operas.

Our friends make "General Hospital" seem like an outpatient clinic for the simple and the sane. I could write a "Bloomfield" or a "Grosse Pointe" that would make "Dallas" appear scripted by Mr. Rogers and Captain Kangaroo.

Sometimes in the course of every day, my wife and I will sit down and compare notes on what we've heard from our friends about their lives, which my wife calls, "As the Stomach Turns."

The one who gets to talk first is the one with today's "You aren't going to believe this" yarn. Some days we both have such juicy gossip we have to flip a coin to see who goes first.

The other evening I had a pair of honeys to tell. One friend thinks he's turning queer again and another is having an affair with her boss' husband. Wouldn't you like the details after hearing those headlines?

But mine had to wait. Lynn's was better. People we know are splitting. She's moved out, taking with her all the kids — hers from another marriage, the two they had together and two of his from a previous marriage. Why? He's a sicko and wants to make porno movies with his family.

Weird friends? Of course they're weird. So, I bet, are yours. Think about it a minute. The whole world's weirding out, isn't it? Around here in particular it's epidemic. Maybe I cultivate the weirdos more than most. I suspect that I may be some sort of weirdo magnet, as I do seem to attract a motherlode of them in all Baskin-Robbins flavors.

These aren't people I hang out with necessarily, you understand. Same with your weird friends. But you know 'em well enough that they bring you into their most intimate relationships and their lives.

Their weirdness then becomes a part of the general jumble of things you think about. And once you get involved in a weirdo's life, it is extremely difficult to untwine yourself from their compelling dramas and melodramas.

With most of them I can't wait till the next telephone call or encounter because I know I'm going to get another enthralling chapter in bozo bizarreness I couldn't possibly imagine.

And Christmas brings out the best — or worst — in them, doesn't it? I think sometimes they're copycats. At least my friends are.

Last Christmas was the suicide one. Several tried it, one to excess, which created unbelievable grief among many. The year before I had a hospital-White Christmas of heart attacks, strokes and bypass operations. Three years ago, runaway kids on drugs seemed to be my friends' Yuletide theme.

No pattern seems to have developed this year. Oh, there are the usual half-dozen folks we know who are getting divorced. But that's sort of standard and normal these days.

I welcome a boring Christmas this year. Uh-oh. Phone's ringing. Have a strange feeling it's a toe-ringer.

— *Dec. 24, 1981*

Out of my mind
on a Monday moanin'

Teachers fear the principal who fears the superintendent who fears the school board which fears the parents who fear the children — who aren't afraid of anyone.

All rush hour traffic seemstomovelikethis.

Just what does a wet martini taste like?

Odds for in people: It's 10-1 you'll forget where you parked your car after a show. 5-1 you'll discover just the item you were shopping for after you've spent all your money. 3-1 you'll not find a parking place the first time around the block. 6-1 your luncheon menu will be duplicated at home for dinner. 2-1 you're in a small town if the only ethnic food available is at the pizza parlor. Even money that the 11 o'clock news will have something on it to irritate you.

Don't most people really live on the "autoskirts" of a city?

Isn't it funny how nothing is impossible to the guy who doesn't have to do it himself?

Road maps tell a motorist everything but how to refold them.

Is an attorney-at-law ever "at" anything else?

If you're offered today's world on a silver platter, take the platter.

The average standing ovation is 10 percent genuine and 90 percent people afraid not to.

Most people don't know when to let go of a helping hand.

Shorts are either getting shorter or girls are getting longer.

If it lasts longer than the payments on it, you've made a good buy.

Real beauty belongs to the girl whose face looks the same after she washes it as before.

Moments that are magic: The first sip of a cold glass of milk. An unexpected check enclosed. Being able to roll over and go back to sleep. A soothing sun on an aching back. Free samples in supermarkets. An egg roll that's crisp and juicy. Smelling bread baking. A Tiger home run. Wriggling bare toes in scrunchy white sand.

I sometimes get mixed up in my hipness and say "Right out!" and "Far on!"

Housewives ask: Why do husbands get so mad when you leave the red ring around the bologna? Why do husbands say wives look prettier when they're pregnant? Why do husbands want to take the good and newest car to work just to park it all day in the parking lot? Why do husbands gawk at women in shorts and braless tops but forbid you to wear such things? Why do husbands get mad when you answer the school question your child has asked the husband who doesn't know?

Once upon a time, man needed rest after work. Now he needs exercise.

Believe me, no one can tell the difference between Southern fried chicken and Northern fried chicken.

You know your kids are growing up when they order a bigger meal than you do.

The trouble with a farm is that no matter where you sit you're always looking at something that needs doing.

In any argument, the man with the greater intelligence is always wrong because he didn't use his intelligence to avoid the argument in the first place.

I can instantly tell what sort of person she is by the way she talks to waitresses, wash girls at the beauty parlor, female order taker at drive-up windows, etc.

People who seem to have more fun doing their job than anyone else are those on the line-painting road crews who get to hang down off the back of trucks and pick up those yellow rubber cones.

Have you noticed: Tennis balls don't bounce as high as they used to and the courts are getting wider. Newspaper prints gets smaller and stairs steeper. You never get around to finishing "Playboy" magazine by the time the next month's issue arrives. Radio music is louder and public speakers much quieter.

I wouldn't dare try to interpret this statistic: the Bible refers to 3,017 men by name, but only 131 women.

Why is it we stock our shelves and cupboards with things "too nice to use?"

Returning vacationers always overestimate the amount of money they spent and underestimate the amount of weight they've gained.

SEASONS & HOLIDAYS

Spring things: How it is at this time of year

Spring is a puzzle, a paradox, a predicament, a pleasure. Spring is cause and effect — a seed and a leaf. A flower bud can wait a week or a month, if need be. Only buds can gauge this.

But man can't wait. He's impatient. Child of the sun, man's blood quickens by some strange shifting of the season's tides. Sensing May, man wants June even before April is over.

He would pick violets in overshoes and topcoat. At the sight of the first green leaf, he talks about the cool shade for summer.

Only man would rush the inevitable, but that's the way it is in the spring.

Spring is a fever of fun and frolic, fine fashions and freedom. Spring is a tonic of trees, trinkets, tickles and tippy-toe. Spring is a peekaboo game of the heart played by the ageless, the aging and the aged.

Spring is a glorious contradiction — rosebuds by day and blankets by night. Spring is a puppy running-rolling through the grass, stopping to sniff a just-opened jonquil.

Spring is the twong! twock! of the tennis court and a new crack jagging along the concrete. Spring is pants cuffs filled with new clipped grass. Spring is a young father nursing a fragile kite aloft for his three-year-old son.

Spring is snugging too much winter into last summer's Bermudas. Spring is the new-green golf course covered in pastel-colored golfers beset with hooks, slices and shanks.

Spring is chalking the sidewalk for hopscotch and finding a flat tire on the bike in the garage. Spring is rain on your day off and falling in love with every other young face you see.

Spring is a $2.95 bag of fertilizer and whistling out of tune. Spring is an airless volleyball, a triple bogie and checking water skis for splinters.

Spring is stopping on the way home from the store to let the kids clatter through the park and ride that lopsided go-round thing. Spring is cold cuts back on the dinner menu and milk shakes on Sunday drives.

Spring is small boys with skinned knees and little girls with chocolate ice cream on the front of a pretty white dress. Spring is looking for the barbecue grill and finding part of it.

Spring is taping broken baseball bats and cleaning the outside of windows. Spring is wondering if you can afford an air conditioner. Spring in spilling a can of green paint in the bleachers at the Little League park.

Spring is letting the sun cook your knees and feeling your face get pink and tight. Spring is a curvesome cutie in cerise capris underhanding a softball to her date in a roll-a-bat game.

Spring is a young couple in a front seat lover's knot and an old couple strolling by, trying not to look but unable not to steal a glance.

Spring is a college textbook's pages fluttering on a faded quilt, forgotten by the owner wading calf-deep in a water fountain.

Spring is a box camera shuttering at shaking objects, capturing blurry images to file away until winter. Spring is a chrome-and-fender tributary flowing to the water's edge, depositing car-cramped people shaking off winter's silt.

Spring is loafers without socks and a stiff breeze starching flags in red-white-and-blue salutes. Spring is apartment house pooches towing owners around the block. Spring is the sun summoning a worm for a prospecting robin. Spring is cab drivers taking off caps, turning radios to ball games and letting the sun soak scalps.

Spring is lights at night sparkling in high buildings — cardboard cutouts with holes punched in them on a backdrop of pink evening sky.

Spring touches us all with sun-tipped fingers and windblown kisses. Spring makes the old feel young, and the young feel different, as if something were about to happen.

Spring is people looking at people looking at people.

And spring is too short. Always.

— April 28, 1969

Sounds and sights of summer, season of rare delights

Summer is a symphony of sights and sounds, sweet and sour, silly and serious, s'wonderful and strange . . .

It's kids throwing browning baseballs and tanning tantrums . . . It's an anemic geranium bowing politely in a tin can garden on the window ledge of a cheap rooming house . . . It's squirrels, pigeons and other strange birds, wearing tight pants and sullen faces, strolling through parks.

It's the clean click of a short iron kissing your ball to the green for a gimme bird . . . It's the way a three-year-old girl's tummy pooches out the front of a swimming suit . . . It's the exciting recording . . . It's that midafternoon stretch and yawn that makes it possible to finish the day.

It's fat, lumpy cows dotting hillsides along interstates, getting homogenized or whatever it is they do . . . It's smoke from a thousand barbecue grills sending up rare or well-done semiphores to the nose . . . It's teenagers parked in shopping center lots, rear doors open and bare feet sticking out of front windows. It's little children with ice cream rivers running down faces and playsuits.

Summer is the feel of cool shaded marble and the comedy of a single raindrop on your nose tip . . . It's little old ladies sitting pinch-faced on front stoops, keeping a weary and wary watch on passing motorists. It's the puzzlement of a mosquito's course and the crunch of an opener in a can or the zipping of a pulltop.

It's the thwick-thwick sound of revolving water sprays and the giggle-shrieks of dancing, scampering children . . . It's travel folders spreading like crabgrass on kitchen tables and figuring where budgets are the most stretchable . . . It's secretaries sunning legs in noon sun and bosses sneaking a peek . . . It's the effortless thwong-thwack of a lazily lobbed fuzzy white tennis ball . . . It's the sliding of saddle leather against a horse's back as a rider dismounts.

It's the tail-wagging, tongue-lolling greeting of a wet dog who has run deep in tall wet grass . . . It's the pre-dawn gathering of males in an all-night eatery to plan the day's fishing or golf. It's standing in line at dusk for a cone of that soft, air-pumped ice cream or frozen cola you eat with a straw.

It's that single moment after dawn when the cloud cover gives one final hug and mist swirls off the water like spun-sugar candy . . . It's clouds curling like black fists and a jagged lightning unzippers the sky which fights back rainy tears.

Summer is the heavy, strong sound of road equipment as it carves away a "progress sculpture" and the awful still quiet when it stops . . . It's talking about the heat and iced tea and diaper rash and how to keep a Band-Aid on . . . It's a kid at camp trying to think of something to write home today he didn't write yesterday.

It's wondering whether those boats on the highway are pushing the people or being pulled by them to the lakes and rivers . . . It's that thin trickle-tickle of the day's first sweat running down your side. It's a cabin cruiser nosing into a cool wave and the bronzed-bodied bikinied miss waving to all riverfront lookers . . . It's roadside stands with green tomatoes sucking the red from the sun . . . It's tippy-toeing tender feet on a cooking white beach and sticky blacktop.

It's a wad of cycles cruising between shimmering mirages on highways, watched by sidelined mouth-opened cars letting radiators unboil . . . It's a young lady drenched by a sudden shower, trying to regain her poise when crying is so much easier . . . It's an undershirted beer belly, the sound of a transistor describing a sharp single to left . . . It's the sun nailed still and bleeding on a whitewashed sky . . . It's the cool breath of an air-conditioned theater lobby.

Summer is little legs pumping twice as fast to keep up with grown-up bike riders . . . It's a little boy running off a diving board holding his nose and posing like an akimbo frozen statue. It's a first-dating young lad, checking tie, hair and shoes before ringing the doorbell . . . It's a slapping paddle sampling a swift river's current.

It's a Little Leaguer taking off for first and his too-big pants taking off for the ground . . . It's girdles left in bureau drawers and skinny, old-men legs hanging out of $2.98 Bermudas . . . It's cold cuts and short cuts . . . It's an ember-pink back being salved in tempo with whimpers . . . It's brass-and-leather sandals leaving funny tan marks on feet . . . It's face-down females burning away all their feminine softness, as rock-and-roll blares music to blister by.

It's slipping into clean, cool sheets after showering away a gritty day . . . It's panting dogs under drivewayed cars . . . It's a giggle of girls and a prance of boys around the pool or lake . . . It's just right for bream-fishing, baby-burping and buying a bag if ice . . . It's hot awnings and contagious yawning.

— June 25, 1970

Nut-brown, gold and scarlet, colors in the autumn song

You feel it as you step outdoors, taste it in a steamy cup of coffee . . .

You smell it on the sharp wind's wings and see it in the going-away costumes of the leaves.

You hear it as the acorns crack along sidewalks.

The dying leaf, trembling at the branch end, becomes something majestic and sad.

Trees dress in a million splendid robes of gold and scarlet, brilliant yellows, vivid reds, and a prism of shattering shades from olive, pea and sapphire to apricot, fox, lemon, topaz, plum, bronze and cinnamon, all moist and glistening in the early morning sun.

Anxious squirrels pursue their nut-brown world with full-clenched paws and silvery tails — scampering and sliding across the pebbly surfaces of slanted roofs and clattering down drainpipes and limb-walking treetops.

Leaves are a singing shower from lemon-scarfed sycamores and maples and the blue-green-mufflered hemlocks.

The early frost nips the hills and turns the country into a sideshow of colors.

Lengths of pipe and rusty chain clang forlornly on empty playgrounds — broken swings tolling summer's sad requiem.

Another leaf falls — and the sad enchantment chokes you.

Clock alarms shudder while the darkness begins to hide the graceful sweep of silent circling hands.

Sundown is earlier as evening acquires an edge, then a sharpness — a subtle suddenness which becomes a shout.

A pyracantha's green berries blush in an amber embarrassment before the cast deepens into a vivid, burning pinnacle.

Burnt-red speckles fleck the sweetgum.

Leaves whip crazily, lose their grasp and jerk aimlessly in windwhirls, dancing the last silent waltz of the season.

Mothers hopefully ramble in closets and boxes for last winter's boots for this winter's young feet.

The ends of the tall blond's long hair swing gaily as she laughs at the joke told by the husky slave who walks her to the car in the school parking lot.

The colors climb down slowly from the Upper Peninsula and into the plains and valley lows.

It lasts for a few precious weeks, before the cold breath of winter turns it all to a hazy gray and misty blue.

The autumn song . . . How does it go?

Furnaces hum back to life, summoned by automatic thermostats.

Back fence chatter turns to the cost of children's coats.

A wild football plummets into a carefully pruned azalea and

catapults the irate homeowner off the porch to berate the erratic street-game punter, shirttail flying.

Days are gorgeous and glaring — each made for framing to save forever.

But a leaf flutters down . . . and another.

So very sad and beautiful. So very brief.

Marshmallows are plopped into paper cups of thick, sweet cocoa or become toasted black globs at stick-ends in a yellow-orange flame.

The fallen fruit of stately oaks pops in the burning leaves.

A wire-broom rake makes scratchy noises along concrete drives — a leafy lyre collecting mounds of crisp and rustling beauty.

Service stations explode in anti-freeze signs and winterize reminders.

Sap pockets snap sharply in crackling logs as fireplaces become small family room forges.

Another leaf falls to the carpet, tended by laughing rakers.

In the stadium, a drum major's whistle brings spangled troops to a halt and the slapping crackle of leather heels coming together echoes to the end zones.

Seams rip on mothball-smelling trousers and there is a comforting sigh of expelled breath when it happens.

The first frost comes silently — at dawning, the flashing tarnished landscape is paled by the white crystalline coat.

Too soon the trees will stand naked and shivering — as the September song ends, the October prelude fades and November's dim melody begins.

But there is a mood now — a challenge, an irresistible call to questing hearts.

At the moment the days aren't cast in loneliness.

The fervid, electric autumn has begun.

It, too, will pass sadly, stripped of its intoxication, its fascination.

Too brief . . . too beautiful.

Sept. 17, 1968

This one's unfair, depressing, irritating

Well, I've finally got myself a winter story.

For the first 13 years here, it was my lot in life to remain silent when a bunch of Michigan winter pros had a good conversation going about such things as snow and ice.

Best I could muster was an 18-inch snow that fell overnight back in the early '70s. But every time I mentioned that, the winter pros would look at me as if to say, "Oh, that one. Pesky, but no big problem. A two-maybe-three-dayer."

I mean these Michigan winter pros talk about shoveling out from an overnight four-footer. Snowed-in for weeks. Drifts three stories high. One open lane down Woodward with 12-foot snow banks on both sides.

I always figured they were exaggerating a tad. Michigan folk have been known to exaggerate about such things. After all, Paul Bunyan is from here.

No more will I doubt a Michigan winter pro. This spring, I'm going looking for Babe, the Blue Ox.

Yes, sir, when this ol' dude gets into the winter of his years and there's a roaring February fire a'going, I'm gonna tell all the young 'uns to gather 'round my knees, cause, children, let me tell you 'bout the winter of '82!

You don't know how embarrassing it is not to have a severe winter to talk about. You feel so inadequate, so amateurish. You feel like your training wheels are exposed. You're an outsider. You don't really belong.

But no longer do I feel this way. This is the braggingest winter you'll ever want to see.

On Super Bowl Sunday I was driving Ernie and Lula Harwell to a breakfast with the Erskine Caldwells because Ernie was a little fearful of negotiating the icy streets in his rolling Farmington Hills subdivision.

The Tiger broadcaster and his wife wintered in Dunedin, Fla., for 16 years before deciding they'd make this their year-round home to be near their children.

I was commiserating with them over their rotten timing. "But look at it this way," I said. "If you get through this winter unscathed you get credit for four winters."

That was Jan. 24, if you'll recall. Since then we've had a couple of weekends and all last week of weather that causes me to update Ernie's credit.

If we survive the winter of '82, folks, I think we should get credit for a lifetime of winters. And I don't care how bad it was back in '33 or '51 or '64, this one ain't no baby winter.

This is your first-class, heavy-duty bad winter. Maybe the depth of the snow hasn't set records. Maybe the number of subzero days is less than average. Statistically, perhaps it's not yet a world champ, but it's a ranking contender in so many ways.

Something about Michigan being hit with a blizzard winter when our economic climate is close to an all-time worst seems horribly unfair. We hardly need this, now do we? On the unfair scale, the winter of '82 ranks in the top two or three easy. That automatically helps make the winter of '82 a high-ranker on the depression scale. Bad enough the state's limping, but we're now limping, too.

This winter, for me anyway, was a high anxiety rating in several areas. For one, I keep hearing how it's going to be even worse in March. You, too? Gulp!

And how about the driving? That's what I'm going to remember the most or the worst or whatever because behind the wheel my anxiety level approaches an all-time record.

It's those impossible-to-see-around-and-over mounds of snow at every intersection, at every juncture in the road! So you have to keep nudging the nose of your car out beyond the safety limits to see if it's clear to enter traffic.

If that's not bad enough, when you finally attempt to enter a street your car slips and slides and then fishtails dangerously and your heart stays in your throat all the time. Right? Thought so. A full 10 on the anxiety scale.

It's also a winter high on the irritation scale. One classic example comes to mind. There's so much snow that when they do scrape your street it leaves a three-foot overflow at the end of your driveway which has frozen solid. Need I say more?

Unfair. Depressing. Anxiety-ridden. Irritating. These are only a few of the reasons why I think we have a world-class winter on our hands. I'm sure you can add dozens of your own reasons why this one's going down in our memory books, if not the record books, as certainly one of the most talked about winters ever.

— Feb. 11, 1982

How many times are you on my Valentine list?

Valentines to . . .

People who really listen to you when they ask for advice.

People who work outdoors in all this cold and ice to keep us warm and lighted.

All those folks at Channel 4 who are trying to make a change — and we all know how hard that can be.

Disc jockeys who give us the time and weather information often.

Businesses that operate on honesty and integrity.

Salespeople who are "help people" first and foremost.

Old songs that stir memories and cause one to drift back through first brushes with the song.

People who deliver newspapers, mail and parcels in weather you and I wouldn't be caught dead in.

Amateur theater groups who give their all for a few weekends a year and relatives' raves.

Good disco dancers who make the fever worth watching.

The Michigan Music magazine, which gives local unknowns a chance to be written about.

People who read and ponder on what they read.

Michigan farmers who have hung in there despite insurmountable odds and little public support for their plight.

Photographers who preserve the things in life we should see but don't.

People who take time to write others notes of thanks or appreciation for even the smallest things.

People who give, share and care.

Editors who save writers' necks and make our words read the way they're supposed to read.

Supermarkets with enough people to bag groceries during rush peaks.

People who let you in in long lines of not-going-anywhere traffic.

Service station attendants who clean your windows without being asked.

Cartoonists who make us laugh as well as think.

Twenty-four hour drugstores.

All parents expecting their first children — brave new pioneers in the toughest of all professions, parenting.

People who bring you chicken soup when you're sick even if you're too sick to eat it.

Movies with happy endings and songs with clean lyrics.

Volunteers who work on the many worthwhile projects around here and all they get for it is tired.

Anyone with a positive attitude.

Teachers, for hanging in there, too.

Public broadcasting — Channel 56 and WDET-FM — for providing alternatives that keep us hanging in there.

Everyone who is hanging in there.

Snugglers everywhere.

The public relations directors of the Detroit professional sports teams, who have some of the toughest jobs around.

People who give a 1958 day's work for a 1978 dollar.

Those who know the future must begin today.

People who don't smoke in public.

Smile-wearers.

Middle-aged Americans. They deserve it.

Entertainers who never forget the audience that put them on top.

Fathers-in-law, because no one ever seems to bother about them.

People who can laugh at themselves.

Preachers' wives who have a tough role that takes a rare quality.

Wives of policemen and firemen, even tougher role.

People who know that making a life beats making a living.

Young people who don't have to be reminded they are still young.

Nutritionists who are helping bring our appetites to their senses.

People who have the right words at the right time when we didn't even know we needed those words.

Every single one of you reading this — just because.

— Feb. 14, 1978

A mother's hug is a miracle drug

Maybe she's someone you know.

A funny sort of mixture — maybe the funniest. Strange, too. So many uses. Like a human Swiss Army knife.

She's the healer of bloody noses and skinned knees and only she always has been able to kiss-it-and-make-it-well instantly. A hug that is a miracle drug.

She mends chipped nails, busted tricycle wheels, split dolls and little people's broken hearts. She has that touch and is also the softest touch around.

She's a master chef without a cookbook, a pinch of this and drop or two of that, and a dash of love that blends it all together.

She's dignity with a wet diaper in her hand, cookie flour on her cheek and a dried Spaghetti-O on her blouse.

She has the curiosity of a new neighbor, the suspicion of an investigative reporter and all the temper of a first sergeant to be avoided at all costs when it is triggered.

Only she can wither you with a look or melt you with a smile — and does, periodically, to keep you on your toes. And there's no price on a surprised grin from her.

She opens, starts, tightens and loosens things with knives, scissors, can openers, hot water, teeth, raps against the sink, screwdrivers with chipped ends and husbands with the same.

Only she is allowed suddenly to decide she's not very hungry when all the meat for dinner is gobbled up by her family and the unexpected visitor.

By now there's no mistaking her — the woman we all honor Sunday. We give her one day a year and she gives us 365. And will 'til she dies. Don't forget it. Sometimes she won't let you.

Where can she be found? Everywhere. In fresh produce . . . bargain basements . . . beauty parlors . . . at this year's club dance in last year's dress . . . in shopping centers . . . looking for a parking space at Little League . . . on a racquetball court . . . in church . . . visiting someone in a hospital . . . working on a PTA project . . . at the polls during elections and in the stands during ball games and concerts.

She has the patience of Job but lets you know what a job it is, too. She proves this in countless ways; scraping the same carrots off the baby's chin four times and putting them back in his mouth; reading the same bedtime story 43 times straight . . . letting her son's rock group practice in the basement . . . letting the nine-year-old cook and the three-year old wash dishes.

What does she like? Lots of things. Gossip, for starters . . . young people who dress neatly and act properly in public . . . boys with socks pulled up and girls with dresses pulled down . . . soap operas, quiz shows, talk shows . . . something extravagant she'd never dream of buying for herself . . . seeing her children happily married . . . early morning disc jockeys . . . window-shopping . . . and warmed-over coffee.

She hates, most of all, girdles or clothes that bind . . . pecks on the cheek . . . a man with a spare tire wearing a tight T-shirt . . . anyone's shirttail hanging out . . . knowing she hasn't had time to shave her legs in three days . . . any age ending in zero . . . staying on diets and budgets . . . her best friends' furniture . . . fashion models . . . mail she can't open . . . ironing (ranks right behind girdles, by the way) . . . cleaning up after she has just cleaned up . . . hot weather . . . wet days . . . movies that don't end right . . . and books that do.

This wonderful person I'm talking about is the only one in the world who can spend hours tweezing, squeezing, plucking, vibrating, combing, brushing, polishing, painting, rubbing on and rubbing off and still come out looking very much like she did before she started it all.

Because to you, she never really changes. Close your eyes and you'll see her — that lady who always seems to have an extra buck or quarter when you need it, but never has change for the parking meter or any money in the house for the paperboy.

She becomes everyone else's memory about birthdays and anniversaries (to cousins, even), but never remembers to keep enough gas in the car or milk in the house.

She's a do-it-yourself kit in denims, with a hairpin for a tool chest. Some things will open or operate only for her.

She'll see the movie first, then read the book — shocked at the carryings-on, but eagerly turning the pages.

She makes great fried chicken, bad coffee, the best lopsided cake going, and her homemade soup is the only kind you'll eat without questioning it.

She seems constantly to be rearranging furniture and never is satisfied with the way any room looks. She can move, entirely by herself, a couch that it took three husky men to bring in.

She's always worrying that you're eating not enough or too much. Then she sends you out the door with bags of goodies she just happened to buy too many of.

She can spend an hour on the phone with a friend and answer "What did she have to say?" with "Oh, nothing." And mean it.

She's a mixture all right — a mix of heart, horse sense, fun, dreams, hopes, pride, work, plans, play, dedication and determination. And she spends every minute of every hour of every day loving you. And don't you forget it ever.

— May 7, 1977

For a day, at least, the `old man' becomes dear father

In millions of families this weekend, the father is going to open a present, receive a kiss and hug, and be honored in a curious custom of our culture which dictates that a day must be set aside for each and everything.

Unfortunately, in most of these families, father becomes just father again next week — a fellow to get some money from, to tell some troubles to, to get mad at because he's the safest one around to get mad at, and to get some work out of when there's a moment handy. Next week, this great man of the hour fades back into the woodwork, a fixture not unlike the TV set, the breakfast room and table and the shower curtain.

What is this man made of? This father, this man of the hour? Well, fathers, to begin with, all began as little boys who somehow grew tall and strong and were then called men. But parts of them remain little boys forever.

Like little boys, fathers possess a quality of aloof independence — coupled with a desire to be pampered and needed at the same time. At the same moment a father can impose strict discipline and melt with affection.

A father is a creature of contradictions, more so than mothers. A father will deny that he can fix a formula or change a diaper or wash a dish. But you can find him in quiet moments rocking the baby, brushing back his son's hair and helping a daughter button up.

A father's husky hands are quick and sure at mending broken toys and lifting children up to see parades or into high windows, but the very same hands fumbled with a daughter's corsage pin or the hooks on his wife's dress.

Father, it seems, is best changing flat tires, securing Christmas trees, grilling steaks, taking out the garbage, hiding Easter eggs, packing a car for a vacation and bringing home surprises after a solo trip out of town. A father always seems to be listening to someone's problem, handing out ticket money, puzzling over your school homework and telling you to get a haircut.

Father's the one who tells the children they can't have a dog, then brings a puppy home, gets up with him when he whines and forever after sees that he's fed, wormed and cared for.

At the end of a busy day, you can find father turning off the lights, checking the door locks and standing quietly in the doorway of his children's room. And those children are secure in their sleep and sweet dreams just because there is a father in the house.

But how many of us realize what a father is until it is too late? Our view of father changes so drastically as we grow up, especially as we become fathers ourselves.

The father-son relationship is unlike any other family relationship. It is more competitive, and is nearly always baffling. From the start, mothers and daughters have a common feminine bond between them. It's unique, and theirs to cherish. A mother-son is patently predictable. The father-daughter relationship is equally predictable, although they never understand each other as well as the mother and son do.

But time — and only time — can make sons see our fathers plain. This view is never accomplished by the daughter and, in the case of a son looking at his mother, is next to impossible. Father is usually the only member of the family who is eventually looked on as an ordinary human being.

It is sometimes difficult to remember that father is a man and his weaknesses are not confined just to him, but are inherent with the masculine nature. As a boy reaches the plateau of life known as manhood, he has the strong inclination to overcome, physically and mentally, his father. And, later on, a lot of men feel cheated when they realize they can do this easily or that father is really "overcomeable" on any basis. We hold it against him, the individual, rather than realizing every man somehow meets defeat some time in some place in some way.

Mothers are never held up to this rigid expectation and inspection by sons. He understands and makes jokes about mother's weaknesses, but father's weaknesses embarrass him. I went through a period of feeling vastly superior to my father. All sons do. I'm thankful my feelings didn't last long. For many it does and eventually turns into a wall which even time and understanding never completely eliminate.

Before his death, my father and I came to understand each other and appreciate each other's individuality. In the last seven months of his life when only he and I and the doctor knew he had cancer, we grew even closer. There was something firmer, more realistic and even calmer about our relationship. It was as if I had located the rest of myself. I think this is the real meaning of father. Identity. If we never come to see our father as a human we have a lesser grasp of our own individuality. Fathers are men. We who are also men find this out too late to take full advantage of it, for it is indeed a joyous revelation. Often it comes so late one can only go to the graveside and say simply, "Father, now I understand."

— June 18, 1971

The Halloween long ago when seven goblins grew up

I don't believe in witches or any of that silly stuff anymore, but once upon a time my best friends at Halloween time were goblins, vampires, skeletons, pirates, frogs and their scary cousins.

We were pretty hip hobgoblins. When we went trick-or-treating it was for real. If the folks came across with bad apples or hard candy, they got tricked anyway.

It was goodies or else. Some of our milder tricks were putting lawn furniture in trees and on roofs.

We discovered along the way that you can run faster and hide better in skin-tight black costumes. Sheets were for sissies or girls who couldn't run fast, anyway, except for Betsy, who lived two doors down and could run faster and hit harder than any boy I've ever seen then or since.

And we didn't mess around with those little brown bags. We carried full-size shopping bags or daddy's old army duffel bag. We were in this thing for the loot.

The entire campaign was planned down to the last door to knock and trick to pull. You'd have thought we were planning how to end World War II, which we did on other days.

Little Ray, a freckle-faced spook, scouted the neighborhood for low-hanging clothes lines, and those almost invisible wires around flower beds and bushes.

Balding Harry — the only 10-year-old in the world who was losing his hair — charted the course. Harry was the one who also got to play navigator when we engaged in B29 runs over Berlin and Tokyo. He had a way with maps and rules.

Betsy, who was the fastest, and I, the fattest, were the doorbell ringers. I could see the logic in having the fastest do this job, but I have never figured out why I was chosen. Maybe we figured fat little boys and deep-voiced little girls were the most appealing. Kids somehow sense these things without anyone telling them.

Betsy's voice was exactly like the "belly-deep" of a pond frog. Grown-ups used to give her dimes just to talk, so they could laugh and say, "Isn't that cute?" She was the richest kid on the block.

There were seven little monsters in our pack, seven chocolate-thirsty little vampires. We wanted goodies from every place we hit, with one exception: The mean old lady who lived at the end of the street in the shriveled little house.

We always saved her house for last. It presented problems because there wasn't a thing we could do to the outside of that place that would have hurt it. Vandalism would only have improved it.

We had to devise devilish means of making her mad at us. On non-Halloween days we could pass by and whisper and she'd call the police that we were noisy enough to wake the dead.

Our parents never told us to leave her alone. They couldn't get along with her, either. She hardly ever came outside. Her groceries and things were always delivered. I never saw her in the yard. She didn't even have a phone and only a half dozen times did anyone ever see her drive this old, old car that gathered dust in her garage.

There are times in the course of growing up when one of life's big lessons hits you, but it is years later before you realize it. This happened to our little gang of ghouls the Halloween we rigged up the mean old lady's steps so that she would fall when she ran out to shoo us away.

We stood out in the yard and chanted about her being a witch and how she drank blood and kept toads. Enraged, she started toward the steps to shout at us but she never did. She got this real funny look on her face and dropped to her knees with her head hung down and her shoulders shaking.

We started to run, but Betsy cried, "Why, she's crying!" You know how girls are. Betsy ran up the steps and put her hand on the mean lady's shoulder. She took Betsy's hand and they walked inside the house.

A little bit later Betsy same out alone and started walking down the street by herself. She didn't say anything as we crowded around and asked what it looked like inside that creepy old house.

Finally, Betsy said, "She showed me her daughter. She's big as my mother and just as old. But she talks like a baby and she isn't, you know . . . right."

No one said very much after that and we divvied up the candy and went home. The next year when Halloween came up one suggested we go trick-or-treating. For some reason it just didn't seem fun any more.

— *Oct. 29, 1968*

Thankful thoughts and thoughtful things

Thanksgiving 1968.

Let us give thanks for . . . drugstores that stay open all night . . . coffee perking on a cold morning . . . new vaccines and vitamins . . . freckles . . . paper clips . . . newly waxed floors . . . snow tires . . . the way a warm puppy feels . . . walking barefoot in the sand . . . popcorn popping . . . logs crackling in a fireplace . . . the sound of a school playground at recess . . .

And peanut butter sandwiches . . . diapers that snap instead of pin . . . night-blooming jasmine . . . laundry bleach . . . the sweet sleep of a baby . . . the roar of the crowd at kickoff . . . any song from the '20s . . . the distant whistle of a train . . . the melodies of mocking birds . . .

(But what about the man who has a wrinkled, hardened candy apple in the back seat of his car? He bought it at the State Fair to take home to his young son. The apple was never delivered. The son was a victim of a hit-and-run driver.)

Be thankful for . . . car pools . . . no-press pants and wash-and-wear shirts . . . teething biscuits . . . driver-training courses . . . movies with "Adults Only" labels . . . the "Peanuts" folk . . . the ever-improving canned soups . . . Brownie Scouts and Girl Scout cookies . . .

And blinker signal lights . . . pizza . . . pediatricians who make house calls . . . Bozo and Oopsy the clowns . . . the way velvet feels . . . the sound of soft rain on a windowpane . . . the tooth fairies . . . places that will cash your check . . . cars that don't stall at red lights, and drivers who don't honk behind you when they do . . .

(But what about the woman and her 16-year-old daughter who sit alone today in a suburban home's dining room? They will hold hands and try to find it in their hearts to give thanks. The booming bass voice that asked the blessing for 16 years is no more. And the mother and the daughter will forever wonder why the end came with a bullet in the brain at the end of a lonely road. As long as they both shall live they will wonder.)

Be thankful for efficient ice-cube trays . . . goldfish swimming in tanks . . . the sight of a sailboat swift on the lake . . . people who listen well . . . contour sheets . . . hairdressers who don't try to sell you the works when all you want is a shampoo-and-set . . . doctors who answer your questions . . . supermarket bag boys who pack with both hands . . . salesclerks who don't stab you with their eyes when you don't buy . . .

And expressways . . . jars and packages adults can open, but children can't . . . salt shakers that pour even when it rains . . . crisp crackers . . . a silent telephone during naps . . . the way beautifully finished wood looks . . . the creaky sound of fine leather goods . . . the taste of cotton candy . . . false eyelashes and makeup . . . the way air smells after a rain . . . fresh-baked bagels . . .

(But what about the lady who lies in a darkened room, a silent 85-pound shadow of her once jolly 145 pounds. This is what cancer can do. It can also make her husband and children forget how to smile.)

Be thankful for mitten clips . . . Winnie-the-Pooh . . . sock hops . . . tree houses . . . cardboard boxes . . . mothers who don't mind volunteering for school work, fathers who mind but do the work anyway . . . family plans on airlines . . . chocolate-covered almonds . . . spaghetti that winds up just right . . . the egg and toast running out at the same time . . .

And parents who leave you alone when you don't want to talk . . . zippers . . . stop-and-go traffic lights . . . typewriters . . . locks on bathroom doors . . . rubber bands . . . early morning disc jockeys . . . neighbors with workshops and power tools . . . bobby pins . . . power steering . . . the sound the ocean makes . . . birthday parties and no one crying . . .

(But what about the man in his late 20s who said goodby last night to his four-year-old daughter who wouldn't stop hugging his neck and asking him, "Why, Daddy, why?" There is no way to explain the divorce papers Monday morning and the way lives ravel.)

Be thankful for Saturday morning TV cartoons . . . butter pecan

ice cream . . . charge cards . . . trading stamps . . . yo-yos . . . the way
a baby smells all powdery after a bath . . . the trust of an eight-year-
old . . . the pride of an 80-year-old . . . firemen and policemen . . .

And turkey and dressing . . . founding fathers . . . football on
television . . . people who don't mind laughing out loud . . . strangers
who smile and speak . . . mail carriers . . . sweaters and loafers . . .
miniskirts . . . holiday decorations . . . candles that don't drip . . .
naps on the couch . . . songs that whistle easy . . . the feel of new
money . . . little, hugging arms.

Many, many things and many, many thanks.

But also, too many people who have lost their reason to be
thankful.

Let them remind us today to be truly thankful for the little things
we somehow forget. If only they could forget them.

Thanksgiving 1968.

— Nov. 28, 1968

America the bittersweet has memories in all moods

Once upon a time there was a Thanksgiving . . ..

The young man stood at the edge of this valley and looked down
to the stubble of grain that once flowed gracefully from the banks of
the tiny stream that laced the valley like a small vein. The life's
blood of the grain came from the stream and the tall young man was
thankful.

He was thankful the harvest was in and stored. He thought of how
hard his family had worked. His heart filled with love for his faithful
and dutiful wife and the three images of their love and affection —
two fine sons and a lovely daughter. They were all sound of body and
limb, maybe a little restless in their will, but the young man
remembered that so was he once. He thought about his family and
was thankful.

They had worked hard and were ready for the harsh winter that
was beginning to breathe heavily from the north. In his bones he felt
the coming winter wind could be as bad as the winter before. He
hoped not. That winter had seen many of the young man's friends,
relatives and neighbors die. It was a sad spring thaw when the
community leaders buried the dead. Small children, old people,

brave young fathers, pregnant mothers — the harsh winter hadn't been selective.

The young man knew the fall hunting had been successful, too. The tanned hides and salted meat were stored. The people had worked harder this fall, haunted by the bitter memory of the last winter. The young man was tired in body, but he was at peace in his mind because he had done everything he could to be prepared. And he was thankful.

His eyes lifted to the sky and he was humbled by the vast grayness. He offered his thanks to the giver of his fortune — his God in heaven.

He fought back the tears that welled in his eyes. He could not remember when he had cried last. He learned early in his new life that tears accomplished nothing. Tears showed weakness and this was something you couldn't afford to show as you carved out a new life in this wilderness.

But they weren't tears of sadness or weakness. He knew they were tears of joy, tears of hope and thanksgiving, tears of promise. And he was thankful.

He thought of his neighbors and knew that they, too, had prepared for this winter. Together they had worked side by side, laboring long and hard toward a common goal — survival. He was thankful that he had friends who helped each other, good people, a strong people.

The wind began to blow and the young man shuddered slightly as he watched the smoke curl lazily from fires below, fires giving warmth and peace to his family and friends. He thought of the coming celebration when all would get together and share their happiness and remind each other of their good fortune to be living in a land that offered so much for those who worked for it.

Thinking of these things humbled the young man. In the back of his mind he couldn't forget the winter that he had almost defeated them. The winter took his father and mother, parents who wanted so much for him and his family. He remembered how hard they had labored, fighting fierce battles with the elements, the animals and strange, greedy human beings. He was thankful for such courageous parents.

The young man thought of the protection he had prepared for evils other than the elements. The young man wished with all his heart that he would never have to touch those stored weapons, but knew there were always people about who made weapons necessary.

As he thought of this and frowned, his eyes swept to the far edge of the valley and he saw something that cause the blood in his veins to stop cold.

Bitterness ran through him and his mouth filled with an angry taste, as he saw a thin line of people and wagons moving slowly into his valley. Dark, wispy smoke rose from a thin red-orange line of flame that meant they were again burning the stubble ahead of them. That was their warning — get out! They had come to take his land, as they had taken his father's land before him. They did not want to share. They wanted it all.

The young man looked toward the heavens once again. This time his eyes filled with tears of anger as his heart asked for the strength to fight. Thanksgiving in the year 1835, and slowly the young Indian brave turned and went down to his village in the valley to prepare for the invasion of the settlers. He was thankful he had the strength to fight.

— *Nov. 26, 1970*

Recalling oodles of reasons for giving thanks any day

Some big, some small — a lot of things to be thankful for on Thanksgiving 1972:

The Wishbone . . . girls with long legs . . . icemakers . . . paper towels . . . anti-freeze . . . waterproof gloves . . . efforts toward world peace . . . buttons that smile . . . Greg Landry and Charlie Sanders . . . the Better Business Bureau . . . Wayne County Sheriff Bill Lucas.

Hot chili . . . salt-stick bagels . . . macadamia nuts . . . power steering . . . laundries that put things on hangers . . . frozen grape juice . . . tooth fairies.

Paper cups . . . radial tires . . . Playboy magazine . . . non-dairy creamers . . . bookmarks . . . trash compactors . . . early morning paper boys . . . hair blowers that really get your hair dry . . . Carole King songs . . . Scotch tape . . . mini-theaters . . . maxi-coats . . . Mary Tyler Moore . . . sirloin strips . . . Doritos taco chips.

. . . Baskin-Robbins' imaginative flavors . . . nail clippers . . . scented candles . . . "church keys" . . . Mott's Clamato and Beefamato juices . . . plastic spoons . . . overhead cams . . . pantyhose . . .

charcoal briquets . . . color TV . . . eye shadow . . . taped cassettes
. . . .coloring books . . . Magic Markers . . . lasagna.

. . . Chocolate-covered almonds . . . Joe Falls' column . . . playing
Under Judd Arnett's Government . . . Marc Beltaire's Worst Joke
. . . musk oil . . . Frank Angelo's interviews with interesting people
he meets . . . Tom Opre's outdoor writing . . . aerosol sprays . . .
emergency rooms . . . ham-and-egg sandwiches . . . Coney Island
hamburgers . . . immediate seating.

. . . Vinyl rainwear . . . garlic dressing . . . 24-hour tow trucks . . .
massages . . . back rubs . . . broken parking meters . . . paper clips
. . . warranties . . . defrosters . . . up-to-date area maps . . . water
boys . . . french fries sliced by hand . . . cottage fries well done . . . elevators without music . . . stereo . . . jazz organ music.

Chinese food . . . Suzanne Pleshette . . . Peter Falk as "Columbo"
. . . new typewriter ribbons . . . aluminum foil . . . Baggies . . . on-
side kicks . . . Lem Barney . . . calendars with extra months . . . Dave
Bing . . . pierced ears . . . zippers.

. . . Tiny time pills . . . Vitamin C and E . . . knit shirts . . . Levi's
. . . bikini briefs . . . Supp-Hose . . . electric tools . . . no-lead gas . . .
polyester material . . . wire-rim glasses . . . direct dialing . . . appeals
courts . . . gummed labels . . . car rentals . . . layered look.

. . . Instant replay . . . copy machines that never break down . . .
square pizza with everything except anchovies . . . pencil sharpeners
. . . postage meters . . . pedestrian zones . . . vanilla wafers . . . latex
paint . . . Sears T-squares . . . meatloaf sandwiches . . . anything
wholesale . . . penicillin . . . free parking . . . Saturday morning
cartoons.

. . . Insulated clothing . . . opening nights . . . Santa Claus . . .
grilled cheese sandwiches and cold milk . . . carbon paper . . . season
tickets . . . DSR Flyers . . . Hudson's . . . nuns . . . digital clocks . . .
John Kelly's laugh at 7 a.m. . . . Detroit's young music market . . .
Virgin Mary cocktails . . . Sanders' hot fudge sundaes . . . Vic
Tanny's whirlpools.

Kids old enough to go to the rest rooms by themselves . . . rest
rooms you don't mind your children going to by themselves . . . off
ramps that are easy to get off . . . Girl Scout cookies . . . velvet coats
. . . the Raleigh House . . . Cobo Hall and Arena . . . wigs . . . art re-
productions . . .

. . . Humorous TV commercials . . . full-page newspaper ads in
color . . . Time magazine's "Man of the Year" . . . K mart . . .
supermarkets with plenty of checkout personnel at crunch time . . .

Easter Seals . . . Pine Knob . . . mental health agencies . . . high-rise apartments . . . low-rise hip-huggers . . . George C. Scott . . . the Red Wings' Johnny Wilson . . . flavored Clorets . . .

. . . Mailmen . . . junk mail . . . Astroturf . . . Bach . . . radio talk shows . . . being able to laugh at ethnic jokes . . . Southern accents . . . Dave Brubeck . . . finding lost car keys . . . non-smokers . . . generous tippers . . . themed Christmas trees . . . discount stores . . .

. . . Fisher Theatre . . . Tiger Stadium hot dogs . . . El Nibble Nook . . . Greektown . . . turtlenecks . . . Topinka's . . . country music . . . sun tan lotion . . . Miami Beach . . . Peter McWilliams' poetry and books . . . crying at Marcus Welby's endings . . . butterscotch pudding . . . Johnny Carson and Dick Cavett . . . no bills in today's mail . . .

. . . No busy signal on second dialing . . . well-marked residential streets and big numbers on homes . . . new hairdos . . . puppies . . . zero population growth . . . POW bracelets . . . 12-year-old daughters . . . five-year-old sons . . . getting close to 40 and not caring. Singing along with your car radio . . . windshield cleaner fluid that works . . . Howard Johnson fried clams . . .

. . . Turkey and dressing . . . Win Schuler's cheese . . . The Vineyards . . . Clock restaurants . . . people who sign their letters . . . political differences . . . non-censored TV stations . . . the Detroit Free Press . . . Mr. Whipple . . . Snoopy . . . running quarterbacks . . . the United Foundation . . . Flip Wilson . . . Archie Bunker . . . Jack-in-the-Box tacos . . . Hot Sam pretzels . . . Kennedy Square . . . Christmas . . . human beings . . . curiosity . . . laughter . . . today.

— Nov. 23, 1972

Tinsel, trees and the mistletoe shortage

Out of my mind on Chris'mas Moanin'

If getting rid of those real Christmas trees doesn't bug you, I'll guarantee you it'll at least needle you a little.

Does anyone save tinsel?

Is there a mistletoe shortage, or have I just missed out on walking under a lot of it this year?

The word is Hanuka pronounced "Ha noo kah." And a happy

eight days to you.

Isn't it funny how people who ridicule gift-giving send big gifts to those people who can help them in business?

How is it those people who have everything always wind up getting something they don't have?

Why is this the only day of the year when eggnog seems right?

If you're the average American home you had turkey on Thanksgiving and ham today, and dishwasher troubles one of the two.

How many of you parents woke up at 5 a.m. today to watch the faces of your children only to have them drag down about 9:30 or 10 o'clock?

I've noticed that those who claim Christmas is overcommercialized usually have mates who take care of all the shopping, so what gives them the right to say anything?

I don't know about you, but I don't care to look at another put-together toy for the rest of my life.

And I couldn't look another piece of fruitcake in the hard little citron eyes if I had to. I hate citrons.

Why do people put so much liquor and wine in sweets at Christmas?

Why do people put so much liquor into themselves at Christmas?

Isn't it amazing how no other holiday comes slower or passes faster than Christmas?

If I had a penny for every battery purchased in just the Detroit area for electronic toys today I could take a trip around the world for a couple of years.

Let's hear it for all those who are working today. May your stockings be stuffed with double time.

I've been amazed at how many people wanted money this year instead of gifts.

How many of you will eat something today you can't stand because you don't want to hurt someone's feelings?

Just think, we can now listen to the radio for at least 320 days without hearing any Christmas carols.

Someone will play one new record or tape over and over and over and over again today until you'll hate it forever.

There will be one thing — a gift, an incident, an accident (hopefully minor), a kid's statement — that will mark this Christmas for you and that's the way you'll remember it.

Anyone who looks at you lovingly today and says, "You shouldn't have," is so very, very glad you did.

Some kid today will have more fun with the box and peanut-shaped Styrofoam packing the toy came in than with the toy itself.

Half of you will play those video games so long at one stretch your eyes will start watering. Mine do.

We're going to be all fouled up the rest of the week, thinking tomorrow is Monday.

Some parents of young children will discover today that their kids discovered the secret of Santa Claus, but kept quiet about it because they were afraid once they knew, he wouldn't come.

You will spend at least 16 minutes on phone calls out of town to loved ones and friends. I haven't eavesdropped at your house, huh?

Someone will leave presents atop their car and drive off that way. I've pulled this number before.

After opening dozens of toys and unwrapping that many packages, some kid is sure to ask, "Is that all there is?"

Someone should come up with a National Recycle Your Christmas Wrapping Paper and Boxes Campaign for Dec. 26.

The height of irony is to give your parents billfolds at Christmas, kids.

But at some family gathering, the two relatives who never got along will set no precedent and continue to carp at each other.

Today will be full of a million pregnant pauses while someone gets a group together for a photo then fouls up the camera.

Count on this, too: Christmas or no Christmas, the joggers will be out there today doing their thing. Don't they ever take a day off?

Sometime today you will hear from someone you least expected to hear from. This invariably happens at Christmas.

You will get at least one gift in the mail you can't figure out, and on top of that, can't figure out who it's from.

Guaranteed to happen: Some little miss will fall asleep in her family's pew, with her Christmas doll tucked lovingly under her chin.

And before I forget, Merry Christmas, and thanks for sharing a moment with me.

— Dec. 25, 1978

Pushing death in a glass with a toast

I am an alcoholic.

This will be my 18th Christmas season without a drink.

It hasn't been easy.

Know why?

You should. You're to blame.

I'm going to lay a guilt trip on you because you deserve it.

And you may not even be aware of what you are doing.

In the past few days I have received several dozen invitations to Christmas parties and telephone calls asking me to attend this party and that.

In every single instance, the writer or the caller has made an emphatic point that the drinking will start at so-and-so time so don't miss it.

Do you know how unfair this is to alcoholics?

Obviously not or you wouldn't be so insistent.

It's a given today that drinks will be served at almost any affair. I've come to accept this and deal with it in my own way.

But my resolve over 18 years ago when I quit drinking was stronger than all the persuasive powers you possess.

Once I admitted that I could not handle the stuff, that I was physically allergic to it, I put the desire for booze out of my life so that I would be able to have a life I could enjoy.

I've belabored you with this story countless times. It's probably the one subject I've written more columns about than any other.

I used to write the I'm-an-alkie column as a form of therapy, I suppose. For sure, the first three or four were a form of that.

But I have long since gotten over that.

In the past few years I've written this type of column, perhaps, as a way to help others who have the same problem. I have a thick file of letters from many of you who have said a column on alcoholism here helped you at a critical period in your life.

Lately I've been writing this sermon in an effort to let you help those who share the problem I have.

Some will say that since I've been dry for 18 years, I should refer to myself as a reformed alkie or some other phrase that isn't so harsh.

Alcoholism is harsh. Extremely so. I am convinced you never

become an ex-alcoholic. Once you fess up to being an alcoholic and quit drinking does not mean you are no longer an alcoholic.

You will always be one. You have to accept this. You must accept this or you will never be able to eliminate this personal problem.

But today I'm addressing myself to the public problem of alcoholism. Hopefully it will sink in.

You, the public, are a major part of the problem.

At this time of the year this is especially so. This is when the alcoholic is most vulnerable, because everywhere the alkie turns there is a drink being offered, a toast being raised and booze being poured to celebrate the holiday season.

All of this emphasis on drinking has become so ingrained in the American way of life that you are probably not even aware you are pushers of the worst kind.

Maybe an innocent pusher, but a pusher none the less.

Your idea of a pusher is some sleaze hanging out in some school parking lot selling kids dope. Some slime getting people hooked on drugs.

My idea of a pusher is not that at all.

The pusher I dread is the happy-faced, hail-fellow sort who says to one and all, "Can I fix you a drink?" The party-thrower whose bar becomes the center of the party's activity. The nice person who asks, "What'll you have?" The person who is trying to make you feel at home by shoving a drink in your hand.

Have you pushers of booze ever stopped and asked yourself one simple question: Could the drink I'm offering someone be the drink that kills?

Drink does that you know. Oh, yes. Each drink served this time of the year is a potential killer. You say that's a little extreme. I say it isn't.

Every drink poured, every drink profferred, every drink consumed during the holiday period could be the very one that will do the drinker in.

Too many of us don't realize we are allergic to the stuff. Too many of us don't want to admit alcohol is a poison. After all, bottles don't carry a skull and crossbones on them.

Too many of us don't realize that those we offer this poison may not even be aware of their allergy. Think about this when you tell someone, "Come on, one drink is not going to hurt you."

Think about this when you plan your holiday festivities . Think about this when you stock your bar with more care than you do anything else. Think about this as you greet your guests with the inevitable, "Let me fix you a drink."

You hardly let them get their topcoats off before you ask this question. And most of you aren't even aware it has become so automatic. It has become part of the way we live and, also, part of the way we die.

Maybe you have no problem with booze. Good for you. You are blessed. Others aren't so fortunate.

For this Christmas and holiday season would you think about those less fortunate, those who have an alcoholic affliction?

I'm not saying make your party a dry one. I'm not saying have an unstocked bar. I'm not saying that at all.

All I'm asking you to do is let your guests, your friends, the people who drop by, ASK for a drink. Then it's their problem. Just quit insisting people should have a drink. Just quit making THE DRINK the uppermost thing.

Just this once, take booze out of the center of Christmas and the celebration of the holiday season. Just this once, don't be a pusher. Please.

— Dec. 18, 1979

Yes, Santa Claus, there is a Virginia

Dear Santa Claus,

You haven't asked, but I'd like to tell you something, anyway, because I'm afraid some of the talk you may be hearing could be confusing.

I mean, you probably think Christmas makes more people mad than it does happy. With all the "Bah-humbugging" going on around Christmas these days about prices, items out of stock and the overcommercialism of the season. I thought maybe you'd like to know we don't all feel that way.

There are some people who will call you all sorts of things.

They say you are a foreigner, a smuggler, a tax evader, a housebreaker, an insurrectionist, an illegal immigrant, a saboteur, and some of the fringe folk think maybe you are a commie or worse.

Oh, yeah, lots of learned folks try to put down your myth and put down what you do. People who can't find the right size or color have been know to take your name in vain.

But they just don't really understand, do they, Santa Claus?

That's why I'd like to tell you about a little girl you should know. She's only five. And she has eyes so blue you can see stars in them during the day, a nose that points up even when she looks down, and a little lisp that makes every word a blown kiss.

She's just learned to tie her shoes "real good" and most of the time she can handle the buttons on her blouse by herself, but sweaters and zip coats give her problems.

She's even getting the hang of combing the tangles out of her own hair, no small accomplishment, let me tell you. But you know all these things. She says so.

She likes things like puppies and kittens, the kids next door (sometimes), big girls everywhere, bubble bath, her mother's eye makeup, high heels to pretend in, walking holding hands, dresses with ruffles, and flannel pajamas with feet in them.

But most of all, Santa, she likes you.

I guess she has seen you probably a dozen times at least this year. In a dozen different places and in a dozen different shapes.

But she isn't suspicious about that. No, sir.

After all, you're magical and that explains everything.

She's just as sure you exist as she is that her baby dolls like lots of sugar in their tea.

Some of the wiseacre kids in her kindergarten bah-humbugged you. "They don't believe in sharing crayons, either," she explained about them.

She says she has already told you what she wants you to bring her. Her parents sure hope so because a "magic doll with a rash" and a "house with stuff" are awfully vague.

But she says you know and for her parents not to worry. "Santa never forgets and always understands little children," she explains.

She isn't old enough to understand overcommercialization, and if she did, she wouldn't care.

To her it's all candy and cookies, colored lights dancing in Scotch pines, carols on the radio, people being nice and mysterious packages in closets and under beds to shake when no one is looking or listening.

To her it's a house full of kissy relatives and dressing up to go shopping with her mother and stories about baby Jesus and the manger and animals.

To her the month of December has been one great long day, and

Christmas eve will be about the scariest and most wonderful night of the year.

You see, Santa, I can sort of remember what she's going through.

I went through the same thing. You start living for Christmas along about August. Halloween and Thanksgiving are nice diversions, but just diversion. Christmas is the biggie. The biggest.

And she really has been "trying to be good." Maybe ever her "goodest" Christmas yet.

I'll never forget the feeling. The closer it got to Christmas Eve, the "gooder" we had to be. "Santa Claus doesn't come to see bad little boys and girls," they said. We knew they were right, too.

Sometimes I thought I'd never even make it to Christmas. One year I got so good I was afraid I would be snatched off to heaven before Christmas could get there.

I'd always been told about good little children who were snatched up to heaven because they were so good God wanted them to be by His side. I believed those stories then and believe them to this day.

She has been that extra-special good that little girls can sometimes be. And she'll tell you that her older brothers and sisters have been "good mostly, too."

She doesn't want you to forget them. And she doesn't want you to forget the poor children she keeps hearing about who do get forgotten this time of year.

There are only five days left. It will seems like five years.

And she hasn't the slightest doubt that you will come. She knows just what cookie she's going to leave you, and your milk will be in her favorite glass.

You see, Santa Claus, there really is a little girl who believes in you. In fact, Santa, there are millions and millions of them. And I've got a hunch there always will be.

Your friend,
Bob Talbert
— *Dec. 20, 1983*

Some things you could do to make this your best year

"This is the beginning of a New Year. God has given me this time to use as I will. I can waste it or use it for good. What I do today is important, because I'm exchanging a day of my life for it. When tomorrow comes, this day will be gone forever, leaving something in its place I have traded for it. I want it to be gain, not loss; good, not evil; success, not failure in order that I shall not forget the price I paid for it." — Lea Aronson, Detroit, 1971.

Heavy words.

Important words.

Meaningful words to make 1971 a meaningful year.

Lea Aronson, a Detroiter with a heart, says invest each day. How?

Let's look around and think about things, big and small, you can do for Detroit in 1971.

GET INVOLVED: The next time you see someone in trouble — a stranded motorist, a puzzled pedestrian, a wandering child, etc. — stop and help. If you suspect a crime is in progress somewhere, report it. Don't be afraid to get involved.

WRITE A FAN LETTER: When a public official does something you endorse and feel worthwhile, sit down and write a thank-you note. Public officials hear from the "knockers" every day. Thank yous are unexpected, appreciated and encouraged.

GLAD-HAND A VISITOR: During the year you'll see a conventioneer — look for the lapel badges. Walk up to this visitor to our town and tell him you're glad his group picked Detroit to have a meeting.

CLEAN UP: It's a little thing, but it helps. Keep your car clean. Dirty cars add to the blighted look of downtown.

PICK UP: Every day pick up a piece of trash you didn't create and put it in the proper receptacle. If a couple million hands do this every day what a sparkling place this could be.

ATTEND A MEETING: When's the last time you attended a Common Council meeting? A school board meeting? A PTA meeting? A church meeting? Any public hearing? Try one a month.

QUIT SMOKING: A very personal plea from me to you and from all those who love you, too. And if you don't smoke, don't start.

HOLD A SIT-IN: Organize a party in your home for the teenagers in your neighborhood. Quit talking about young people and start talking with them. And young people, when you're invited to such a party be big enough to attend.

PLANT A TREE: There are plenty of places that need them. If your yard is concrete, check the roof. Why not a garden there?

OBEY A TRAFFIC LAW: Read the signs, obey 'em. Heed the lines, stay in 'em. Limit yourself to the limits.

LET SOMEONE IN: Freeway courtesy is contagious. You couldn't possibly be in that big a hurry not to let someone in line from the feeder ramps or switch to your lane ahead of you, or let them out of the parking lot ahead of you.

HOLD A GARAGE GIVEAWAY: Forget about the profit, it's usually only a few dollars anyway. Turn your garage giveaway into an attic and basement thing, too. Give the stuff to places and people who can use your dust-gatherers.

USE YOUR PULL: Pull up weeds, particularly those on vacant lots that become eyesores. Organize your friends and see how much pull you can have.

QUIT HORNING IN: Save those auto blasts for real emergencies, not momentary bursts of anger.

REMEMBER THE MAGIC WORDS: "Thank you" and "please."

PASS THE GOOD WORD: Surely everything isn't bad. Somebody you know is doing something right. Your mailman, the cop on the beat, the service station attendant, the school bus driver, somebody. Tell 'em so.

SHARE A TREASURE: Detroit is a virtual treasure chest of great little unknown shops and restaurants people keep as their own private domain and secrets. When you discover such a spot, share it with others.

TAKE THE TIME AND THE KIDS: At least once a month, take the time and the kids somewhere you've never been — one of those "we'll go there some day" places. Maybe you've been there before, but not lately; Greenfield Village, Cranbrook, Belle Isle, Detroit Institute of Arts, etc. But go with your kids. If you don't have any kids of your own, borrow some.

SHOW UP: Whether it's caroling in Kennedy Square, appreciation day at the ball park, a parade down Woodward, an open house at school, a free band concert, etc., try showing up once and you'll find twice is even better.

SMILES: Happiness is contagious. Wear a smile on your face and a happy thought on your heart. Detroit will love you for it.

— *Jan. 1, 1971*

Here's my list of New Year's resolutions

In 1974, I hereby resolve:

To stop eating chocolate-covered nuts.

To be as honest with myself — at all times, at all costs, and above all, when it hurts the most.

To never draw to an inside straight.

To not get mad at my six-year-old son who has a green belt in United Tai Kwon Do and can put me to my knees in a second.

To give more of my time and money in things that have been too bothersome, too much trouble and too insignificant in the past.

To wink at every pretty girl I see.

To be curious about one thing every day and pursue it until I can satisfy my curiosity.

To keep the weight off I plan to lose in the next two months and get down to 200 pounds of lean and mean me.

To look people straight in the eye when I talk with them and especially when they talk to me.

To absolutely not read those lifestyle stories that never ask anyone the questions except the Nederlanders, the Schoeniths, the Fords and anyone else hanging out in Grosse Pointe or the London Chop House.

To get such a kick out of my work that it will become contagious.

To stop anyone who bad-mouths the city and the urban crisis and make them give me a specific example of something bad that happened to them — not something or someone they heard about.

To not interrupt a story-teller by telling the joke's heart or punch line.

To find more and more tolerance within me about everything, and particularly the things I don't understand and don't espouse.

To make sure my 14-year-old daughter is listened to more than she is talked to.

To write a fan letter to someone in public life who has done something worth praising — and a letter makes you take the time to say thanks.

To not eat two helpings of anything I like.

To make sure any statement I make is clearly understood as my opinion only, and not the gospel for everyone else.

To make sure my shoes are shined and my fingernails are clean.

To fight fear at every level of society — the feat of the lazy and the lousy and the easy-way-outers.

To not talk when I have my mouth full.

To show up whenever I say I will no matter how small the event is and quit telling people "maybe" — give 'em a yes or a no right from the start.

To tell people good things about themselves, even if they're strangers — like "You have beautiful eyes" or "Gee, that's a nice coat."

To not tell restaurant owners how to run their restaurants.

To share with you as many treasures around town and country that I can discover.

To attend meetings of civic, school, political, religious or informative nature.

To make up my bed every day.

To take criticism with a better attitude and not try for an immediate defense.

To demand total honesty from everyone because that's what they're going to get from me.

To clean up my conversational language.

To pick up things — trash, empties, scraps of paper, junk, etc. — that I see and didn't make, but know someone has to make a move to clean up and fix up.

To speak to high school assemblies as often as I can work them into my schedule because that's the future of us all.

To get up when the alarm goes off the first time and start smiling that very minute.

To share smiles with everyone I see, morning noon and night.

To adopt at least a couple of causes, little known ones, and work through them until results are gotten.

To brush my teeth, use a water pik, and gargle daily.

To take a 30-minute nap every day.

To seek every possible way to eliminate impatience in every aspect of my life.

To give half the money I win in the Michigan Lottery to charity and the other half to my children.

To not take anyone's word for something without first checking that something out thoroughly.

To try not to wax so enthusiastically about things I like because I sometimes sound like a cheerleader or a constant standing ovation.

To admit mistakes at once — and admit them in print, too.

To give advice only when it's asked for or when it must be given.

To be interested in whatever it is you're talking about even if I know it's not something I really care about — I'll be interested in your interest.

To work harder every day in every way to make me and you and Detroit and wherever you live and whatever you do and this column more meaningful and worthy.

— Jan. 1, 1974

Out of my mind
on a Monday moanin'

Small children always look out of place in sport cars.

I've got to believe the world's really fouled up when barbers, cab drivers and disc jockeys don't have ready solutions to all the problems.

Politicians always have four speeches: the one written down; the one they actually say; the one they wish they'd said, and the one they're quoted as saying.

A record number of twins are born today, which must mean that with the shape of the world what it is, kids are afraid to come into it alone.

Drivers who swing left before they can make a right turn or swing right before they can make a left turn should swing all right — by the neck.

The best gossip in the world is hearing something you like about someone you dislike.

The bore is always sure, and the sure are always boring.

How much you do is important, but how well you do it is what counts.

People who live in stone houses shouldn't throw glasses.

A broken reputation can be repaired but everyone will always watch the spot where the crack was.

The easiest way to go into debt is to keep up with people who already are.

Pseudo-intellectuals are the sort of people who enjoy anything until it becomes popular.

Love is when the happiness of another person is necessary for your own happiness.

Do teenagers realize that someday they'll know as little as their parents?

No matter how small a town is you can always find someone to give you the wrong directions.

Anyone who thinks marriage is a 50-50 proposition doesn't understand fractions or the opposite sex.

When someone starts a conversation with "I really don't know where to begin," they really mean they really don't know where to end.

No hydrogen bomb can make a noise as loud as the first rattle in your brand new car.

How can kids' shoes wear out so fast when we seem to drive them every place they go?

That life begins at 40 must explain why some men who hit 50 start acting like adolescents.

You're still young if you can wake up in the morning with a pain and honestly believe it will go away.

If you spend as little the day after payday as you do the day before payday, you'll make it all right.

If your average daily luncheon bar tab tops your food tab you've got troubles.

Seven million Americans suffer from pains in the back at least 50 million give them.

"Ya know" is America's verbal dial tone.

Every time you stretch the truth someone's bound to see through it.

Some women spend a lot of time looking for a husband — particularly after they marry one.

It's easier to believe a lie uttered a hundred times than the truth the first time you hear it.

The trouble with this country is that all the stupid people are sure of everything and all the intelligent people are full of doubts.

One of life's happier moments is when your kids get to the age where you don't have to pretend to them that you know everything.

If they could do it over again, whoever picked the way marijuana smells would probably pick again cause that stuff doesn't get it in the aroma league.

Boys' names I like the very best all begin with the letter J: Jason, Jarrad, Joshua, Jethro, Justin, Josh, Jeremiah, and Jonathan.

Has there ever been a book that was soon to be a minor movie?